LIBRARY OF HEBREW BIBLE AND OLD TESTAMENT STUDIES

677

Formerly Journal for the Study of the Old Testament Supplement Series

Editors
Claudia V. Camp, Texas Christian University
Andrew Mein, University of Durham, UK

Founding Editors
David J. A. Clines, Philip R. Davies and David M. Gunn

Editorial Board
Alan Cooper, Susan Gillingham, John Goldingay, Norman K. Gottwald,
James E. Harding, John Jarick, Carol Meyers, Daniel L. Smith-Christopher,
Francesca Stavrakopoulou, James W. Watts

IMAGINED WORLDS AND CONSTRUCTED DIFFERENCES IN THE HEBREW BIBLE

Edited by
Jeremiah W. Cataldo

LONDON • NEW YORK • OXFORD • NEW DELHI • SYDNEY

T&T CLARK
Bloomsbury Publishing Plc
50 Bedford Square, London, WC1B 3DP, UK
1385 Broadway, New York, NY 10018, USA
29 Earlsfort Terrace, Dublin 2, Ireland

BLOOMSBURY, T&T CLARK and the T&T Clark logo are
trademarks of Bloomsbury Publishing Plc

First published in Great Britain 2019
This paperback edition published in 2021

Copyright © Jeremiah W. Cataldo and contributors, 2019

Jeremiah W. Cataldo has asserted his right under the Copyright, Designs and
Patents Act, 1988, to be identified as the Editor of this work.

All rights reserved. No part of this publication may be reproduced or transmitted
in any form or by any means, electronic or mechanical, including photocopying,
recording, or any information storage or retrieval system, without prior
permission in writing from the publishers.

Bloomsbury Publishing Plc does not have any control over, or responsibility for, any
third-party websites referred to or in this book. All internet addresses given in this
book were correct at the time of going to press. The author and publisher regret any
inconvenience caused if addresses have changed or sites have ceased to exist,
but can accept no responsibility for any such changes.

A catalogue record for this book is available from the British Library.

Library of Congress Cataloging-in-Publication Data
Names: Cataldo, Jeremiah W., editor.
Title: Imagined worlds and constructed differences in the Hebrew Bible /
edited by Jeremiah W. Cataldo.
Description: 1 [edition]. | New York: T&T Clark, 2019. |
Series: Library of Hebrew Bible/Old Testament studies, 2513-8758; volume 677 |
Includes bibliographical references and index.
Identifiers: LCCN 2019016129 | ISBN 9780567683519 (hardback) |
ISBN 9780567689801 (epub)
Subjects: LCSH: Bible. Old Testament–Criticism, interpretation, etc.
Classification: LCC BS1171.3.I44 2019 | DDC 221.6–dc23
LC record available at https://lccn.loc.gov/2019016129

ISBN: HB: 978-0-5676-8351-9
PB: 978-0-5677-0037-7
ePDF: 978-0-5676-8350-2
eBook: 978-0-5676-8980-1

Series: Library of Hebrew Bible/Old Testament Studies, 2513-8758, volume 677

Typeset by Deanta Global Publishing Services, Chennai, India

To find out more about our authors and books visit
www.bloomsbury.com and sign up for our newsletters.

CONTENTS

Chapter 1
INTRODUCTION
    Jeremiah W. Cataldo   1

Chapter 2
SOCIAL SCIENCES MODELS AND MNEMONIC/IMAGINED WORLDS:
EXPLORING THEIR INTERRELATIONS IN ANCIENT ISRAEL
    Ehud Ben Zvi   9

Chapter 3
THE ASSASSINATION OF AMON AND THE CRISIS OF ASSYRIAN
IMPERIALISM
    Bradley L. Crowell   27

Chapter 4
NEHEMIAH'S SOCIOECONOMIC REFORM: PRINCIPLES AND
ACCOMPLISHMENTS
    Kyong-Jin Lee   43

Chapter 5
VEILED RESISTANCE: THE COGNITIVE DISSONANCE OF VISION
IN GENESIS 38
    Carolyn Alsen   59

Chapter 6
THOSE AT EASE HAVE CONTEMPT FOR MISFORTUNE: BIBLICAL
APPROACHES TO CHALLENGING ANTI-POOR SENTIMENT
    Matthew J. M. Coomber   83

Chapter 7
A TASTE FOR WISDOM: AESTHETICS, MORAL DISCERNMENT, AND
SOCIAL CLASS IN PROVERBS
    Mark Sneed   111

Chapter 8
BIBLICAL STRATEGIES FOR REINTERPRETING CRISES
WITH "OUTSIDERS"
   Jeremiah W. Cataldo   127

Chapter 9
MULTINATIONALITY AND THE UTOPIAN PROJECT: THE CASE OF
ACTUALLY EXISTING ISRAEL
   Roland Boer   145

Notes on Contributors	161
Bibliography	163
Author Index	178
Subject Index	182
Biblical Index	185

Chapter 1

INTRODUCTION

Jeremiah W. Cataldo

Where are we going?

It is a troublesome thing that the role constructed, cultural memory has played in the formation of the biblical texts remains an under-explored area of academic inquiry. True of both the past and the present, the ways in which groups imagine the world as they believe it *should* be and the ways in which they construct identities and boundaries of difference in response to that imagining are important indicators of ideological, and frequently specifically political, intentions. In that vein, with respect to the Hebrew Bible, descriptions of a new "Israel," of a restored nation and its monarchy, are nearly all utopian—projected desires for a stabilized sociopolitical community. In such contexts, the ways in which the distinction between member and nonmember are articulated are products of an imagined world, or community, in which the desired order reflects the deeply rooted values and desires of the community—that is core to how restoration as a biblical concept has been interpreted by more modern readers.[1] The distinction between member and nonmember gets measured out in spheres of politics, economics, and society (for instance, in the issue of gender relations) to the point that insiders are considered safe and outsiders threatening. To *imagine* a community, as Benedict Anderson described in his work *Imagined Communities: Reflections on the Origin and Spread of Nationalism*, is to orient, through narrated or acted out beliefs and behaviors, institutions, meanings, values, and relationships, toward realizing an intended sociopolitical state, one that takes on an objective quality for the community's members. While some such worlds are entirely utopian, some, if not most, are also directly grounded in real concerns and strategies. And in some cases, an imagined community may provide the basis for revolutionary action. Certainly, for those familiar with social-scientific methods, these premises are familiar. They are foundational to much theory on collective identity; they are also frequently

---

1. Yet one should acknowledge that the vocabulary of "restoration" overlooks the fact that the imagined result is in fact utopian.

overlooked, ignored, or unknown by biblical scholars. There is still too often a greater dependence upon a view that the texts depict the sociopolitical world as it was, rather than one that prioritized cultural memory, values, interpretation, and utopian desire(s) as primary motivations behind the authors' writing. That dependence seems to forget that authors cannot help but react with or against the sociopolitical world and dominant identity as imagined within their communities. And it is that imagination that provides the moral and value frameworks—even the moral credibility—that authors assume when they write their texts, whether they be texts of the Bible or of modern fiction.

One might say, then, that the writing of texts is a political act. As one of its functions, even merely in its structure and presentation, it reinforces or challenges dominant aspects of sociopolitical identity. Imagining community and identity means more than articulating it within text. It means understanding how values and behaviors reflect it outside of individual and group intention or agenda, and how cultural memory is confirmed and preserved by it.

Toward that end, the intent of this volume is twofold: to introduce readers to an important area of study and to the work that has already been done in it, and to set up strategies for connecting studies of the historical contexts and literatures of the Bible to parallel issues in more present contexts. Can we better understand, for instance, the desire of the minority and the imagined world that drives her? Or can we better understand the powerful impact of prejudice as a basis for preserving differences between "us" and "them"? Such questions will be explored in related ways by each of the contributions in this volume. Each contribution will focus on one or more elements—social, economic, or political—that have shaped or influenced dominant elements of cultural memory and identity within the biblical texts.

This volume emerged primarily out of the work of the Social Sciences and the Interpretation of Hebrew Scriptures section of the Annual Meeting of the Society of Biblical Literature during its sessions from 2014 to 2017. To varying degrees, Anderson's theory presented a rhetorical framework for the contributions collated here. His articulation of *imagining* community identified general processes and strategies that can be found in all cultures, historical and modern. However, making the connection between studies of the biblical contexts and Anderson's theory, which focused on modern examples from nation-states and their cultures, requires flexibility to explore particular cultural ideas or events under a general pattern of constructing identity, which reflects how a group imagined the dominating contours of its sociopolitical world.

Each of the contributions here is part of a larger argument, where the collected volume embodies an exploration of the complexity and multiplicity of imagining community and constructing social worlds. Some of the works focus on specific events or people while others identify cultural or political trends or patterns. The micro and macro perspectives are equally important for understanding how communities are imagined by their insiders and what they appear to be from an outside perspective. In all cases, the emphasis is upon understanding different aspects of how identity is both imagined and expressed in support of a shared cultural understanding of the sociopolitical world. That shared understanding operates as the framework through which identity is internalized, which also, concomitantly, sets up strategies by which that identity is outwardly expressed through group behavior, action, and sociopolitical movement.

But such movements are oftentimes inadequately understood. Biblical scholars often continue to prioritize the world(s) of the biblical text as causative over sociopolitical processes that shaped them. That is, in part, why Ehud Ben Zvi calls to question tendencies to overlook the importance of social-scientific models, which are often abandoned by those who reject cross-historical and cross-cultural comparisons and who default lazily to accusations of universalism. He argues that models from the social sciences employed in historical analyses are productive; they have shed much light on the historical worlds of past societies. In addition, they seem to work well, and at times even better, within imagined social worlds that exist(ed) only in the shared, social memory of a particular, ancient or modern, group (or sets of such groups). They are not complete solutions but helpful tools. He first discusses a number of substantially different, illustrative examples concerning the world of memory about ancient Israel that existed among the literati of late Persian/early Hellenistic Yehud/Judah. Then he explores the question of why these models not only work within imaginary/remembered worlds but at times fit these remembered/construed worlds even better than their counterpart "historical" or "actual" worlds, as the latter are reconstructed by historians. It is a critical issue as it re-orients academic focus upon the literati's role in shaping not only how historians interpret biblical portrayals of Israel past but also how the same literati imagined the Israel of the future. Toward that end, Ben Zvi highlights the roles that constructed differences, which are preserved in cultural memories, played in (re-)imagining sociopolitical worlds.

That idea is critical to understanding both the formation of the biblical texts and how they are interpreted. What the authors or editors say, what they preserve in memory, how they describe individuals and behaviors reflect the constructed sociopolitical world—often those of the authors/editors themselves. Moreover, it is one that reflects one of Anderson's main points: that bitter disputes in politics often drive how a sociopolitical body, or its representatives, imagines itself as a, or in a, community. Brad Crowell addresses this issue by zeroing in on the brief narrative of Amon. As he argues, this narrative highlights aspects of failed pro-Assyrian policies championed by Amon and his father. The failure of such policies was confirmed with Amon's assassination by his own servants. At its heart, it conveys a conflict experienced in the Judean court between imperial realities and desired political identity, between both insider and outsider and also between subgroups competing to articulate a dominant collective identity, which prompted a popular uprising with the intent to install Amon's son, Josiah, on the throne. Crowell argues, then, that this brief and under-studied narrative provides significant insight into the various factions and imperial interests that developed in the wake of declining imperial influence and, consequently, the increase in local or national social and political interests as newly viable ways in which to articulate *in a constructive fashion* society and social-political identity. Employing theoretical works on the sociology of empire and on the expression of "national" community, Crowell shows how the tumultuous reign of Amon was a product of an "imperial crisis," by which he means the internal fracturing that occurs as empires fail, on the periphery of a declining empire. On local and regional levels, the ideals of community and collective identity were reimagined in light of such bitter and threatening sociopolitical experiences.

Kyong-Jin Lee's analysis of Neh. 5:1-13, the passage of Nehemiah's "socio-economic reform," carefully turns our focus to how perceptions of economic fairness and performance impact fundamental aspects of social and political identity. She begins by viewing Nehemiah through the methodological lens of classical economic and sociological theorists, who argue that diffuse and decentralized institutions in a society provide a profitable environment, particularly for economic actors who pursue self-interest single-mindedly. According to them, the marketplace is an unrelentingly rational ground, disconnected from a moral conscience or restraint. Economic or other related gains are made by emphasizing differences. Consequently, communal ethics do not always play an influential role in the changes that a political economy undergoes. She makes an important distinction: where ethical and legal injunctions pertaining to debt did exist in the cultures and traditions of Persian-era Yehud, the rationality of a developing market economy, one driven by profit-maximizing behaviors, trumped the code of kinship, creating divisions based on social-economics above family or shared humanity. In other words, the demands of an emerging rational marketplace facilitated by imperial conquest began to supersede traditional ways in which communities came to understand the collective sociopolitical identity that previously defined them. This shift entailed, Lee argues, a more pronounced dependence upon sociopolitical and economic institutions to play a key role in minimizing uncertainty in human social interaction, in part by codifying or institutionalizing distinctive aspects of cultural identities. This is particularly the case when institutions reduce uncertainty in economic transactions, whether the mechanisms by which they do so are informal (norms of behavior, societal codes of conduct) or formal (laws, rules). However, institutions do not always maximize efficiency, and over time institutional design, even if only on the level of an *imagined* design, can promote the bargaining power of certain social groups by capitalizing on differences and defining a hierarchy of power, which includes preservation of that hierarchy through a controlled sense of moral obligation. She argues that amid a deficient central power, elites enjoyed enhanced bargaining powers and, eventually, expanded their economic influence and prosperity over the subaltern, whose own sense of moral obligation preserved the distribution of roles that supported the elite. Consequently, what began to take shape was a community as it was imagined by the elites or more specifically, as Ben Zvi argues, the literati.

Centralizing power around a dominant identity, however, also tends to produce feelings of disenfranchisement, oppression, and inequality for those left on the margins. While some individuals may accept, and oftentimes many *do*, the role that dominating forces acting upon their sociopolitical world have given them, others resist and react through social deviancy. That is a focal point in Carolyn Alsen's contribution, which overlays a sociology of social deviancy and public visibility as an optic on the symbolism of Tamar's veil in Genesis 38. According to Alsen, the veil becomes a polyvalent symbol, capable of multiple visual social meanings: accessible through the concepts of veiled and unveiled, covering and uncovering, and the social risk of deviating from dominant social norms. Alsen's careful use of that optic shows that for Tamar, the veil was a tool, within a patriarchal world, that could overturn imposed lines of gender difference, which Tamar accomplished through her own ethical self-objectification and her objectification of Judah—the woman objectifying the man—in the pursuit of sexual activity. In other words, Tamar's veil, when considered through a sociology of social deviancy and public visibility, symbolized her taking control of her own (re)presentation of otherness before Israelite, and even later biblical, ideologies of sexual and social deviancy. Consequently, her "unveiling" at the conclusion of Genesis 38 was an act of deviancy that threatened the dominant norms of the Israelite community, reimagining it through a rearticulation of collective identity. Tamar's actions, Alsen shows us, are best interpreted against the grain of an imposed dominant narrative of imagining community. And that exposes an aspect that Anderson doesn't acknowledge in his own work, that minority groups within a dominant culture offer details of a different imagining or view of community than what might be imposed upon them—a point that Roland Boer would also address from a more modern perspective.

Where Alsen shows us an impact of constructed identity upon the minority individual, Matthew Coomber takes us from the individual to the oppressive aspects of institutions. As he maintains, in any centralization of power, and consequent oppression of a subaltern, one must ask what motivated the rulers, those who took from the impoverished for their own personal gain? In what ways was the national community, as they imagined it, different from how those they ruled imagined it, especially in light of the increasing economic burdens shouldered by those of the lower class? In exploring the processes by which communities are imagined, Coomber weighs the benefit to biblical studies of Susan Fiske and Paul Piff's research on class division, which argues that (economic) privilege affects individual and collective psyches by validating class through cultural-economic differences, resulting in contempt and "unethical" behavior directed toward the impoverished. Through that, Coomber carefully exposes the restrictive side of imagined communities by illustrating how the social psychology of wealth-poor divisions can open new levels of interpretation in texts that condemn economic abuses. His contribution reminds us to consider what many biblical scholars who apply sociological theory often fail to acknowledge: that *every* social and political process produces some detritus—which for Alsen was embodied in the minority figure—that influences the longitudinal direction of dominant social and political developments.

Mark Sneed peers into the space between the individual and the institution by analyzing how class and distinction are ideologically manifest in a text that teaches the individual to behave in a manner consistent with the dominant collective ideal.

He brings together elements of three theoretical schools to Proverbs: philosophical, sociological, and literary. The philosophical involves the recent trend in using virtue ethics to tease out how Proverbs attempts to develop moral discernment in its readers. He draws upon Pierre Bourdieu's notion of "taste" as a social force in difference to show how Proverbs promotes a taste for aesthetics, and that that, in turn, *distinguishes* its addressees from the rest of Israelite society morally and socially. In his book *Distinction*, Bourdieu, Sneed argues, offers observations about the petite bourgeoisie in France that resonate strikingly with the intended audience of Proverbs. This social class in question compensates for its lack of economic capital by emphasizing its own moral superiority over others, which is visually and ideologically expressed through aesthetics (as cultural capital). Sneed argues that both the literary sophistication in Proverbs and the book's preoccupation with morality serve to aid its addressees in acquiring a taste for a type of wisdom largely inaccessible to the rest of Israelite society and, thereby, compensating for their less than aristocratic status. In doing that, they create a map for reimagining the value hierarchy of the community.

The final two contributions lay out possible points of connection between the historical and the modern. Where the previous contributions emphasized the historical context of the biblical texts, the latter two focus on the "so what" of whether interpreting the texts through social-scientific methods might have modern relevance and importance.

To do that, Jeremiah Cataldo tackles Benedict Anderson's theory on imagined communities and how prejudices shape them. For him, this theory, as well as how it inadvertently exposes prejudice, provides an important optic through which to interpret the strength of the Bible as a religious-cultural symbol relevant for renegotiating the dominant Western, and Judeo-Christian, discourse, a dichotomized discourse, on the identities of minorities, such as immigrants, refugees, and foreigners. Clarifying the depth of the symbolic value and role of the Bible permits one to reimagine "community" as a body constructed through relational discourse and not fashioned in subordination to a preexisting or objective ideal or object. The value of that revised strategy is a better understanding of how borders are defined and enforced. Yet that strategy also requires an understanding of the historical context that provides the foundation for the biblical texts—it explains the values and agendas that shaped the texts and that have largely become adopted in Judeo-Christian insider-outsider discourse. Cataldo focuses on that foundation by setting Anderson's theory into conversation with sixth- to fifth-century BCE biblical literature—literature that wrestled with the realities of immigration and the threat of foreigners for *imagined* communities. Engagement of those realities set the tone for resistance against imperial authorities. With that in mind, given how the subject of immigration has become something of a global concern, does the Bible, Cataldo asks, have anything helpful to say on the matter?

Where Cataldo focuses on prejudice as a reflection of difference, Roland Boer, in the spirit of Benedict Anderson's work on imagined communities and the role that imposed and constructed differences play in the formation of such communities, applies the theoretical concept of nationalism to biblical articulations of "Israel."

Where prejudices facilitate difference, nationalism facilitates community. Boer makes that argument by focusing on the process of imagining community: Israel, he argues, was the product of an intersection of nationalities and one in which "actually existing Israel" was a simultaneously utopian/dystopian project. As part of a cross-cultural, theoretical approach, important for social-scientific inquiry, Boer picks up the intense debate over "nationalities" at the turn of the twentieth century in Austria, Russia, and elsewhere, finding currents of similarity between the biblical project and more recent situations. He knowingly avoids anachronism by defining "nationalities" in a way that would satisfy Anderson: what is often meant in usages of the term is what are now problematically called "ethnic groups" within states, or kingdoms. Each state is made up of such nationalities, so when one speaks of nationalism, one speaks of distinct political and cultural identities within a state. Nationalism, in other words and as Anderson argued, is an *imagined* framework for political communities that holds a constructive, if not utopian, intent: building a world in which the threat of difference is controlled. All said, each of the contributions in this volume contributions in this volume pursue that idea from different perspectives. And each of them plants a seed for future conversations.

Where do we go from here?

What this volume offers is not a conclusion but a strategy for beginning. Not only must we rethink conventional interpretive angles and assumptions about what it meant to be Israelite or Judean in the historical context of ancient Israel/Judah, but we must also, because of the Bible's importance for many modern communities, rethink what it really offers in the way of incontrovertible truths or facts. Failure to do so is one reason, for instance, why R. S. Sugirtharajah published *Still at the Margins: Biblical Scholarship Fifteen Years after the Voices from the Margin*.[2] The fact that we are still trying to discern the relevance of the Bible for marginal groups is telling, if not indicting. That we still tend to assume that the Bible's portrayal of its historical contexts is factually accurate is myopic. Part of the problem is the very terminology, "Bible," which demands that historical, cultural texts be read with modern sentiments of theology and historiography and very often be guided by "metaphysical prejudices" regarding divine causation within the natural and historical world(s).[3] In response, this volume begins the conversation about reimagining communities of the Bible. And it pays close attention to what our responsibilities are in light of that reimagining.

---

2. Rasiah S. Sugirtharajah, ed. *Still at the Margins: Biblical Scholarship Fifteen Years after Voices from the Margin* (London: T&T Clark, 2008).

3. I first came across the phrase "metaphysical prejudice" when reading Yoram Hazony, *God and Politics in Esther* (Cambridge: Cambridge University Press, 2016), 202.

Chapter 2

SOCIAL SCIENCES MODELS AND MNEMONIC/ IMAGINED WORLDS: EXPLORING THEIR INTERRELATIONS IN ANCIENT ISRAEL

Ehud Ben Zvi

Introduction

Undoubtedly and unsurprisingly from a methodological viewpoint, models and concepts from the social sciences have shed much light on contemporary societies and also on historical worlds of the ancient past/s. The reason that they work effectively for contemporary societies as well as reconstructions of ancient historical ones, including ancient Israel, is that matters as diverse as ancient communities, kings and other political leaders, prophets, priests, literati, prophecies, laws, marriage, divorce, temples, cultic practices, historical narratives, and group memories share one thing in common: they are all social entities of one sort or another and, therefore, are all amenable to approaches from the social sciences.[1]

Even more, these very approaches often work well for imagined social worlds that existed only in the shared, social memory of a group or set of groups in antiquity.[2] This is especially important for analyses of those texts that depict constructed memories of what an (ideal) political community should look like. At times, the mentioned methods not only work in these worlds of constructed and

---

1. My use of the term "social entity" reflects an understanding of it in line with the following: "A social entity is not a fixed thing with stable properties.... It is rather a continuing swirl of linked social activities and practices, themselves linked to other 'separate' social traditions" and that all "social facts are carried by socially construed individuals in action." Citation from D. Little, "The Heterogeneous Social: New Thinking about the Foundations of the Social Sciences," in *Philosophy of the Social Sciences: Philosophical Theory and Scientific Practice*, ed. C. Mantzavinos (Cambridge University Press, 2009), 154–78 (159); and cf. also A. Abbott, *Department & Discipline: Chicago Sociology at One Hundred* (Chicago, IL: University of Chicago Press, 1999), esp. 222–23.

2. They work also in memory worlds held by groups in other societies, including contemporary ones, but the focus here is in ancient Israel.

shared memory, but seem to work far better within them than in the "counterpart" historical worlds, which for ancient contexts are typically reconstructed by historians.

To illustrate my point, I will first draw attention to several substantially different, illustrative examples that all together serve as an indication that the issue raised above is not marginal, but a major one for future research. Then I will begin to explore the implications of these observations and suggest some research paths to which they lead. On the whole, the goal of this contribution is to draw attention to these matters and encourage further conversations and explorations on them.

A set of diverse examples

The case of well-known social constructions and structures

There is no denying the presence and underlying importance of more broadly understood social constructions such as honor-shame, patron-client, and "the house of the father" (and in some cases, its subdivisions into "houses of mothers") in numerous narratives or worlds of memory.[3] Social-scientific and comparative studies on all the above are relevant and provide good heuristic tools for studies of both narrative worlds and most likely "historical" societies in ancient Israel in which all the above played important roles.

The reason for congruence in these cases is relatively simple: communities imagined worlds in terms of what they implicitly construed as "natural" and therefore, such social constructions were part and parcel of the world of communities, across time and both in their "real" world and their worlds memory and imagination. Although relatively easy to understand, these cases are certainly not meaningless. They do provide us crucial information about that which was so

---

3. Concerning honor and shame, see, for example, S. Olyan, "Honor, Shame, and Covenantal Relations in Ancient Israel and Its Environment," *JBL* 115 (1996), 201–18; and in relation to, for example, Esther see, for example, T. Laniak, *Shame and Honor in the Book of Esther* (SBLDS, 65; Atlanta, GA: Scholars Press, 1988); and L. Klein, "Honor and Shame in Esther," in *Feminist Companion to Esther, Judith and Susanna*, ed. A. Brenner (Sheffield: Sheffield Academic Press, 1995), 149–75; for multiple cases of narratives and prophecies involving accounts of past or future mutilations of enemies, see T. M. Lemos, "Shame and Mutilation of Enemies in the Hebrew Bible," *JBL* 125 (2006), 225–24. Examples may be easily multiplied. On imagined/construed patron-client relationships, see, for example, J. Schäder, "Patronage and Clientage between God, Israel and the Nations: A Social-Scientific Investigation of Psalm 47," *Journal for Semitics* 19 (2010), 235–62. On literary constructions of the house of the mother, see C. Chapman, *The House of the Mother: The Social Roles of Maternal Kin in Biblical Hebrew Narrative and Poetry* (New Haven, CT: Yale University Press, 2016). The motif of the house of the father is ubiquitous in the Hebrew Bible narratives, wisdom texts, poetry and prophetic literature.

"natural" as to be transparent to particular communities, and even so "natural" that it permeated and constrained their social imagination.[4]

The case of state (and chiefdom) formation

The next example is, appropriately, of a different type. Rather than socially construed non-dynamic constant conditions and transparent continuity, this example unequivocally relates to change and discontinuity. Without entering much into the details and shortcomings of various theories of state formation[5]

---

4. Cf. "What is familiar is what we are used to, and what we are used to is what is most difficult to know. The greater discovery lies in becoming aware of our most basic assumptions, so that we can question them and make them strange," D. Nirenberg, 527th Convocation Address University of Chicago, "A Time of Mind," available at http://eventbeat.org/the-527th-convocation-address-the-university-of-chicago/.

The larger issue of constraints on imagination cannot be discussed here. It suffices to mention that such constraints are based on cognitive matters (e.g., humans cannot really imagine what seven dimensions may look like) and on the basic fact that imaginaries (just like memories, for that matter) are not construed by individuals or social groups in a vacuum. Imaginaries are strongly grounded on the world of knowledge held among those construing them, that is, the imagination agents, and on their group's social mindscape social, political, and cultural circumstances. Moreover, imaginaries have to relate in some way directly or indirectly to the world of those that imagine them, if the act of imagining is to have some epistemic function and thus help those involved in to learn something.

The range of research on these and the related and much larger matters concerning imagination, usually with an eye into the present, may be exemplified by the following works and the works cited in them: *Knowledge through Imagination*, eds. A. Kind and P. Kung (Oxford: Oxford University Press, 2016) and see especially in this collection, A. Kind, "Imagining under Constraints," 145–59, and N. Van Leeuwen, "The Imaginative Agent," 85–110; the journal issue introduced by J. Latimer and B. Skeggs, "The Politics of Imagination: Keeping Open and Critical," *The Sociological Review* 59 (2011), 393–410; R. Carter, "The Limits of Imagination," in *Human Nature: Fact and Fiction: Literature, Science and Human Nature*, eds. R. Headlam Wells and J. McFadden (London: Continuum, 2006), 128–43; G. Currie, "Imagination and Learning," in *The Routledge Handbook of Philosophy of Imagination*, ed. A. Kind (New York: Routledge, 2016), 407–19; N. Fletcher, "Imagination and the Capabilities Approach," in *The Routledge Handbook of Philosophy of Imagination*, ed. A. Kind (New York: Routledge, 2016), 392–404.

5. Those advanced by E. Service (see, e.g., *Origins of the State and Civilization: The Process of Cultural Evolution* [New York: Norton, 1975], along with the emphasis on chiefdom as the stage between tribal and state political organization) and thus also those of, for example, C. Renfrew (see, e.g., "Beyond a Subsistence Economy: The Evolution of Social Organization in Prehistoric Europe," in *Reconstructing Complex Societies An Archaeological Colloquium*, ed. C. Moore [BASORSup, 20; Cambridge, MA: ASOR, 1974], 69–88) had a significant impact on studies of ancient Israelite history. See, for example, J. Flanagan, "Chiefs in Israel,"

and without any need to accept unilineal, evolutionary paths,[6] it is safe to say that there is a wide agreement that transitions from chiefdom to state usually involved, inter alia, a shift toward sociopolitical complexity, which often includes the development of state bureaucracy, law, and the ability to enforce it, "urban" centers; strong and permanent armies; more complex redistribution systems than those of chiefs (including tax systems and an ability to administer them); building, and tendencies toward enhancing the role of, central temples and administrative centralization.

Are these not all part and parcel of a world of memory in which a polity that we may call today a "state" emerged out of clashes between two original chiefs, Saul and David, during the late reign of David and especially Solomon, from the perspective of ancient readers of Samuel and Kings?

Surely, when the literati who read the books of Samuel and Kings recalled and imagined Saul, David, and Solomon, the polity that their readings evoked shifted from one in which features consistent with models of chiefdom are dominant to one in which features consistent with a polity we may call "state" are obviously prevalent—obviously using our own terminology.[7]

In addition, we may consider the influential model of Carneiro, which argues that warfare (or the threat thereof) played an important role in the establishment of chiefdoms.[8] David's kingdom is often, and with good reasons, characterized as a "chiefdom." Certainly, Saul's kingdom as portrayed in the book of Samuel qualifies as a "chiefdom." This being the case, it is worth noting that the narrative communicated by the book of Samuel and the set of socially shared memories encoded and evoked by this book about the establishment of Saul's kingdom, and even David's, conform with Carneiro's model. In fact, one might approach the emergence of the short-lived "chiefdoms" of Gideon and Jephtah, as portrayed in Judges, in the same manner.

in *Social Scientific Old Testament Criticism. A Sheffield Reader*, ed. D. Chalcraft (BibSem, 47; Sheffield: Sheffield Academic Press, 1997), 136-61.

6. The models mentioned above have been critiqued on these grounds.

7. For the present purposes, it is not necessary to enter the debate about archaeological data dealing with the emergence of states in the Southern Levant during the Iron Age or reconstructions of "historical" Iron Age Sauls, Davids, or Solomons, or whether the wars of David were constructed and remembered in terms associated with those of Hazael in the ninth century (see, e.g., N. Na'aman, "In Search of Reality behind the Account of David's Wars with Israel's Neighbours," *IEJ* 52 [2002], 200-24) or whether the portrayal of the Solomon of Kings was based on Omride sources portraying Omride kings (see E. Axel Knauf, "King Solomon's Copper Supply," in *Phoenicia and the Bible. Proceedings of the Conference held at the University of Leuven on the 15th and 16th of March 1990*, ed. E. Lipiński [Studia Phoenicia, XI, Leuven: Peeters, 1991], 167-86).

8. R. Carneiro, "Chiefdom: Precursor of the State," in *The Transition to Statehood in the New World*, eds. G. Jones and R. Kautz (Cambridge: Cambridge University Press, 1981), 37-75 (63-65).

2. Social Sciences Models and Mnemonic/Imagined Worlds

To be sure, scholars of previous generations have been very much aware that the narratives in Samuel, Kings, and Chronicles as well portray a world and sociopolitical processes that conform, to a significant extent, with some widely known general social-scientific models.[9] These scholars, however, have been challenged, over time and inter alia, because they relied on the "historicity" of literary texts much later than the putative time they were portraying. Moreover, these texts often had a long redactional history. Today, even if one were to argue that these texts might contain a kernel of historicity, few historians would take them as reliable sources for historical reconstructions of the process of state formation for the historical, Iron Age kingdoms of (northern) Israel, first, and Judah later. Moreover, the process of state formation portrayed in these sources is not that of either one of these historical kingdoms, but of the Israel that serves as the main site of memory and character in the Primary History (Genesis–2 Kings), the Deuteronomistic History Collection (hereafter, DHC), or the book of Chronicles, and which is a social and ideological construction that evolved much later than the establishment of these kingdoms.

I would like to stress that I consider neither the narratives nor the world they evoke as reliable sources for reconstructions of the events that led to the formation of the state polities referred to as the kingdoms of Judah and Israel. They are products of imagined identities, not intentional historical reflections. But the basic observations made above still hold true; the narratives in the DHC

---

9. Jim Flanagan wrote about thirty-five years ago as follows: "To summarize militia, kinship ties, redistribution, and appeals to religious legitimacy all figured as strands in the warp and woof of the social, political, economic, and religious fabric of the day. Studies of the cultural evolutionary and succession patterns of other societies have described similar transitional circumstances and have concluded that such times were periods when the society was led by chiefs. The descriptions drawn from those non-Yahwistic and primary societies fit the evidence found in the literature of Yahwistic, secondary Israel. In fact, most of the elements on Renfrew's list of twenty characteristics of chiefdoms cited above can be documented in Israel. These indicate both the presence of chiefs and the absence of a strong centralized monopoly of force equipped with laws during the time of Saul and the early years of David. Since the parallels between Renfrew's list and the biblical evidence are not random, and because the evolutionary process outlined by Service is clearly evident in Israel, the cross-cultural comparisons are valid and productive. They have helped us understand the processes at work in ancient Israel and have aided in dismissing conjectures about the immediate transition from tribal league to full-blown monarchy." (See J. Flanagan, "Chiefs in Israel," 136–61; citation, 157–58; the original article was published as J. Flanagan, "Chiefs in Israel," *JSOT* 20 [1981], 47–63; and was republished in additional volumes, for example, C. Carter and C. Meyers, eds. *Community, Identity, and Ideology: Social Science Approaches to the Hebrew Bible* [Winona Lake, IN: Eisenbrauns, 1996], 311–34 and J. Exum, *The Historical Books* [Biblical Seminar, 40; Sheffield: Sheffield Academic Press, 1997], 142–66.)

and Chronicles, and the worlds of imagination and memory that they shaped and evoked when these books were read—both separately and in a way in which each one informs the other—do indeed show some degree of coherence with what one would anticipate from models of processes by which chiefdoms end up becoming state polities.

Whereas these narratives and worlds of memory may not be a good mimetic reflection of historical processes in the Iron Age, the fact that they conform in broad strokes with what models in twentieth- and twenty-first-century social sciences project is still a very meaningful piece of information. Moreover, the fact that the relatively simple, uni-directional, and teleological manner in which the narrative in these textual sources moved first toward chiefdom and then to a state polity is far more consonant with both the simplified lines of "theoretical models" and with construed narratives of social memory that existed among the much later literati who produced, reproduced, redacted, and read, and reread these texts than the far more complex, chaotic historical realities.

It is worth noting in this context that relative lack of complexity in comparison with historical "realities" tends also to characterize social memory.[10] Since both social memory and socio-anthropological models involve simplification, even if for different reasons, their confluence in the case mentioned above is not necessarily perplexing. Before discussing these matters further, a few additional examples/case studies are needed.

The case of prophetic (and a few other) figures of old

The next case focuses on prophetic figures of memory that were evoked through readings and rereadings of the Prophetic Book Collection (hereafter, PBC) or the DHC in the late Persian/early Hellenistic period and some common socio-anthropological characterizations of prophets. For instance, prophets are considered a type of "intermediary" between the deity and humans. This holds well for prophets in general and for the prophets of memory evoked by the literati's reading of the PBC, DHC, or Chronicles. The same holds true for the distinction between central and peripheral prophets, which is also at work within the world of memory of these literati.[11] In addition, the Elijah and Elisha of memory that were encoded in the book of Kings and whose memory was evoked through rereadings

---

10. See, for instance, N. Yoffee, *Myths of the Archaic State: Evolution of the Earliest Cities, States, and Civilizations* (Cambridge: Cambridge University Press, 2004), 91–100, and his comments about the construed and remembered dynastic cycle and the unification of China.

11. For instance, the Nathan of memory and the Isaiah of memory conform—in the main, in the case of Isaiah—to general matters present in central prophets, and the Elisha of memory to those of peripheral prophets. On central and peripheral prophets in this context, the foundational contribution has been R. Wilson, *Prophecy and Society in Ancient Israel* (Philadelphia, PA: Fortress, 1980). See, for example, how this distinction is used in

of the book clearly show some well-known shamanistic behaviors.[12] Likewise, there can be little doubt that the prophetic characters of memory were imagined, for the most past, as "spontaneous" diviners, that is, a class of diviners who do not need to use a particular form of learned technical knowledge, except in some cases trance-inducing techniques (see 2 Kgs 3:15; cf. 1 Sam. 10:5; 1 Chron. 25:1) and unlike "technical diviners" such as astronomers or priests using the ephod.[13]

When Lester Grabbe discussed and summarized a well-known case in which comparative anthropological studies substantially impacted research on prophecy in ancient Israel,[14] he stated:

> The prophetic persona of Handsome Lake has many parallels with those of the OT prophets. He had a divine call to preach to his people at a time of crisis in the community. . . . His message was not necessarily a popular one but called for repentance and a change of life on the part of hearers. . . . Several of his messages were received in visions, at least one seems to fit the characteristics of an apocalypse. . . . His message was a moral one.[15]

Everything cited above fits well the prophets of memory evoked through readings and rereadings of the PBC by the mentioned literati.[16] In fact, what he states in the text above seems to fit these prophets of memory much better than the average historical prophet of the monarchic period. For one, there is no reason to assume that the prophets of the monarchic period lived or spoke only or mainly at times

---

relation to Micah in P. Reddit, *Introduction to the Prophets* (Grand Rapids, MI: Eerdmans, 2008), 274–75.

12. See, for example, T. Overholt, *Cultural Anthropology and the Old Testament* (Minneapolis, MN: Fortress, 1996), 24–68. Grabbe elsewhere draws on social sciences models of prophecy when he compares the prophets populating the texts of the Hebrew Bible ("the Israelite prophet") and Joseph Smith, the Latter-Day Saints' prophet. See L. Grabbe, "Joseph Smith and the *Gestalt* of the Israelite Prophet," in *Ancient Israel. The Old Testament in Its Social Context*, ed. P. Esler (Minneapolis, MN: Fortress, 2006), 111–27.

13. Cf. J. Stokl, *Prophecy in the Ancient Near East: A Philological and Sociological Comparison* (Culture and History of the Ancient Near East, 56; Leiden/Boston, MA: Brill, 2012), 9–10.

14. See, for example, T. Overholt, "Prophecy: The Problem of Cross-Cultural Comparison," *Semeia* 21 (1982), 55–78 and T. Overholt, *Channels of Prophecy: The Social Dynamics of Prophetic Activity* (Minneapolis, MN: Fortress, 1989).

15. L. Grabbe, *Priests, Prophets, Diviners, Sages: A Socio-Historical Study of Religious Specialists in Ancient Israel* (Valley Forge, PA: Trinity Press International, 1995), 97.

16. It is worth noting that Grabbe himself refers to them as the "OT prophets" rather than as "ancient Israel prophets" in the text cited above. This said, there are also plenty of prophets (נביא) portrayed in texts of the Hebrew Bible and whose memory was shaped and communicated through the literati's reading and rereading of the respective books and texts that do not fit well with Grabbe's description. See below.

of crisis, nor that they mainly called the people to repentance and were unpopular because of that. Moreover, one has to keep in mind that the topos of the rejected prophet is also a variant of the "one against the many" topos (and cf. Micaiah, Elijah, to a significant extent, Jeremiah). This ideological and literary topos often serves legitimization purposes.

Legitimation may also occur through vision narratives. There is no denying that some flesh and blood prophets may indeed have experienced visions/dreams in the ancient Near East (including, of course, ancient Israel), but the prophets whose visions are always reliable and uncontestable are those (archetypal) characters populating the memory landscape of the literati who read the relevant texts within the context of their authoritative repertoire.[17] The visions here serve to legitimize the (literary and memory-world) messenger, but above all, the message that such a messenger conveys. Memories of these visions play important roles as sites of memory by themselves and their contribution to the memory landscape and to the social mindscape of the group was to socialize it to some "godly" messages.

In addition, Grabbe and others tend to focus on the images of prophets construed in the PBC. As mentioned earlier, there are plenty of prophets (נביא) portrayed in texts of the Hebrew Bible, written memories about which were shaped and communicated through the literati's reading and rereading, who do not fit well with Grabbe's description (e.g., Gen. 20:7; Exod. 15:20; Num. 11:24-29; Deut. 13:2-6; 1 Sam. 9:9; 10:10-13; 22:5; 1 Kgs 14:1-18; Isa. 3:2; Mic. 3:5; Lam. 2:14; 1 Chron. 25:1 and notice also the way in which these literati remembered, e.g., Ahab's prophets [except Micaiah], Elisha, Hulda, Hananiah, the son of Azzur, and so on; cf. the later Noadiah).

In addition, the emphasis on prophets who are not listened to by their contemporaries is indisputably present in the PBC but is just one "voice" among others in Chronicles. In fact, the memory of the monarchic past encoded and communicated by Chronicles includes many prophetic voices that were listened to.[18]

To be sure, one may argue that this memory is not necessarily reliable for reconstructing the historical circumstances in the kingdom of Judah. But the books in the PBC are much later than the putative time of the prophet and represent the outcome of a very lengthy compositional and redactional process, which is impossible to track with any certitude. Further, the characterizations of the monarchic-period prophets in the PBC sets them apart from much of what we know of other prophets in the ancient Near East,[19] a fact that cannot but raise

---

17. This is so, because the literati construed and remembered the implied authors and narrators of texts within their core repertoire as reliable characters.

18. See E. Ben Zvi, "Chronicles and its Reshaping of Memories of Monarchic Period Prophets: Some Observations," in *Prophets, Prophecy, and Ancient Israelite Historiography*, eds. M. Boda and L. Wray Beal (Winona Lake, IN: Eisenbrauns, 2013), 167–88.

19. Cf. M. Nissinen, *Ancient Prophecy: Near Eastern, Greek, and Biblical Perspectives* (Oxford: Oxford University Press, 2017), esp. 189–216.

questions about the "historicity" of their portrayal. These kinds of concerns are not restricted to the PBC. For instance, the Elijah and Elisha narratives, at least in their present form, should be dated to the Persian period. And few scholars would consider literary personages Nathan or Samuel, as characterized in Kings and Samuel respectively, to be reliable guides for the reconstruction of historical prophets at the time of the formation of the Iron Age kingdoms of Israel and Judah.

It is not surprising therefore, that as in the case of state (and chiefdom) formation, one of the main critiques raised against colleagues who use "social sciences" models for historical studies of monarchic-period prophets is that they root their analysis on an assumed "historicity" of, in most cases, the characterization of prophets in the PBC, and less frequently on selected characterizations of particular prophets in the DHC (e.g., Samuel, Nathan, Elijah, Elisha).

One might argue that such a critique may be addressed, even if one were to accept at least some of the concerns about the reliability of these characterizations for the purpose of reconstructing historical prophets in their putative periods, by maintaining that these characterizations were rooted in well-known aspects of realia from ancient times, even if these characterizations were indeed the outcome of long editorial processes and were informed by the eventual circumstances of the readership of the relevant books, as they emerged in their final compositional versions.

The same type of response may be advanced against critiques of using socio-anthropological analysis for characters that clearly existed in literary and memory worlds such as Qohelet.[20] In other words, one might claim that even if Qohelet is a character in the book, his characterization and the related memory evoked by reading the book are deeply rooted in the actual realia of a sage or sages.

For the present purposes, it is crucial to note that within this framework, it is only to be expected that the worlds portrayed in these books would include social roles, agents, and processes that fit corresponding, in type, socio-anthropological models and concepts. This is so, because within this argument (a) models and concepts "work" in the "actual" world, (b) since the world of memory encoded in the relevant texts is mimetically rooted in the former, therefore (c) these models and concepts must "work" on the world of memory evoked by reading the relevant texts.

The problem with this approach is that social memory rarely mimetically reflects the "actual" world. Communities do not remember events and characters in particular ways only or even mainly because they just "happened" that way. This is so because the shaping of social memories involves, inter alia, ongoing processes of selection, remembering and forgetting, attaching significance by plotting characters and events in larger (implicit or explicit) core narratives or metanarratives, and creatively developing sites of memory and their own network of connections.

---

20. Cf. M. Sneed, *The Politics of Pessimism in Ecclesiastes: A Social-Science Perspective* (SBLAIL, 12; Atlanta, GA: SBL, 2012).

Moreover, socially constructing and remembering what "happened" always brings the present of the community to bear and by necessity the use of social-ideological lenses that draw attention to some matters and away from others and thus, not surprisingly, the past is always the presently remembered past. In addition, as is well known, transculturally communities may, did, and continue to, construe, remember, and celebrate past events, personages, and circumstances that "historically" never happened. There is plenty of historical evidence for these social processes. A simple cross-cultural case one may mention in this context is the Passover story told and retold every year.

In addition, and using again the example of prophets, the comprehensive world of memory shared by the literati who read and reread their entire corpus of authoritative books included a general construction of what a prophet is that emerged strongly informed by the PBC, but which stood in sharp contrast with general conceptualizations of prophets in the ancient Near East and in other memories held by the literati (compare and contrast the PBC prophets as a whole with those in Chronicles or in the DHC [e.g., a prophet like Joel with Hulda, or the singer prophets in Chronicles]), or for that matter Neo-Assyrian and Mari prophets, and notice, inter alia, that many of the prophecies of the PBC prophets tend to focus on a utopian, far away future of "the people," their characters are encoded in a particular and unique literary genre, "the ancient Israelite prophetic book," and their words are expressed in such a matter that contain signposts to words appearing in other sections of the book associated with them, and other texts within the core corpus of texts of the literati.[21]

It is worth noting also that the vast range of prophetic characters populating the comprehensive memory-scape of the community is far more diverse and chaotic than the often narrow sets of collections of texts at the center of many social-scientific studies. However, the mentioned models work well within the particular worlds of memory evoked by each of these sets.

To be sure, one may argue that this is just because people imagine worlds on the basis of what they know and that "naturally" they would construe prophets as diviners and so on. Although there is an element of truth in this argument (see above), this is certainly not the entire story.

For one, in the world of the relevant literati prophets could be imagined as singers (see 1 Chron. 25:1-8) or individuals who recorded (and interpreted) monarchic history (see 1 Chron. 29:30; 2 Chron. 9:29; 12:15; 13:22; 23:32; 33:19), and conversely books consisting of historical (royal) record included prophetic texts (2 Chron. 20:34; 32:32; 33:18).[22] None of the above is necessarily the most common role of the prophets from a socio-anthropological perspective or transculturally.

---

21. Cf. Nissinen, *Ancient Prophecy*.

22. See Ben Zvi, "Chronicles and Its Reshaping of Memories of Monarchic Period Prophets."

In addition, at times the prophets of memory were imagined in even more significant ways unlike those of actual monarchic polities, such as when remembering them as focusing much of their message on an ideal future set at a fully indeterminate period well beyond the period of the relevant king, or in ways that strongly communicate a "historically blurred," vague, and potential "trans-historical" context.[23] Most significantly, in all these aspects, many of the prophets included in Chronicles but absent from the DHC (e.g., Shemaiah, Azariah, the son of Oded, Jahaziel, the son of Zechariah, Oded) and whose prophecies and, thus, their portrayals in the book are considered to be unreliable sources for historical reconstructions of the monarchic period, with good reason, fit much better with the usual models or roles of a prophet than many of the prophets in the PBC. In other words, worlds of memory may or may not conform with social-anthropological expectations about prophets in ancient Near Eastern societies and the distinction between one case and the other is not grounded on matters of historicity or lack thereof.

In addition, it is worth keeping in mind that prophetic characters were never imagined as standing alone, but rather as part of a closely interrelated system that included many other figures of memory (e.g., kings, "the people"). As in all systems, grammars of preference shaping the memories associated with some members could not but impact the way in which others were remembered. These systemic considerations constrain the ways in which prophets may or may not be remembered in particular cases, narratives and general metanarratives.[24] In none of these cases, the constraints are based on adherence to "historicity" in our contemporary terms.

The case of memory agents and transfer of social roles across time

This case relates to the social role of "memory agents." Such agents are at work in any social group.[25] The literati who composed, edited, read, and reread texts belonging to their authoritative repertoire clearly served the social roles of actual, historical "memory agents" in their societies. But, for reasons that deserve a separate discussion, they construed themselves as not worthy of being remembered and

---

23. See E. Ben Zvi, "Balancing Shades of 'Historical', 'Historically-blurred', and 'Trans-historical' Contexts and Temporal Contingency in Late Persian/Early Hellenistic Yehudite Memories of YHWH's Words and Prophets of Old in the Prophetic Book Collection and its Subcollections," forthcoming in a collected essays volume to be published by Mohr.

24. See E. Ben Zvi, "Memories of Kings of Israel and Judah within the Mnemonic Landscape of the Literati of the Late Persian/early Hellenistic Period: Exploratory Considerations," forthcoming in *SJOT* 33 (2019), 1–14.

25. Cf. "reputation entrepreneurs" in the works of the influential sociologist Gary Alan Fine. See, for example, G. Fine, *Sticky Reputations: The Politics of Collective Memory in Midcentury America* (New York: Routledge, 2012).

erased themselves, as it were, from their own texts.[26] These texts, however, evoked and construed social memories of characters of old that were worth remembering as those explicitly and saliently fulfilling the social role of "memory agents" for both their putative world and that of the literati.

One finds them, most obviously, as the speakers proclaiming purported historical, social memory résumés (e.g., Joshua 24; 1 Samuel 12; Ezekiel 20; Psalms 105, 106; Nehemiah 9).[27] In this context, it is worth mentioning also the numerous related calls to remember the past in particular ways that existed within the world of memory of the literati and which were encoded in texts such as Deut. 6:20-25; 26:5-9. In all these instances, remembered, but not-historical (in the professional sense) characters served, at least on the surface, the necessary role of socially authoritative "memory agents," and were accepted by the community as such.

The case of expelled wives and children

Whereas the previous example refers to social roles in two worlds, this one deals with processes of social causation at work in non-historical, mnemonic worlds. Elsewhere I joined several other scholars in the field and raised major concerns about the "historicity" of the narrative of the expulsion of foreign wives and children reported in Ezra 9–10. I argued that in some circles such a mnemonic narrative served to remember and explore seemingly utopian circumstances, as per the understanding of the group, as well as the limitations of that utopia.[28] This said, since what is at stake in the story concerns matters of social identity and both boundary markers and *makers*, and particularly in times envisioned as "crisis time," it is not a surprise that the underlying sociopolitical process in the world of the text, taken more or less literally, have been explained productively in terms of a number of socio-anthropological models, many of which may actually complement each other.[29]

Moreover, these explanations are usually supported not by the text of Ezra 9–10, per se, but by the world evoked by their co-texts, that is, when Ezra 9–10 is read in the context of Ezra-Nehemiah. Since both Ezra 9–10 and Ezra-Nehemiah represent a closing stage of a long and complicated compositional and redactional textual process, one may correctly argue that the process led, in a way

26. The situation changes dramatically by the time of Ben Sira.
27. On these see, for example, C. Newsom, "Rhyme and Reason: The Historical Résumé in Israelite and Early Jewish Thought," in *Israel's Prophets and Israel's Past: Essays on the Relationship of Prophetic Texts and Israelite History in Honor of John H. Hayes*, eds. B. Kelle and M. Moore (LHBOTS 446; London; New York: T&T Clark: 2006), 293–310.
28. On all these issues, see E. Ben Zvi, "Re-negotiating a Putative Utopia and the Stories of the Rejection of the Foreign Wives in Ezra-Nehemiah," in *Worlds That Could Not Be: Utopia in Chronicles, Ezra and Nehemiah*, eds. S. Schweitzer and F. Uhlenbruch (LHBOTS, 620; London: Bloomsbury T&T Clark, 2016), 105–28.
29. For a summary of many of these approaches, see Ben Zvi, "Re-negotiating," 105–10.

unbeknownst to those involved, to a final text and memory world that fits well with certain transcultural social processes that can be modeled and explained through the mentioned socio-anthropological models. In other words, the outcome of the generative grammar governing the redactional processes was a text and a socially shared memory that is explainable by socio-anthropological approaches, despite its lack of "historicity."

The case of a supposed split in the inner group

As I discussed elsewhere, the Pentateuch encodes and communicates the foundational, "national" collective memory of two historical groups that saw themselves as "Israel," and which participated in shaping the collection, namely Yehudites and Samarians. Usually, in cases of two groups that construe themselves as sharing a common past, the existence of the two groups is explained and remembered as the outcome of a split in an original group. Often in such instances, the post-split groups tend to claim that they (but not the other) represent the proper continuation of the pre-split group and frequently—though not always— express a hope for a future re-unification, in which the "wrong" side will recant and be re-incorporated into the "proper" group.[30]

The story of the Pentateuch and, one may say with some reason, the entire Hebrew Bible, and later related literature informed by books and texts included in these collections fit extremely well into this model. Israel was one and split up. Each side blames the other, and often delegitimizes its claims and post-split memories. Expressions of hope for a future re-unification appear and are usually construed as narratives of appropriation, in which one side adopts finally the "proper" path, that is, the path that characterizes one of the two groups, but not the other. There are good historical and socio-anthropological (including social memory) reasons for the wide distribution of these models.

---

30. I discussed this in E. Ben Zvi, "The Pentateuch as/and Social Memory of 'Israel' in the Late Persian Period," in *The Oxford Handbook of the Pentateuch*, eds. J. Baden and C. Nihan (forthcoming, 2019). Examples of the mentioned strong tendencies include the case of Christianity and Judaism sharing the Old Testament/Miqra as a collection embodying the memory of Israel, and despite all their differences, Western and Eastern Germany, North and South Vietnam; North and South Korea. See also the dispute over who is "true" to the (American) Constitution in the process leading to, and even during the American Civil War (cf., e.g., M. Kammen, *A Machine That Would Go of Itself: The Constitution in American Culture* [New Brunswick, NJ: Transaction Publishers, 2006], esp. 95–124). Comparable examples of splits within political parties are myriad and well attested in Europe. The identity, character, and even historical context of the players may be widely different, but the grammars of preference for construing and remembering the foundational events that led to a situation of two groups sharing a past and the usual hopes of unification, identity fears, and the associated processes of "otherization" tend to appear in the vast majority of these cases.

However, the "biblical" main narrative is of an "all Israel" that consisted of the twelve tribes, was together in Egypt, then experienced the Exodus and revelation during its wanders in the desert, and then entered to/conquered the land under Joshua, and so on. This story and the memory of such unified Israel that only eventually split into two, following the end of Solomon's reign over "all Israel," do not reflect history.

In this case, the social memory of "Israel" as agreed upon by the group fits well into transcultural, socio-anthropological models and expectations, but the historical reality as reconstructed by professional historians does not at all. The "all Israel" of the Pentateuch (and other "biblical" texts) is not the result of one unified group that eventually split, but to the contrary, of two groups that under circumstances that cannot be discussed here, eventually grew to understand themselves as one, with a shared memory about themselves and their foundational events.

The point I wish to advance here is that the eventual main narrative of "Israel" about itself and its origins in the Pentateuch fits very well with what one would anticipate from socio-anthropological models and concepts, yet it is non-historical. These models and concepts work here only in a world of imagination and memory.

A later but illustrative case about the role of language in social identity strategies

The last example comes for a later period. As is well known, selective use of language plays an important role in identity strategies. Examples abound and come from various periods and areas of the world. Given the context here, it is worth noting that Diana Edelman has recently explored this matter, from a strong historical perspective, in relation to the early second Temple period.[31]

That said, I would like to draw attention to a rabbinic tradition embodied in Leviticus Rab. 32.5 (and in Song Rab. 4.25), according to which Israel was redeemed from Egypt because they maintained four things. Two of these directly address this issue, namely "language" and "names,"[32] the latter being directly related to the former. I doubt there are many professional historians of ancient Israel who would accept the "historicity" of this mnemonic narrative, but it certainly works well within the parameters of accepted socio-linguistic approaches and their bearings on matters of social identity and of strategies of producing and socially reproducing identity by minority groups across time and space.[33]

---

31. D. Edelman, "Identities within a Central and Peripheral Perspective: The Use of Aramaic in the Hebrew Bible," in *Centres and Peripheries in the Early Second Temple Period*, eds. E. Ben Zvi and C. Levin (FAT, 108; Tübingen: Mohr-Siebeck, 2016), 109–31.

32. The other two are "gossip" and "licentious" sexual behavior. A discussion of why these two were also included is beyond the scope of this contribution, as much as is of interest in itself.

33. Language distinctiveness is often a key marker of social identity (see the importance of speaking Greek in the Hellenistic world), both for insiders and outsiders. In general,

Implications and further research

The preceding examples may be easily multiplied.[34] Paraphrasing Qohelet, there is no end to examples, and the multiplications of examples is a weariness of the flesh. I am certainly not interested in wearing out the reader. I hope that the examples above suffice to make the point that socio-anthropological or social-scientific models and concepts may work not only for "historical" worlds, but also for worlds of imagination and memory. Moreover, given that socio-anthropological models require, by necessity, process simplification, at times they may work better in worlds of memory than in "historical" worlds. Historical worlds are always chaotic, whereas the models tend not to be. Remembered worlds are often less chaotic than "real" worlds, due to cognitive reasons, and therefore may provide a better playground for the aforementioned models to work. The same holds true in terms of a reduction in the number of agents and their interactions.

This being so, and given our focus on ancient Israel, what are the implications and potential paths for future research that emerge from these considerations in terms of the use of "social-scientific" approaches in our field? The following remarks are meant to open a wide discussion on these matters.[35]

(a) The historicity in the sense of "mimetic external referentiality" of narratives about the past cannot be proven by arguing that the processes and events that it portrays fit with general explanatory models and expectations derived from cross-cultural, socio-anthropologic studies.

(b) Conversely, claiming that the historical prophets of the monarchic period were not as portrayed in the PBC, or that the process of state formation in Israel and Judah did not proceed as described in Samuel (and Kings), or that Israel was not historically a unified group that split into two does not require that we abandon socio-anthropological models and concepts. In fact, we may find much of interest in the work of scholars who used social-scientific models a generation ago.

---

it is usually agreed that the ability to maintain heritage languages in minority contexts contributes to the development of a strong sense of group identity and boundaries, and that the latter, in turn, contribute much to the ability to maintain the heritage language, and thus shaping a positive feedback loop. Edelman writes, reflecting a long tradition in scholarship, "language is often a marker of group identity ... language is one means by which group identity is often defined and expressed. . . . It cements solidarity among members by eliciting feelings of belonging, appreciation and attraction." See Edelman, "Identities within a Central and Peripheral Perspective," 110–11.

34. For instance, one may discuss the choice of Jerusalem as the city located in a peripheral space or cognitive dissonance in the prophets of memory and their putative worlds.

35. The oral presentation out of which this contribution emerged was given in a forum about the future of social-scientific approaches in our field.

(c) These models and expectations have indeed much to contribute to the study of mnemonic narratives and the imaginary worlds of memory that they construe, even when they are devoid of "historicity."

(d) As mentioned above, and given that theoretical modelling is by inner necessity a simplifying process, the mnemonic narratives, which by themselves, tend to simplify complex events and processes so as to make them memorable and reduce the associated cognitive costs, might resemble these models more than historical events/processes as professional historians are able to reconstruct them (e.g., less chaos, fewer characters, and so on).[36] Further, whereas memories evoked within particular contexts and through the reading and rereading of certain books or sections thereof may activate worlds of memory in which certain models work well, memories evoked in other contexts and through the reading and rereading of other books or passages may activate other worlds of memory, in which this does not hold true.

(e) The previous consideration raises the issue of how the comprehensive social memory of a group, which includes all these worlds of memory, balances these worlds and how socio-anthropological models and concepts may heuristically help us to imagine and construct these balancing processes.

(f) Imagination has its limits. The world of knowledge of those shaping imaginary worlds is to a significant extent constrained by their own world of knowledge, social mindscape, and of course, social memory. This means both that (i) "realities" in the present past of the remembering group influence their construed worlds of memory, though in a highly mediated way, namely via its reflections in memory, including, and in some cases mainly via, shaping and evoking memory texts, either oral or written and (ii) all other sociocultural "realities," and matters of social location and ideology in the present also influence their construed worlds of memory. Both (i) and (ii) may serve as mechanisms through which models from the social sciences that might have worked in these "realities" are transferred, at least partially, to the community's world of memory.[37]

---

36. From a different perspective, one may approach these matters from the perspective of the difference between "history" and "historical narrative." To address this perspective in this context requires a full discussion on historical methodology and on the relation between social memory and professionally written historical narratives, which cannot be carried out here. For my own position on some of these issues, see E. Ben Zvi, "Clio Today and Ancient Israelite History: Some Thoughts and Observations at the Closing Session of The European Seminar for Historical Methodology," in *"Even God Cannot Change the Past": Reflections on 16 Years of the European Seminar in Historical Methodology*, ed. L. L. Grabbe (LHBOTS, 663, London: Bloomsbury T&T Clark, 2018), 20–49.

37. Cf. the case of the Book of Mormon and notice the role of the present past of the community in which the book emerged (i.e., their "biblical past") contributed to the shaping

(g) Within the social mindscape of the group, there exist underlying generative grammars of preference or dis-preference for social production and reproduction of narratives about the past, including both matters related to basic features of plots and, inter alia, underlying, implicit rules concerning basic expectations and conceptualizations of causality and the potential ways in which the latter may be instantiated. When the community shaping its world of memory implicitly, likely in ways unbeknownst to them, internalized expectations that we today relate directly or indirectly with those to which social-anthropological approaches lead us, the latter are likely to, in one way or another, be understood as "at work" in the world of memory of the group, even if they never formulated them. The literati followed some transcultural models we have now about how certain social and political processes and roles tend to develop. It seems that in these cases our socio-anthropological models represented, at the very least, an approximation of the "natural" order, that is, "the way things are/work out" from the perspective of the literati, and thus, by shaping their memories accordingly, they increased the memories' verisimilitude within their ideological discourse, world of knowledge, and social mindscape.

(h) The "natural" rules of the world may well be transparent to the literati. There is a need for socio-anthropological studies that emphasize that which was transparent in their social mindscape and how it influenced the worlds of memory.

(i) The community imagining and remembering a past and past characters and processes must be able to feel connected with, and emotionally care about the past world they are creating in their own present; it must be able to "engage" as it were and this requires that which is "natural" and thus "invisible" in their world to be so in the other. The outcome is the creation of a partially shared realm either conveying a sense of underlying continuity or, at the very least, shaping a conceptually in-between area in which the same basic rules apply. In other words, it requires the construction of sites of memory that serve as transtemporal bridges. Through this process the imagined, remembered past may be influenced by the interpretive framework of social models and roles at work in the present of the literati, as it imagines itself, and vice versa.

(j) Social memories are most often shaped as explicit or implicit narratives. The mnemonic narratives of a group (including their characters and plots) do not exist in silos, but informed each other, and all together create a system or world of memory, which by necessity is also an imaginary, literary (in the widest sense of the term) world. This being so, cross-cultural and cognitive studies on (a) (imaginary) world shaping, (b) the ways in which they serve necessary social roles, as social memories in ancient Israel, providing

of other memories of their (later) past, and eventual future, and how both were associated with the identity, location, and ideology of the group.

playgrounds on which members of the group may safely explore various ideas and (c) the ways in which texts may induce readers to care about characters that are a product of social imagination. All the above types of studies may make an important heuristic contribution to the study of the intellectual world of ancient Israel, even if these studies are focused on contemporary societies and their sociocultural production.[38]

Instead of a conclusion

In sum, there is much work before us. Socio-anthropological approaches are as needed now as they were one or two generations ago for studies of ancient Israel. This said, a wider focus is also needed. Conversations as the one I hope to initiate with this contribution represent a step in that direction.

---

38. For example, M. Wolf, *Building Imaginary Worlds: The Theory and History of Subcreation* (Routledge: New York, 2012); I. Jaén and J. Simon, eds. *Cognitive Literary Studies Current Themes and New Directions* (Austin: University of Texas Press, 2012); B. Vermeule, *Why Do We Care about Literary Characters?* (Baltimore, MD: John Hopkins University Press, 2010).

Chapter 3

THE ASSASSINATION OF AMON AND THE CRISIS OF ASSYRIAN IMPERIALISM

Bradley L. Crowell

The Deuteronomistic Historian (Dtr) lodges the account of the brief reign of Amon son of Manasseh between two of his history's most elaborate narratives. After his condemnation of what Dtr portrays as Judah's "most evil king," Manasseh (2 Kgs 21:1-18), and before his lengthy and effusive praise of what he portrays as Judah's "most righteous monarch," Josiah (2 Kgs 22:1–23:30), Dtr inserts the short story of the assassination of Amon, who was killed after only two years on the throne (2 Kgs 21:19-26).

It is curious that historians and biblical scholars have seemingly neglected the story of Amon and his rapid demise at the hands of his anonymous "servants." For some of them, Amon is considered "biblically insignificant," an "insignificant appendix," a "relatively unimportant footnote," or perhaps simply "unlucky" to have lived between Dtr's "great reformer," Josiah, and his "great counter-reformer," Manasseh.[1] Except for a brief 1953 article by Abraham Malamat, the majority of scholarship that discusses this narrative is focused on the enigmatic "people of the land" who killed the conspirators and installed Amon's son Josiah on the throne.[2]

Rather than overlooking it, I maintain that the brief narrative interlude of Amon's reign provides important insights into social and political conflicts fundamental to maintaining social order under imperial rule, specifically in

---

1. Cf. C. Begg, "Jotham and Amon: Two Minor Kings of Judah According to Josephus," *Bulletin for Biblical Research* 6 (1996), 2; G. Hens-Piazza, *1-2 Kings* (Nashville, TN: Abingdon Press, 2006), 378; I. W. Provan, *1 and 2 Kings* (NIBC; Peabody, MA: Hendrickson Publishers, 1995), 267–68; H. Spiekermann, *Juda unter Assur in der Sargonidenzeit* (Göttingen: Vandenhoeck & Ruprecht, 1982), 161.

2. Cf. E. Nicholson, "The Meaning of the Expression *'am hā'āreṣ* in the Old Testament," *JSS* 10 (1965), 59–66; L. S. Fried, "The *'am hā'āreṣ* in Ezra 4: 4 and Persian Imperial Administration," in *Judah and the Judeans in the Persian Period*, eds. O. Lipschits and M. Oeming (Winona Lake, IN: Eisenbrauns 2006); J. T. Thames, "A New Discussion of the Meaning of the Phrase *'am hā'āreṣ* in the Hebrew Bible," *JBL* 130.1 (2011), 109–25.

this case the Assyrian imperial strategies of territorial control and hegemony.[3] Like other minor rulers subjected to the Assyrian empire, Amon fell victim to sectarianism and popular anger prevalent during the empire's decline during the last part of the seventh century BCE. As is typical of declining, overextended empires, the Assyrians refrained from engaging in the political activities of their marginal satellite polities and focused on strengthening their core, or center. Within that historical and political context, the assassination of Amon was not an isolated event in a marginal polity of the Assyrian empire; it was neither a religiously motivated killing to place the "divinely ordained" Josiah on the throne, as Dtr suggested in his History. The assassination of Amon was an event that was part of a larger pattern of reactions to imperial saturation and social fracturing that began under Manasseh—a pattern identified as an "imperial crisis" within the field of the sociology of empire.

The declining Assyrian empire and the increased power of both the Egyptians and Babylonians made the end of the seventh century BCE a time when some minor rulers grasped at opportunities for territorial expansion and increased prosperity, but the possibility that the competing regional powers would violently intervene to contain or eliminate those minor rulers was always present. The rulers of the small, minor satellite states in the southern Levant were forced to navigate between the Assyrian imperial demands for tribute and fealty, the coalition-building politics of neighboring states, and popular internal movements that supported either independence from or subordination to another regional or imperial power. In the small highland state of Judah, this political morass of demands led to a fractured and complex sociopolitical world marked by shifting loyalties and ideologies over, what Benedict Anderson terms generally, "the imagined community" upon which sociopolitical authorities are based.[4]

While Manasseh complied with Assyrian imperial demands, which lead to an extended period of relative peace and prosperity, the time of his reign was mirrored by turmoil in the Assyrian homeland. His 55-year reign (ca. 697–643 BCE) began during the rule of Esarhaddon (r. 681–669 BCE) and extended into the reign of his son Ashurbanipal (r. 668–627 BCE). Manasseh was mentioned positively in Assyrian inscriptions by both of these emperors: he contributed building material to Esarhaddon for the construction of his palace (Nineveh Prism A v 54; BM 121005; Leichy, RINAP 4.1, col. v 54), and he provided support to Ashurbanipal during his invasion of Egypt around 667 BCE (Rassam Cylinder C, I 24–45; BM 091026; Luckenbill 1927 §793–840). But during the later reign of Ashurbanipal

---

3. B. J. Parker, "Power, Hegemony, and the Use of Force in the Neo-Assyrian Empire," in *Understanding Hegemonic Practices of the Early Assyrian Empire: Essays Dedicated to Frans Wiggermann*, ed. B. S. During (Leiden: Nederlands Instituut voor het Nabije Oosten, 2015), 287–97.

4. As discussed throughout B. Anderson, *Imagined Communities: Reflections on the Origin and Spread of Nationalism* (revised edition; London: Verso, 2006).

a series of rebellions around the empire exposed internal weaknesses within the sprawling empire. Tirhakah, the ruler of Egypt, who had only recently been pacified by the Assyrians, rebelled in 666 BCE prompting Ashurbanipal to undertake two additional campaigns to Egypt to defeat the rebels and solidify his rule there. Over the next decade, Ashurbanipal countered a rebellion in Tyre and fought to maintain control of Elam, Tabal, and Urartu. By 652 BCE, Ashurbanipal's brother, Shamash-shum-ukin, who Ashurbanipal placed in control of Babylon, was in open rebellion, taking control of Assyrian outposts and villages in his territory. Elam split into factions during the years 648 and 647 BCE leading to a civil war provoking another campaign by Ashurbanipal. The empire was still together in 643 BCE when Amon came to power, but it was fracturing and the benefits of the so-called *pax Assyriaca*, including the prosperity it promoted, were no longer assured.

Internally, Manasseh's pro-Assyrian stance met a vitriolic response from the religious innovators associated with the Yahweh-alone movement and the Deuteronomistically influenced prophets and priests who were prominent in Hezekiah's royal administration.[5] The stance of Hezekiah's religious advisors was opposed to cooperation with the empire, a position that had tragic results for Jerusalem and its environs under Hezekiah. During his reign, Manasseh isolated the influence of such religious advisors and permitted the more traditional worship of popular deities. With that seeming abandonment of Yahweh, he also cooperated with the Assyrian economy and politics. The conflict between the pro-Assyrian and anti-Assyrian factions close to the royal, and still Davidic, families led to larger conflicts in society. At the same time, the prosperity and growth of Judah during Manasseh's reign suggests that the majority of the people benefitted from those policies and kept the peace, whether or not they agreed with or even cared about Manasseh's political strategies.[6]

Amon came to power when he was twenty-two, after the death of Manasseh who was considered by the Deuteronomists to have been his father, although he could have been his grandfather since Amon was born when Manasseh was

---

5. See recently B. D. Thomas, *Hezekiah and the Compositional History of the Books of Kings* (FAT 2: 63; Tübingen: Mohr-Siebeck, 2014), 178–206.

6. The overall prosperity of the kingdom of Judah during the reign of Manasseh is well documented. See the important studies of I. Finkelstein, "The Archaeology of the Days of Manasseh," in *Scripture and Other Artifacts: Essays on the Bible and Archaeology in Honor of Philip J. King*, eds. P. J. King, M. D. Coogan, J. C. Exum, and L. E Stager (Louisville, KY: Westminster John Knox Press, 1994), 169–87; Y. Thareani-Sussely, "The 'Archaeology of the Days of Manasseh' Reconsidered in the Light of Evidence from the Beersheba Valley," *PEQ* 139.2 (2007), 69–77; W. S. Morrow, "Were There Neo-Assyrian Influences in Manasseh's Temple? Comparative Evidence from Tel-Miqne/Ekron," *CBQ* 75 (2013), 53–73; E. A. Knauf, "The Glorious Days of Manasseh," in *Good Kings and Bad Kings*, ed. L. L. Grabbe (JSOTSup 393; London: Bloomsbury, 2005), 164–88.

fifty-five years old (2 Kgs 21:19).⁷ The subtle Deuteronomistic agenda in the text focuses on his maternal lineage, tracing his legitimacy through his mother Meshullemeth to his grandfather Haruz of Jotbah, possibly to emphasize her connection with an Edomite territory (Num. 33:33-34; Deut. 10:7) or with a town in Galilee captured by Tiglath-pileser III in 732 ([Ia]-a-bi-te) and subsumed into the Assyrian province of Magidu.⁸

The bulk of the passage about Amon consists of typical Deuteronomistic phraseology: he did evil in Yahweh's view, walked in the way his father Manasseh had walked, served his idols, worshipped those idols, and abandoned Yahweh (2 Kgs 21:20-22). In the Deuteronomistic rhetoric of apostasy, Amon compares to the worst among kings of the north. For instance, the phrase "he did evil in the view of Yahweh" is a common Deuteronomistic phrase used to denigrate the kings of Israel (see 1 Kgs 15:26, 34; 16:25; 22:52; 2 Kgs 3:2; 13:2, 11; 14:24; 15:9, 18, 24, 28; 17:2) but only used to condemn two other kings of Judah: Jehoram (2 Kgs 8:18) who was misled by marrying the daughter of Ahab, and Manasseh (2 Kgs 21:2, 16), Amon's father, for whom the Deuteronomist reserved the most vitriolic rhetoric. Even within the standardized language of the Deuteronomistic judgments, Amon was deemed a continuation of his father's policies and agendas. The continuation of Manasseh's policies, the religious ones mentioned by the Deuteronomistic authors as well as the political ones that tied the fate of the Judean monarchy to that of Assyria, led to the brief episode in 2 Kgs 21:23-24—one that provides an important window into the political and social factions operating at the end of the seventh century BCE.

Amon was assassinated as a result of a conspiracy among his royal servants, with no description of the manner or process of the conspiracy or the means of assassination. Miller and Hayes catalog the possible reasons for the assassination: religious or cultic change, an internal palace coup instigated by one of Manasseh's older sons, or a nationalistic surge to throw off the yoke of Assyria.⁹ Eventually, the "people of the land," an enigmatic but not uncommon group, rejected the conspirators and, before the anonymous usurper could even take the throne, the people executed the rebels. Amon, along with his father Manasseh, was buried in a family tomb in the Garden of Uzza away from other kings of Judah.¹⁰ This short

---

7. W. B. Barrick, "Dynastic Politics, Priestly Succession, and Josiah's Eighth Year," *ZAW* 112 (2000), 565–66.

8. Ibid., 566–67; Na'aman ("Josiah and the Kingdom of Judah," *TA* 18 [1991], 27–28) favors locations in Idumea due to the prevailing *pax Assyriaca* during Manasseh's rule and the sparse habitation in the Galilee during this period.

9. J. M. Miller and J. H. Hayes, *A History of Ancient Israel and Judah* (Philadelphia, PA: Westminster John Knox Press, 1986), 376.

10. On the Garden of Uzza, see B. Becking, "The Enigmatic Garden of Uzza: A Religio-Historical Footnote to 2 Kings 21:18, 26," in *Berührungspunkte: studien zur sozial- und religionsgeschichte Israels, Festschrift für Rainer Albertz zu seinem 65. Geburtstag*, eds. I Kottsieper, R Schmitt, and J. Wohrle (AOAT 350; Munster, Ugarit-Verlag, 2008), 383–91;

narrative when read in light of recent sociological theory concerning the "crisis of imperialism" highlights some of the more common methods of constructing identity in response to conflict resulting from imperial overreach into the culture and political apparatus of the colonized territory. Applying theories such as that to the narrative in question helps locate it in the transition from the pro-Assyrian Judah to the rise of Josiah, the anti-Assyrian hero of the Deuteronomistic movement.

The assassination of Amon in biblical scholarship

The assassination of what the Deuteronomistic History deemed an "evil"—a categorization largely a product of political differences—king was not unprecedented. Politically motivated assassinations in Israel and Judah began shortly after the reign of Solomon (tenth century BCE) and the division of "Israel" into northern and southern kingdoms: Jehu killed Ahaziah and Jezebel (2 Kgs 9); Jehoash killed the illegitimate queen Athaliah (2 Kgs 11:1-16); and Jehoash was murdered by rebels (2 Kgs 12:21-22), who were then summarily executed by Amaziah (2 Kgs 14:5-6), who in turn was murdered by conspirators (2 Kgs 14:18-19). Yet Amon's assassination was unusual in that his death was not avenged by members of the royal family but by the people of the land. Most commentators, even recent ones, do not explain this text as anything more than a conspiracy against an evil king, in the tradition of Manasseh, which freed the throne for Amon's young son, Josiah.

Malamat was the first modern scholar to submit Amon's reign to a focused examination in his four-page discussion from 1953, in which he started by defining the account an "enigma."[11] Touching upon scholarly discussions of this episode, albeit brief discussions in larger histories of ancient Israel and Judah, he laid out the commonly accepted view of the early twentieth century: Amon was assassinated by the "Religious Reform Party" in response to his religious infidelities. The people reacted by attempting to restore the previous state of affairs that existed under Amon by installing his heir on the throne. Malamat's contribution to the scholarly views of his day, which largely presupposed the accuracy of the Deuteronomistic explanation, was to place this event within a political and military context, one that existed among the larger trends within the ancient Near East.

Malamat explicitly describes Amon's assassination as "an anti-Assyrian repercussion of his foreign policy,"[12] but he relied primarily on the Chronicler's

---

F. Stavrakopoulou, "Exploring the Garden of Uzzah: Death and Ideologies of Kingship," *Bib* 87 (2006), 1–21; J. Gray, "The Desert God 'Attr in the Literature and Religion of Canaan," *JNES* 8 (1949), 72–83.

11. A. Malamat, "The Historical Background of the Assassination of Amon, King of Judah," *IEJ* 3.1 (1953), 26.

12. Ibid.

expansions of the Deuteronomistic *Vorlage* to present Amon as a more ardent supporter of the Assyrian regime. According to 2 Chron. 33:22-23, Amon followed Manasseh in committing evil in the sight of Yahweh, but Amon also sacrificed to Manasseh's non-Yahwistic carved images, an indictment never levelled by the Deuteronomist. According to the Chronicler, what made the final judgment on Amon worse than Manasseh is that the son did not humble himself and repent as Manasseh had done, or at least according to the Chronicler's expansion of the Manasseh episode.[13] Malamat, however, did not explore the Chronicler's theological judgment, rather he placed the conspiracy against Amon within the context of the widespread Levantine rebellion against the imperial reign of Ashurbanipal, which he dated at 640–639 BCE. This revolt was defeated in typical Assyrian fashion with the defeat of the Arabian tribes near Damascus and the destruction of the Phoenician cities of Acre and Ushu (Akko and Tyre), whose inhabitants were either killed or exiled to the Assyrian homeland.

Malamat connected the conspiracy against Amon with that widespread rebellion against Ashurbanipal, pitting Amon's pro-Assyrian policy of supporting the Assyrian rule against the conspirators who wanted to side with many other Levantine states to break free from the imperial reign. For Malamat, this state of affairs continued until other political forces within Judah, such as embodied within the so-called people of the land, who Malamat calls "nobles," desired peace rather than confrontation with Assyria as it became increasingly clear that the western revolt against Ashurbanipal was failing. These "nobles" acquiesced to the empire by removing the anti-imperial rulers and replacing them with more compliant ones. As an example, Malamat cited the Arabian king Uayte (^{1}U-a-a-te), the son of Bir-Dada (K 2802 ii 3; Rm. Viii 2; ix 2), who was removed from the throne by his subjects to avoid reprisals,[14] though this is a difficult and problematic example of a popular rebellion followed by a substitute king.[15]

Malamat assessed the geopolitical maneuvers further by suggesting that it was "not improbable" that Egypt's initial attempts to annex Assyrian satellites in

---

13. See recently E. Ben Zvi, "Reading Chronicles and Reshaping the Memory of Manasseh," in *Chronicling the Chronicler: The Book of Chronicles and Early Second Temple Historiography*, eds. P. S. Evans and T. F. Williams (Winona Lake, IN: Eisenbrauns, 2013), 121–40; G. Knoppers, "Saint or Sinner? Manasseh in Chronicles," in *Rewriting Biblical History: Essays on Chronicles and Ben Sira in Honour of Pancratius C. Beentjes*, eds. J. Corley and H. van Grol (Berlin: De Gruyter, 2011), 223–25, emphasizes that the Chronicler's rendition of Amon is judged more harshly than Manasseh because he rejected the reforms that Manasseh instituted late in his life and reverted to his earlier non-Yawhistic life.

14. Malamat, "The Historical Background of the Assassination of Amon, King of Judah," 27.

15. S. Anthonioz, "Adummatu, Qedar and the Arab Question in Neo-Assyrian Sources," in *Duma 3: The 2012 Report of the Saudi-Italian-French Archaeological Mission at Dumat al-Jandal, Saudi Arabia*, eds. G. Charloux and R. Loreto (Riyadh: Saudi Supreme Commission for Tourism and Antiquities, 2015), 35–36.

the southern Levant was concurrent with the more widespread rebellion along the eastern Mediterranean basin.[16] These surreptitious Egyptian maneuvers are best known through the writings of Herodotus (Book 2, chapters 157–158) who states that the Egyptians began their siege on Ashdod of Philistia in 640–639 BCE. Malamat concludes with the note that the synchronism of events in Assyria, Egypt, and Judah provide proof of extensive military and political activity during the years 640–639 BCE in the southern Levant.

In the same year that Malamat's study placed the assassination of Amon within the context of imperial geopolitics, Frank M. Cross and David Noel Freedman published a brief article arguing that the "reform" of Josiah took place within a similar context, the internal political debates relating to Judah's relationship with the Assyrian imperial rulers. For Cross and Freedman, the "discovery" of the Deuteronomic Code in the temple wall in 622 BCE prompted a religiously inspired revolt to launch "a full-scale politico-religious program for the re-establishment of the Davidic kingdom." Thus, the finding of the legal codes and the initiation of the revolt appear to be more serendipitous than intentional.[17] Based on 2 Chron. 34:6, which narrates Josiah's military activity in the region of Samaria, they argue that the "reform" of Josiah was a revolt. They claim that by 628 BCE, Josiah and his anti-Assyrian supporters had taken control of the Assyrian provinces of Samaria, Gilead, and Galilee. To avoid immediate imperial reaction, they suggest, he did this within the "legal fiction of Assyrian control."[18] Cross and Freedman reinforced that these activities within ancient Judah were less about religious reforms, as the Deuteronomist frames them, than about political maneuvering within the context of the growing uncertainty caused by several shadow empires forming in Persia, Babylonia, and Egypt.

John Gray emphasized the potentially explosive situation in the southern Levant as Assyria was in decline in the region and Egypt was attempting to exert its influence, as suggested by Herodotus (Hist. 2:147-157) and possibly Jeremiah 2.[19] Gray, citing Herodotus, argued that Psammetichus was active in Ashdod during this time and the assassination plot against Amon was planned and executed by Egyptian agents. The "people of the land," in this scenario, referred to "free Israelite subjects" who opposed the pro-Egyptian factions in order to promote "national independence."

More recently, scholarship has focused on some of the more literary and less historical issues of this narrative. For example, Begg showed that Josephus arrived at a more elaborate story by supplementing his primary source text, the Deuteronomistic

---

16. Malamat, "The Historical Background of the Assassination of Amon, King of Judah," 29.

17. F. M. Cross, Jr. and D. N. Freedman, "Josiah's Revolt against Assyria," *JNES* 12.1 (1953), 56.

18. Ibid., 57.

19. J. Gray, *I & II Kings* (OTL; Philadelphia, PA: Westminster Press, 1963), 648.

History, with the longer Chronicles rendition.[20] Rudman focused on the name of Amon, connecting it to a theophoric reference to the Egyptian god Amon rather than connecting the name to the Hebrew root ʾmn "to establish, confirm."[21] For Rudman, Amon's father Manasseh encountered the name on campaigns to Egypt in support of the Assyrian emperor Ashurbanipal in the mid-seventh century BCE.

In his recent commentary, Sweeney connected the conspiracy against Amon to the economic conditions in the Judean countryside that resulted from the imperial reappropriation of land after the invasion of Sennacherib.[22] He tied the assassination to the revolts around the Assyrian empire, especially those in Babylon in 652–648 BCE and Elam in 642–639 BCE, both of which weakened the Assyrian presence at the western extremes. Regarding the revolt in Elam he states it "provided impetus for revolt on the part of the conspirators."[23] For Sweeney, the assassination seems to have been an anti-Assyrian plot with the goal of ending the tribute demands placed on the palace by the Assyrians. The "people of the land" responded quickly because the burden of providing tribute would have fallen primarily upon the rural population. They placed Amon's son Josiah, eight years old at the time, on the throne. Being that young, however, he would have complied with the guidance of the royal advisors, who sought to avoid Assyrian retaliation.

With the articles of Malamat and Cross and Freedman introduced into the general conversation, biblical scholars and historians have noted the reality of multiple possible motivations for Amon's assassination, as well as for the later violent purges of Josiah. This range of possible motivations emphasizes the internal dynastic politics of the Judean monarch instead of interactions between a marginal Judah and its overlord in the Assyrian imperial system. This study attempts to incorporate the events surrounding the assassination with the more general patterns of imperial domination, the "crisis" in subjugated polities caused by imperial saturation and societal fracturing, a situation that was exacerbated by the beginning of the decline of a major hegemonic and territorial empire.

Social and political dynamics of an imperial crisis

Over the past decade, sociologists have begun to rediscover a rich and vibrant tradition of sociological analysis of imperialism, empires, and colonialism.[24]

---

20. C. Begg, "Jotham and Amon: Two Minor Kings of Judah According to Josephus," 1–13.

21. D. Rudman, "A Note on the Personal Name Amon (2 Kings 21, 19–26 II 2 Chr 33, 21–25)," *Biblica* 81.3 (2000), 403–05.

22. M. A. Sweeney, *I & II Kings* (OTL; Louisville, KY: Westminster John Knox Press, 2007), 432–34.

23. Ibid., 433.

24. See, for instance, G. Steinmetz, "Empires, Imperial States, and Colonial Societies," in *Concise Encyclopedia of Comparative Sociology*, eds. M. Sasaki, J. Goldstone,

While this history of sociological involvement in empires and empire-building reveals the complicity of the academic field with the colonial enterprises of the early twentieth century, the research and analysis of sociological patterns and formations were insightful and important for the study of empires and their effects upon colonized and subjected peoples.[25] This sociological approach emphasizes the social, political, and institutional processes by which polities expand to become "imperial states" that extend beyond their borders to acquire resources, control neighboring states, and traffick labor and material for the benefit of the imperial state. Less well studied, but still an important area within the sociology of empires is how these imperial states decline and ultimately fail, the pattern of "hegemonic decline" whereby the "weary titan" slowly loses its ability to influence and hold sway over its once dominated territories.[26] As the empire weakens both internally and in its ability to project power outward, there is a dramatic increase of instability at the peripheries of the empire, especially those areas bordering powerful competing states, resulting in coups, assassinations, popular uprising, and dramatic electoral shifts.[27]

In an important 1936 article, Thurnwald discussed what he called the "crisis of imperialism," a moment in imperial decline that led to the rise of anti-colonial factions in colonial states in Africa.[28] The reason for this "crisis" was what he called the "overbearing insolence of the dominant stratum" which would invariably lead to the rise of anti-colonial factions that opposed not only the imperial system but also the generation of complicit local rulers.[29] Much of Thurnwald's discussion would be familiar to postcolonial critics; he highlights the hybrid African "intelligentsia" educated within colonial structures, the colonial discourse that encourages dependency, and the mimicry of the colonial power by the younger generations. For Thurnwald, the fracturing of the colonized society is a

---

E. Zimmermann, and S. K. Sanderson (Leiden: Brill, 2014), 58–74; G. Steinmetz, "Major Contributions to Sociological Theory and Research on Empire, 1830s–Present," in *Sociology & Empire: The Imperial Entanglements of a Discipline*, ed. G. Steinmetz (Durham, NC: Duke University Press, 2013), 1–50; J. Go, *Patterns of Empire: The British and American Empires, 1688 to the Present* (Cambridge: Cambridge University Press, 2011).

25. E. Kowal, "Sociology and Empire," *Postcolonial Studies* 17.4 (2014), 415–17; G. McLennan, "Complicity, Complexity, Historicism: Problems of Postcolonial Sociology," *Postcolonial Studies* 17.4 (2014), 451–64.

26. Go, *Patterns of Empire*, 167–68.

27. Ibid., 193–96.

28. R. C. Thurnwald, "The Crisis of Imperialism in East Africa and Elsewhere," *Social Forces* 15.1 (1936), 84–91.

29. For a brief biography of Thurnwald, see G. Steinmetz, "Neo-Bourdieusian Theory and the Question of Scientific Autonomy: German Sociologists and Empire, 1890s–1940s," *Political Power and Social Theory* 20 (2009), 100–08; G. Steinmetz, "Major Contributions to Sociological Theory and Research on Empire, 1830s–Present," 30–31; G. Steinmetz, "Empires Imperial States, and Colonial Societies," 65–66.

direct result of the colonial process of creating a new stratification of society, a new class of subjects, whereby the various trappings of colonial privilege—elite items, wealth, prestige, protection—are offered to what Thurnwald labels the "intelligentsia."[30] The "peasants" in this crisis-building situation are employed to produce the necessary surplus to meet imperial demands that then promotes the status of the "intelligensia" within the imperial system. This situation ultimately results in a saturation of imperial culture—symbols, wealth, power, ideology, religion—among the upper stratum of society, what could be termed "imperial overreach." Eventually the situation leads to the "imperial crisis" which could lead to rebellion, violence, protest, or even active and intentional under-production by those who labor to provide the surplus.

The "pattern" of hegemonic decline and the crisis of imperialism that is produced on the empire's periphery can provide a useful paradigm to understand the events within the parsimonious narrative of the assassination of Amon. The late seventh-century BCE crisis of imperialism likely began decades earlier in Judah and slowly built to the point that factions desired to make a dramatic change in political leadership. Manasseh's courting of Assyrian favor with its concomitant increase in wealth, prestige, and power for the political and religious elite, mostly centered in Jerusalem and its environs, resulted in the process that created a new stratification of Judean society, similar to the patterns observed by Thurnwald. This new structure of society spurned a rapidly increasing factionization into groups that supported the royal administration's pro-Assyrian policies, and likely benefited from them, and other groups that rejected the imperial presence and Judah's subservience to the empire.[31] This latter group likely was burdened with the worst of the imperial situation, including taxation, loss of independent decision-making, and intimidation by both pro-Assyrian royalty and Assyrian presence.

The "people of the land"

One of the more enigmatic aspects of this text, but one that goes to the heart of the issues of political factions, imperial subjugation, and the dynamics of social power during the demise of imperial occupation in marginal societies is the identity of the "people of the land," the *'am hā'āreṣ*. The identification of this group is fraught with vague references across the entire corpus of the Hebrew Bible without specific descriptions of who belongs to the group and even whether these references are to the same group. Were they identified as "foreigners," as some scholars suggest based on the reference in Ezra 4:1-5? That passage suggests that they were descendants

---

30. Thurnwald, "The Crisis of Imperialism," 88.
31. See B. Halpern, "Jerusalem and the Lineages in the Seventh Century BCE: Kinship and the Rise of Individual Moral Liability," in *Law and Ideology in Monarchic Israel*, eds. B. Halpern and D. W. Hobson (JSOTSup 124; Sheffield: JSOT Press, 1991), 11–107.

3. The Assassination of Amon and the Crisis of Assyrian Imperialism

of resettled captives by Esarhaddon of Assyria.³² Other scholars argue that the "people of the land" were the impoverished rural villagers, oppressed by both the colonial excess of the Assyrians and Babylonians. According to this scenario, the "people of the land" were the poor who remained in Judah while the elite were exiled to Babylon, only to be oppressed by the returning diaspora who no longer considered them part of "the purified Yehud."³³ Still others view the term as too vague and used in too many different contexts to be a precise sociological term, a generic "everyone" without particular precision.³⁴ To emphasize the difficulty of determining the referent for this vague phrase, some suggest that they were the "landed aristocracy of an area" who comprised the "class of free, landowning, full citizens of Judah."³⁵

When the phrase occurs in Deuteronomistic texts, the "people of the land" do have a certain amount of authority and power. It was this group who participated in a revolt against the usurper queen Athalia (2 Ks 11).

After the assassination of Amon, the "people of the land" intervened to end the rebellion, execute the usurpers, and placed King Josiah on the throne. Later, after Josiah was killed in battle against the Egyptians, it was the "people of the land" who choose and supported the next king (2 Kgs 23:30). It is clear that the ʿam hāʾāreṣ mentioned in these texts seem to have a particular vested interest in maintaining the status quo, often by defending the royal family against opposition or going to battle when the polity is under threat (2 Kgs 25:19). They do appear to have political and social power, though evidence to suggest that they are economically independent or "free" is difficult to identify, especially within the Deuteronomistic corpus.³⁶

This group, which appears in Deuteronomistic texts only after the division of Solomon's "United Monarchy," could also be understood as resulting from this process of imperial saturation and the subsequent societal fracturing. They appear to be a group that, at least within Deuteronomistic texts, benefited from the continuation of the status quo that was contingent upon imperial acquiescence and complicity. The "people of the land" appear to support "pro-Assyrian" policies and rulers. They may have developed a more vibrant membership during the economic "boom years" of Manasseh, an economic incentive that would have turned into a devastating loss if the Assyrian emperor and his armies returned yet again to the

---

32. See, for instance, H. Barstad, "After the 'Myth of the Empty Land': Major Challenges in the Study of Neo-Babylonian Judah," in *Judah and the Judeans in the Persian Period*, eds. O. Lipschits and J. Blenkinsopp (Winona Lake, IN: Eisenbrauns, 2003), 3–20.

33. L. L. Grabbe, *Ezra-Nehemiah* (London: Routledge, 1998), 138.

34. Nicholson, "The Meaning of the Expression ʿam hāʾāreṣ in the Old Testament," 59–66.

35. Fried, "The ʿam hāʾāreṣ in Ezra 4: 4 and Persian Imperial Administration," 125.

36. Cf. Thames, "A New Discussion of the Meaning of the Phrase ʿam hāʾāreṣ in the Hebrew Bible," 109–25.

Levant to reestablish their dominance due to the shifting loyalties of the small highland kingdom of Judah.

Ancient Near Eastern parallels

Royal assassinations were not unusual in the ancient world, particularly in areas with newly established monarchies or where the political order had been controlled by imperial machinations. The history of the Assyrian empire is replete with examples of imperial intervention in local affairs to guarantee compliance from kings who continued to rule in territories that were not deemed profitable or useful to annex entirely. These interventions were typically in response to local movements to replace a pro-Assyrian ruler, as was the case in the Amon episode. This was part of the Assyrian strategy of domination to continue to exploit the subjected polity's resources, labor, and territory for their purposes. This process also involved the fracturing of local politics into factions that either accepted Assyrian domination or rejected and attempted to subvert it. These factions are also major actors in the marginal territories of the empire that were not annexed as they assisted the empire in either maintaining control or disrupted the imperial status quo that the empire attempted to preserve through acquiescent kings and royal families.

The following sections contain a brief recounting of several episodes of imperial management of local political dynamics. These will help provide some insight into the methods of control and the construction of factions that formed as a result of Assyrian intervention. The following examples are not exhaustive but are meant to illustrate the political and social interaction between factional groups that resist their leaders' acquiescence to the imperial culture and the response by other groups to support the empire and attempt to reinstate the status quo. These examples are similar to the "imperial crisis" that facilitated the end of Amon's reign.

Menahem of Israel

In the middle of the eighth century BCE, the polity of Israel was subjected to a series of unstable reigns, some of which were very short in duration. Already the specter of Assyria influenced Israelite politics. Although not mentioned in the biblical text, Tiglath-pileser III (745–727 BCE) was campaigning at the time in northern Syria where he defeated the kingdom of Patina, capturing the city of Kunulua (modern Tell Tayinat).[37] He also quelled uprisings throughout the area including Urartu, Babylon, and Syria. While the Assyrians destroyed kingdoms that were distant from Israel, the royal drama that took place within the Northern Kingdom reflects not only local jockeying for power but different perspectives on

---

37. T. P. Harrison and J. F. Osborne, "Building XVI and the Neo-Assyrian Sacred Precinct at Tell Tayinat," *JCS* 64 (2012), 125–43.

the profitability of colluding with the empire. While there are no references to Zechariah, son of Jeroboam, or Shallum, son of Jabesh, in available Assyrian texts, the political maneuvers that they undertook according to the biblical text suggests an internal factional debate on the relationship of the kingdom to the empire.

There was a series of assassinations in Samaria. Zechariah, who continued the policies of his father Jeroboam, was likely an anti-Assyrian ruler, like his forefathers and even Jehu the founder of his dynasty. He was assassinated in public by Shallum, one of his generals (2 Kgs 15:10). After a reign of only one month, Shallum was assassinated in Samaria by another general of Zechariah, Menahem, who whether pro-Assyrian or not, acquiesced to the demands of tribute from Tiglath-pileser and avoided the potential destruction. Shortly after that round of assassinations in Samaria, the Assyrian emperor received tribute from seventeen rulers in the region, including Raḫiānu of Damascus, Menahem of Samaria and Queen Zabibe of the Arabian tribes (BM 124961, ll. 10b-12; Tadmor and Yamada 2011, text 14, pp. 44–47).[38] Heavy taxation was required to pay the tribute demanded by Tiglath-pileser, a requirement that Menahem fulfilled through heavy taxation of the wealthy in Samaria (2 Kgs 15:19-20). The requirement to pay a "heavy taxation" fomented subversion within Israel and an anti-Assyrian faction brought more assassinations and royal shifts to the already unstable kingdom. As a result, anti-Assyrian sentiments increased along with internal political dissension. Shortly after Menahem died and his son and successor Pekaiah came to power, Pekah, the chief royal armor bearer, killed the newly installed king and seized the throne in 735 BCE.[39] He immediately changed the pro-Assyrian policies of the former kings in Samaria and joined another anti-Assyrian coalition led by Raḫiānu of Damascus.

Hanunu of Gaza

Another parallel to a local factional rebellion in order to replace a pro-imperial king involved the case of Tiglath-pileser III campaigning in the area to ensure compliance with his rule, a campaign directed primarily against the Philistine king Hanunu who ruled from the city of Gaza. In 734 BCE, Hanunu fled to his ally Egypt and Gaza quickly succumbed to the Assyrians.[40] The Assyrians constructed garrisons to ensure continued acquiescence to the empire, making the area of Philistia into a trading station (*bit kari*) and dependent upon the empire. Hanunu was later reinstated by Tiglath-pileser. At the same time, the Assyrians removed the rebellious Israelite king Pekah who conspired with the coalition and replaced him with King Hosea

---

38. G. W. Ahlström, *The History of Ancient Palestine* (Minneapolis, MN: Fortress Press, 1993), 629–30.
39. Ibid., 632.
40. Summary Inscription 4, 8'-15'; H. Tadmor and S. Yamada, *The Royal Inscriptions of Tiglath-Pileser III (744-727 BC), and Shalmaneser V (726-722 BC), Kings of Assyria* (RINAP 1; Winona Lake, IN: Eisenbrauns, 2011), no. 42.

(^{m}a-ú-si-i) who would serve as the final king of Israel.[41] The leniency offered to Hanunu proved counterproductive for the empire. After the death of the emperor, Hanunu allied with Yau-bi'di of Hamath against Sargon in 721 BCE. The coalition was roundly defeated, Yau-bi'di was killed and Hanunu was deported to Assyria.

Azuri of Ashdod

Sargon later was forced to return to Philistia when Azuri, king in Ashdod, refused to pay tribute. In 711 BCE, according to Sargon's so-called Great Summary Inscription (Annals 29-30; Prunkinschrift 62-63) and the Sargon inscription from Tang-i Var, Azuri plotted with other kings to withhold tribute.[42] Azuri's conspiracy against Assyria was understood by the imperial administrators as twofold: first, he withheld the required tribute payments, thus assuaging the anti-Assyrian elements of his population and retaining the surplus collected for tribute within the royal coffers; and, second, Azuri was involved in a larger seditious plan to build a coalition of neighboring royal families in a rebellion against the Assyrian empire in response to its demands for tribute. This last was a far more deleterious program that could have severely diminished Assyria's influence in the southern Levant along the strategic but contested border with Egypt. From Sargon's summary inscription and biblical material, it appears that the young king of Judah, Hezekiah, also broke with the pro-Assyrian policies of his father Ahaz and joined the anti-Assyrian, and probably pro-Egyptian, coalition instigated by Azuri in 712 BCE. Furthermore, the smaller Transjordanian polities of Ammon, Moab, and Edom all joined Azuri's conspiracy as well as the Philistine cities of Gaza and Ekron. After suppressing the disruptive agitations in Babylon and Elam, Sargon marched against Azuri's coalition in his eleventh year.

Azuri of Ashdod and his coalition quickly relented and most of the complicit kingdoms avoided severe retaliatory punishment. The Assyrian response was to remove Azuri and replace him with his brother Ahi-miti, who proved to be more compliant to Assyrian rule. Assyria replaced the rebellious king with a more friendly, pro-Assyrian member of the royal family. Shortly after the compliant king was in office, however, the people of Ashdod engaged in a conspiracy to remove him. In a move reminiscent of the rebellion against Amon, they installed an anti-Assyrian ruler who was a leader of the rebellion but not a member of the royal family.[43] This new usurper, Yamani, once again approached rulers from Judah,

---

41. Summary Inscription 4, 17-18; Tadmor and Yamada, *The Royal Inscriptions of Tiglath-Pileser III (744-727 BC), and Shalmaneser V (726-722 BC), Kings of Assyria*, no. 42; cf. 2 Kgs 17:1-6.

42. For the Tang-I Var inscription, see D. Kahn, "The Inscription of Sargon II at Tang-I Var and the Chronology of Dynasty 25," *Or* 70.1 (2001), 1–18; G. Frame, "The Inscription of Sargon II at Tang-I Var," *Or* 68.1 (1999), 31–57.

43. L. Niesiolowski-Spano, *Goliath's Legacy: Philistines and Hebrews in Biblical Times* (Wiesbaden: Harrassowitz-Verlag, 2016), 21–22.

Moab, and Edom, leading to another response from the empire. Yamani, like Hanunu before him, fled to Egypt only to be returned in chains to the Assyrians as an act of goodwill between the empires.[44] Sargon resettled the cities of Ashdod, Gath, and Ekron, rebuilt them and then organized them under the auspices of a new province with a governor and permanent Assyrian presence.[45] Yamani might have been abandoned by his fellow agitators in Judah, Edom and Moab. Sargon II's inscriptions make no mention of any punitive action against them at this time. This theme of Assyrian interference, coups against compliant rulers, and installation of popular insurgents against the empire reflects a common social and political dynamic on the margins of hegemonic and territorial empires, one that reappears multiple times in the Assyrian annals as well as in the biblical narratives of the time.

The assassination of Amon and the crisis of Assyrian imperialism

The conspiracy against Amon in the late seventh century BCE is illustrative of the pattern of events that occur on the margins of failing empires. The violent overthrow of Amon was similar to other royal conspiracies on the margins of the Assyrian empire, where surveillance and imperial intelligence were less secure and retaliation could be severe but was rarely swift. The sociological analysis of the "crisis of imperialism" suggests that the subordinated rulers and their territories that were compliant with imperial demands began to become more and more saturated with imperial benefits like wealth and power which in turn initiated fractures within the subordinate society. In Judah, this process likely began under the rule of Manasseh whose acquiescence to the empire with the concomitant peace and prosperity would have begun to create more disparity within the social fabric of rural Judah, as well as urban Jerusalemites. The continuation of the policies of pro-Assyrian compliance under Amon, Manasseh's son, would have further divided the culture of Judah. With rebellions taking place around the empire during the early reign of Amon, the stage was set for an opposition faction, an important feature of times of crisis within imperial states, to mount a conspiracy and attempt to overthrow the pro-Assyrian king. But as the pattern of imperial crisis suggests, the societies that exist under imperial subjugation at the moment of crisis do not achieve universal support for one position or the other. In the assassination of Amon, it was another faction, the "people of the land" who likely desired to avoid the severe repercussions that would have occurred as a

---

44. Display Inscription of Room XIV, see D. Luckenbill, *Ancient Records of Assyria and Babylon. Volume 2: Historical Records of Assyria from Sargon to the End* (Chicago, IL: University of Chicago Press, 1927) §79; cf. Nineveh Prism A in Luckenbill, *Ancient Records of Assyria and Babylon*, §30, 62, 194.

45. Ahlström, *The History of Ancient Palestine*, 693.

result of the Assyrian response to the conspiracy, that quickly overwhelmed the conspirators.

The rebellion against the royal family of Judah and the assassination of the sitting king by a group of conspirators close to the royal house suggests that the overthrow of Amon was more than a collection of pro-Yahwistic zealots attempting to reinstate the worship of Yahweh alone after the long, idolatrous reign of Manasseh—a storyline that the Deuteronomists clearly supported. The scholarship within sociological research on imperialism and the groups that form under intense imperial pressure suggest that this event, and others throughout the Assyrian empire at the time, were a product of the saturation of imperial culture and the fracturing of society under compliant local rulers whose power, prestige, and wealth benefit from the imperial control.

Chapter 4

NEHEMIAH'S SOCIOECONOMIC REFORM: PRINCIPLES AND ACCOMPLISHMENTS

Kyong-Jin Lee

Now there was a great outcry of the people and of their wives against their Jewish kin. For there were those who said, "With our sons and our daughters, we are many; we must get grain, so that we may eat and stay alive." There were also those who said, "We are having to pledge our fields, our vineyards, and our houses in order to get grain during the famine." And there were those who said, "We are having to borrow money on our fields and vineyards to pay the king's tax. Now our flesh is the same as that of our kindred; our children are the same as their children; and yet we are forcing our sons and daughters to be slaves, and some of our daughters have been ravished; we are powerless, and our fields and vineyards now belong to others."

Neh. 5:1-5 (NRSV)

The account in Neh. 5:1-13 is frequently referred to as an example of socioeconomic reform[1] by biblical scholars. Three groups of poor and vulnerable Yehudites bring to the attention of Nehemiah the Persian governor a predatory economic system, which dooms them and their family members to a perennial cycle of debt and

---

1. For example, H. G. Kippenberg, *Religion und Klassenbildung im antiken Judäa* (Göttingen: Vandenhoeck und Ruprecht, 1978), 54–77; E. Yamauchi, "Two Reformers Compared: Solon of Athens and Nehemiah of Jerusalem," in *The Bible World: Essays in Honor of Cyrus Gordon*, ed. Gary Rendsburg and C. H. Gordon (New York: Ktav, 1980), 269–92; H. G. M. Williamson, *Ezra, Nehemiah: Word Biblical Commentary* (Nashville, TN: Thomas Nelson Publishers, 1985), 236 ff.; J. Blenkinsopp, *Ezra-Nehemiah: A Commentary* (Philadelphia, PA: The Westminster Press, 1988), 281 ff.; R. Albertz, *A History of Israelite Religion in the Old Testament Period* (London: SCM, 1994), 636 ff.; J. Wright, *Rebuilding Identity: The Nehemiah-Memoir and Its Earliest Readers*, BZAW 348 (Berlin: de Gruyter, 2004), 163–87; A. Fitzpatrick-McKinley, *Empire, Power and Indigenous Elites: A Case Study of the Nehemiah Memoir* (Leiden: Brill, 2015), 172 ff.

exploitation. Presumably some residents had fallen into such severe financial hardship that they could not afford basic sustenance for themselves and their families (v. 2), while others were landowners who had fallen on hard times and had to mortgage their properties in exchange for food during famine (v. 3), and still others had to borrow money in order to pay taxes (v. 4). Persian-era Yehud was a decentralized and diffuse society without clearly identifiable institutions of political or economic exchange, and scholars tend to agree in their assessment that throughout the Achaemenid period, Yehud was economically an underdeveloped province. The local elite—nobles and officials—who controlled the inner workings of this agrarian society in the absence of a state government, played key roles in influencing the political and economic life of the province in cooperation with the agenda of the imperial government. These urban landowning classes seem to have been capturing most of the economic surplus above that required for basic sustenance and were acting as the principal holders of economic, and by default, political, power. In the absence of a centralized government, the local upper-class families found themselves in an advantageous position profiting from many aspects of economic management and administrative upkeep in the province. Needless to say, though biblical scholars' traditional perspectives on the book tend to focus on the ethical, moral, and religious implications of Nehemiah's actions, an economic crisis and reform like the one described in Nehemiah 5 have inherently political implications as well.

This discussion examines the circumstances surrounding Nehemiah's actions in Chapter 5, through theories of economic development and its relationship to and influence on political institutions. Nehemiah's actions and the conditions described in the book would have long-lasting consequences not just in the religious life of the Jewish inhabitants of Yehud, but also on the formation and growth of the Jews as a polity. Moreover, due to Nehemiah's status and limited direct power as a temporary governor, a political theoretical reading suggests that his actions may have been the only effective strategy for enhancing the political and economic power of his suffering compatriots, an outcome that would serve to improve their quality of life as well. This is not to suggest that Nehemiah was aware of these political and economic dynamics, which have subsequently been elucidated so well by modern theorists, but that a better understanding of them will help readers to gain a more holistic understanding of the biblical account and its context.

The precarious conditions of the agrarian community depicted in Nehemiah 5 typify a society whose subsistence depends on agricultural production and is periodically exposed to the worst impacts of natural conditions. In order to survive, but also because of Yehud's political status as an imperial vassal province, its inhabitants were forced to borrow money using their land as collateral and rely on family members' labor to pay the Persian imperial tax.[2] In such a scenario,

---

2. On this latter point, M. Jursa's comment on Babylonia under the Achaemenid rule is pertinent. "While it is hard to generalize for the entire Persian empire, or even for all strata

the wealthy elite act as an informal autocratic government in the community and gradually gain control of the property and labor of those without other economic means, and the political power which attends it. Especially from an economic standpoint, when the productive ability of subsistence farmers is hampered, the province's overall market functioning is impaired. The monopoly held by the elites of Yehud stifled market relations within the province as market participants become trapped in an institutional framework that not only failed to create but barred incentives and means that would enable the development of impersonal exchange outside the already established and limited network of creditors and debtors. In this vicious cycle, borrowers are constricted from expanding their transactional partnership with other possible lenders, and growth across the entire region is limited. Still, the elite of Yehud prefer to keep the majority at the subservient level in order to lord over them. The destitute, therefore, have limited power to contest the unequal distribution of symbolic and material power and resources, further perpetuating the cycle in a situation where the elites continue the predatory practices complained of in v. 5, when the petitioners tell Nehemiah that they feel powerless. The dehumanizing and myopic approach of those in power leaves no room for a hopeful future for this community, a scenario that is only rendered more ironic by the fact that even the elites are in turn subjugated by an imperial oppressor.

To illuminate the nature of the economic and political power that is on display in Nehemiah 5, this discussion uses political theory to understand the role of local elites in the political-economic dynamics of Yehud in the absence of formal government. The nobles and officials, a group of resource stakeholders, are also the de facto incumbent autocratic elite in this Persian vassal province. Contemporaneous administrative records from other vassal territories show that the Achaemenid Empire usually preferred that local governments continue their political and economic activities in a semi-autonomous manner. Persian rulers famously relied on economic and political cooperation from native dynastic leadership to oversee administration of these decentralized systems from a central location and used a "carrot and stick" approach to control indigenous elites. The text of Nehemiah 5 suggests that the elites of Yehud played a key role in the local economic life, as they would have in all Persian provinces.

The present discussion benefits from the theories of American economist Douglass C. North, which are concerned with institutional change, economic growth and the structure of political economies, and for which he was awarded the 1993 Nobel Prize in Economics. Similarly, readers of Nehemiah will benefit

---

of Babylonian society, I do believe that one can make a good case for the argument that the Babylonian elites were subject to increasing demands by the Persian administration; and it goes without saying that discontent among this class was politically relevant" ("Transition of Babylonia from the Neo-Babylonian Empire to Achaemenid Rule," in *Regime Change in the Ancient Near East and Egypt from Sargon of Agade to Saddam Hussein* [Oxford: Oxford University Press, 2007], 90, n. 55).

from an understanding of the works of another Nobel laureate, the Austrian-British economist and political philosopher Friedrich A. Hayek, who received the 1974 prize for his contributions in political theory, psychology, and economics, who explained the role of knowledge in society and the functioning of economic markets. Their works are especially relevant for understanding the situation in Nehemiah 5 because their theories help us to examine how social norms and mores interact with and are affected by property rights, law enforcement, and efficient bureaucracy. So, the question is, how did informal social institutions—also known as slow-moving institutions—impact the economic function and political mechanisms of Yehud?

Through a theoretical analysis of the interconnection between economic elitism and political autocracy in a Persian imperial-political context, this discussion suggests that a politically astute author of Nehemiah 5 attempted to leverage the power of slow-moving institutions by expressing the universal values of kinship and shared humanity rather than the Mosaic injunctions; and, conscious of the full breadth of his readership, he also may have sought to align the account's expression of local economic and political interests with those of the *Pax Persica*. Nehemiah was a political leader whose bi-cultural identity and dual loyalty grant him a unique political vantage point from which to impact the economic performance and political development in a subaltern society by harnessing the power of informal institutions, such as religious ideals and traditional norms governing conduct throughout the society.

Nehemiah had been dispatched to Yehud during the rule of Artaxerxes I (465–424 BCE). It was now almost a century since the issuing of the edict of Cyrus the Great in 538 BCE, which had granted royal permission for the Jews in Babylon to return to their homeland and rebuild the most representative institution of Yehud—the Temple of YHWH in Jerusalem, reconstruction of which had been stalled for eighteen years due to internecine conflicts between the Samaritans and the Yehudites, internal political disorganization, and economic hardship. The book of Ezra, named for another imperial envoy, also depicts an economically and politically depressed Yehud, and scholars generally share Nehemiah's grim assessment of local socioeconomic conditions, arguing that there is little evidence that the Persians were interested in establishing social, political, or economic local power structures in Yehud.[3] At the same time, it is noteworthy that the

---

3. O. Lipschits maintains, "The Persians had no interest in establishing urban centers in the hill country or in developing new social, political, and economic local power structures on the local level" ("Achaemenid Imperial Policy, Settlement Processes in Palestine, and the Status of Jerusalem in the Middle of the Fifth Century BCE," in *Judah and the Judeans in the Persian Period*, eds. O. Lipschits and M. Oeming [Winona Lake, IN: Eisenbrauns, 2006], 30). K. Hoglund concludes, "The overall portrait that emerges in the post-exilic community is of a decentralized, ruralized population spread across the central Judean hill country" ("The Material Culture of the Persian Period and the Sociology of the Second Temple Period," in *Second Temple Studies III: Studies in Politics, Class and Material Culture*, eds.

few instances when the central government exercised any direct influence upon the province's organizational structure were when they provided legislative and material support to rebuild the Temple and walls of Jerusalem. Throughout the Achaemenid period, Yehud remained a backwater province, as the Persians did not attempt to stimulate growth. Yehud at this time was small and poor according to the archaeological evidence,[4] and it is easy to imagine that the central government did not want the province to grow too strong, perhaps fearing that Yehud would ally itself with Egypt, a possibility with well-known precedents that would have alarmed the Persian authorities.

In the fractured, subaltern society depicted in Nehemiah 5, one with weakened or nonexistent formal and informal institutions, the Yehudites' claims of predatory lending practices are unsurprising. The account does not take issue with the practice of lending itself. In fact, within contemporary Ancient Near Eastern agrarian societies, particularly in times of hardship, lending and agricultural credit systems were crucial for survival.[5] The speakers were not

---

P. Davies and J. Halligan [London: Sheffield Academic Press, 2002], 18). J. Elayi and J. Sapin posit that while the far-reaching administrative power of Achaemenids may be assumed, "it is necessary to be aware of the great diversity in local governments and in their socio-economic and cultural aspects" (*Beyond the River: New Perspectives on Transeuphratene*, trans. J. Crowley [Sheffield: Sheffield Academic Press, 1998], 146).

4. See C. Carter, *The Emergence of Yehud in the Persian Period: A Social and Demographic Study* (Sheffield: Sheffield Academic Press, 1999); A. Faust, "Settlement Dynamics and Demographic Fluctuations in Judah from the Late Iron Age to the Hellenistic Period and the Archaeology of Persian-Period Yehud," in *A Time of Change: Judah and Its Neighbours in the Persian and Early Hellenistic Periods*, ed. Y. Levin (London: T&T Clark, 2007), 23–50; O. Lipschits, "Achaemenid Imperial Policy Settlement Processes in Palestine, and the Status of Jerusalem in the Middle of the Fifth Century B.C.E," in *Judah and the Judeans in the Persian Period*, eds. O. Lipschits and M. Oeming (Winona Lake, IN: Eisenbrauns, 2006), 19–52; O. Lipschits and O. Tal, "The Settlement Archaeology of the Province of Judah: A Case Study," in *Judah and the Judeans in the Fourth Century B.C.E.*, eds. O. Lipschits, G. N. Knoppers, and R. Albertz (Winona Lake, IN: Eisenbrauns, 2007), 33–52; J. Ro, "The Theological Concept of YHWH's Punitive Justice in the Hebrew Bible: Historical Development in the Context of the Judean Community in the Persian Period," *Vetus Testamentum* 61.3 (2011), 406–25.

5. See, for instance, D. Charpin, "The Historian and the Old Babylonian Archives," in *Documentary Sources in Ancient Near Eastern and Greco-Roman Economic History: Methodology and Practice*, eds. H. D. Baker and M. Jursa (Oxford: Oxbow Books, 2014), 24–58; J. Dercksen, "The Old Assyrian Trade and Its Participants," in *Documentary Sources in Ancient Near Eastern and Greco-Roman Economic History: Methodology and Practice* (Oxford: Oxbow Books, 2014), 59–112; M. Jursa, "Economic Development in Babylonia from the Late 7th to the Late 4th Century BC: Economic Growth and Economic Crises un Imperial Contexts," in *Documentary Sources in Ancient Near Eastern and Greco-Roman Economic History: Methodology and Practice* (Oxford: Oxbow Books, 2014), 113–38; M. Van de Mieroop, "Credit as a Facilitator of Exchange in Old Babylonian Mesopotamia,"

complaining about transactions among willing market participants, but rather, the usurious practices and use of coercion during hardship which over time resulted in the loss of land and income generation ability. The text suggests that remission of debts as would have been required or encouraged by adherence to the Torah (e.g., Exod. 22:25-27; Lev. 25:35-38; Deut. 15:1-18; 23:19-20; 24:6, 10-13) was not being practiced. Lending practices were not limited by either government enforcement of the Torah strictures or cultural encouragement of Torah lending standards. Thus, the petitioners' claims in vv. 3-5 of having to mortgage their fields, vineyards, and homes, even to the point of selling their children into slavery—the powerlessness expressed here—is an indicator that well-developed institutions and effective mechanism for enforcement were absent in Yehud at the time. That members of a society who largely derived their livelihood from subsistence farming were predictably beset by ecological hazards is no surprise. In the case of subaltern Yehud, however, these were compounded by political uncertainties as well, and the combination seems to have created a uniquely difficult time of economic strain and impoverishment, as evidenced by the distress of the plaintiffs in this account. In normal situations of famine or drought, credit transactions were crucial mechanisms in coping with risks, but without regulating institutions to guard against risks in the spheres of labor and market relationships, lending seems to have gone beyond the normal boundaries into predatory practices.

North, in his definition of institutions, posits that "institutions are the rules of the game in a society, or more formally, are the humanly devised constraints that shape human interaction."[6] The purpose of institutions is not to anticipate or restrict changes as they arise in the economic or political interactions, but to reduce obstacles arising from imperfect and asymmetrical information between parties. North explains that individuals' access to information is generally inadequate and their ability to process information often limited by their mental models. Institutions remove obstacles to market transactions, but they also ought to obstruct corrupt transactions.[7] In classical economics, the individual rather than any collective group is traditionally viewed as the subject of study,[8] and individual decisions are usually focused on maximizing benefits. North disagrees with such a view when he stresses that individual economic decisions cannot be

---

in *Debt and Economic Renewal in the Ancient Near East*, eds. M. Hudson and M. Van de Mieroop (Bethesda, MD: CDL Press, 2002), 163–73.

6. D. North, *Institutions, Institutional Change, and Economic Performance* (New York: Cambridge University Press, 1990), 3.

7. See D. North, *Structure and Change in Economic History* (New York: W. W. Norton & Company, 1981).

8. M. Bunge, "Ten Modes of Individualism—None of Which Works—and Their Alternatives," *Philosophy of Social Science* 30 (2000), 384–406; H. Kincaid, "Methodological Individualism and Economics," in *Elgar Companion to Economics and Philosophy*, eds. J. Davis, A. Marciano, J. Runde, and E. Elgar (Cheltenham: Edward Elgar, 2004), 299–314.

viewed apart from the context of political and other social processes. Therefore, institutions are the product of intentional human action. Societal values play a crucial role in the transactional processes between individuals. Hence, institutions are not necessarily ruled by economic or any other kind of logic.⁹

Thus, institutions play a key role in minimizing uncertainty in human social interaction. This is particularly the case when they reduce risk in economic transactions, whether the mechanisms by which they do so are informal (i.e., norms of behavior, societal codes of conduct) or formal (laws and rules). Both forms require enforcement; however, formal institutions are typically represented and upheld by the state. North explains:

> If formal third-party enforcement is essential, it is important to define exactly what one means by it. In principle, third-party enforcement would involve a neutral party with the ability, costlessly, to be able to measure the attributes of a contract and, costlessly, to enforce agreements such that the offending party always had to compensate the injured party to a degree that made it costly to violate the contract. These are strong conditions that obviously are seldom, if ever, met in the real world.¹⁰

Conversely, the political and economic conditions of a society without a formal governing structure tend to draw on informal institutions. In the absence of a clearly identifiable state government a society's values, beliefs, and social norms undergird the social exchanges of a community.

Hayek, on his part, recognizes how social and political institutions are vital in coordinating human conduct, highlighting not only their benefit, but also their essential role in securing social welfare and optimal economic functioning— so long as the central government exercises limited control. Hayek stresses that cultural institutions and social dynamics ought to be allowed to play their organically constructive role in economic development, and was famously skeptical of big government planning.¹¹ In his work, he consistently warns that over time, an economic—and consequentially political—power imbalance would limit changes in the dynamics of a given society. Governments' economic control and decision-making through central planning should be kept modest because, he concludes, statism inevitably leads to totalitarianism. Individual liberty and self-interest have a valuable role to play in the development of political and economic institutions. Thus, Hayek's note on the relationship between power and institutions is valuable for explicating the imbalance of economic and political power in the

---

9. D. North, "Economic Performance through Time," *The American Economic Review* 84.3 (1994), 359–68; D. North, "Markets," in *The Oxford Encyclopedia of Economic History, Volume 3*, ed. J. Mokyr (Oxford: Oxford University Press, 2003), 432–33.

10. North, *Institutions, Institutional Change and Economic Performance*, 58.

11. F. Hayek, *The Road to Serfdom* (Chicago, IL: University of Chicago Press, 1944); F. Hayek, *The Constitution of Liberty* (Chicago, IL: University of Chicago Press, 1960).

present biblical account. Hayek does not gainsay the role of the government altogether. In fact, the central government, according to Hayek's paradigm, plays a key role in that it ensures a competitive economy through a successful enforcement of laws and rules. He explains that, in theory, the rule of law and corresponding enforcement have the potential to lead to *isonomia*—equality of political rights—for everyone in society.[12]

Hayek insists that just and efficient functioning of any market can be ensured only by the presence and functioning of institutions that safeguard public choices and legal processes.[13] Building on a pragmatic observation originally proffered by the eighteenth-century Scottish philosopher David Hume, Hayek contends that because of the scarcity of resources and many times also the scarcity of generosity, societies are not capable of promoting general welfare unless social institutions safeguard the implementation of justice for their members. Hume noted:

> All the laws of nature, which regulate property, as well as civil laws, are general, and regard only some essential circumstances of the case, without taking into consideration the characters, situations, and connections of the persons concerned, or any particular consequences which may result from the determination of these laws, in any particular case which offers. They deprive, without scruple, a beneficent man of all his possessions, if acquired by mistake, without a good title.[14]

Hayek's own understanding of institutions is well reflected in a personal note he wrote in his final years, which stated, "Restraint is an instrumental condition, not the opposite of freedom."[15] He explains: "The bases of freedom are the restraints commonly accepted by the members of the group in which the rules of morals prevail. The demand for 'liberation' from these restraints is an attack on all liberty possible among human beings."[16] For Hayek, freedom is not the absolute liberty to do as one pleases, rather it is the recognition of the necessity of law and morality to ensure that human interaction is cooperative and orderly. Thus, Hayek underscores the inextricable role of enforcement in institutions. Strong political institutions, even when armed with positive laws, yet devoid of moral obligation or religious

---

12. Hayek, *The Road to Serfdom*, 42–45.

13. Ibid., 45–90. Also, F. Hayek, "The Use of Knowledge in Society," *American Economic Review* 35 (1945), 519–30.

14. D. Hume, "Some Further Considerations with Regard to Justice," in *An Inquiry Concerning the Principles of Morals*, Sec. III (Edinburgh: James Clark, 1809), 359.

15. S. Horwitz, "Hayek and Freedom," https://fee.org/articles/hayek-and-freedom/. Also see Hayek, *The Constitution of Liberty*, 32; F. Hayek, *Law, Legislation and Liberty: A New Statement of the Liberal Principles of Justice and Political Economy* (Abingdon: Routledge, 2012), 14.

16. Horwitz, "Hayek and Freedom."

considerations, cannot guarantee the establishment or preservation of a humane and cohesive society.

> The interests of those who bring about the required adjustments to changes, namely those who could improve their position by moving from one group to another, are systematically disregarded. So far as the group to which they wish to move is concerned, it will be its chief aim to keep them out. And the groups they wish to leave will have no incentive to assist their entry into what will often be a great variety of other groups. Thus, in a system in which the organizations of the existing producers of the various commodities and services determine prices and quantities to be produced, those who would bring about the continuous adjustment to change would be deprived of influence on events.[17]

Here Hayek echoes a conclusion similar to that drawn by Adam Smith, the eighteenth-century Scottish philosopher and political economist, who viewed slavery as economically highly inefficient. Smith argued that slave labor is generally less productive than free labor. According to Smith, freemen work for themselves and therefore work much harder and better for less.[18] "The experience of all ages and nations, I believe, demonstrates, that the work done by slaves, though it appears to cost only their maintenance, is in the end the dearest of any. A person who can acquire no property can have no other interest but to eat as much and to labor as little as possible."[19] In Smith's view, slavery reduces productivity growth because slaves do not have any incentive to innovate and thus slavery has sometimes limited slaveholding societies' economic development throughout history.[20] Despite these disadvantages, according to Smith, masters still prefer domineering over other human beings. Economist Yoram Barzel explains that, in a similar manner, serf rulers "were willing to sacrifice income because the restrictions they imposed reduced the ability of their subordinates to rebel."[21]

Hence, one may see how the absence of established or recognized institutions with the capability to represent and protect individual's selfhood and production can easily unravel into exploitation and unjust distribution of resources and power among the members of a society. In such a scenario, the ownership of the land can be a determining factor in one's ability to exercise the right to self-determination in that the property right, in theory, ought to grant the right to occupy the land, pursue an appropriate development, and benefit from its production and one's own labor. Here, North's theory of institutions speaks to the ways in which economics

---

17. Hayek, *Law, Legislation and Liberty*, 92.

18. A. Smith, *An Inquiry into the Nature and Causes of the Wealth of Nations*, ed. E. Cannan (New York: Modern Library, 1994), I.8.

19. Ibid., II.3.

20. Ibid., IV.9.

21. Y. Barzel, "Property Rights and the Evolution of the State," in *Conflict and Governance*, eds. A. Glazer and K. Konrad (Heidelberg: Springer, 2003), 139.

shapes politics. Political rules give rise to economic rules and vice versa. Property rights and thus individual contracts are specified and enforced by political decision-making. Naturally, the structure of economic interests also influences the political structure. North explains the crucial role of institutions in a functional society when he writes:

> Institutions are the humanly devised constraints that structure political, economic and social interaction. They consist of both informal constraints (sanctions, taboos, customs, traditions, and codes of conduct), and formal rules (constitutions, laws, property rights). Throughout history, institutions have been devised by human beings to create order and reduce uncertainty in exchange. Together with the standard constraints of economics they define the choice set and therefore determine transaction and production costs and hence the profitability and feasibility of engaging in economic activity. They evolve incrementally, connecting the past with the present and the future; history in consequence is largely a story of institutional evolution in which the historical performance of economies can only be understood as a part of a sequential story. Institutions provide the incentive structure of an economy; as that structure evolves, it shapes the direction of economic change towards growth, stagnation, or decline.[22]

Therefore, secure property rights undergird political stability and economic efficiency in society, which in theory, support political efficiency. In reality, however, this self-reinforcing relationship does not always result in the advancement of the collective good. History shows that institutional designs, instead of maximizing efficiency for the broader society, can over time become tools that promote the bargaining power (and hence political power) of certain social groups.

A crucial point for understanding the political-economic context of Nehemiah 5 derives from North's insights into the impact of property rights. He insists that sustained economic growth requires institutions and an efficient system of property rights is crucial for individuals in order to channel their efforts into activities that will yield optimal returns.[23] Property rights serve as one example of how institutions and institutional change influence economic productivity. When in equilibrium, a given structure of property rights (and their enforcement) will be consistent with a particular set of political rules (and their enforcement). Changes in one induce changes in the other.[24] In other words, unstable societies, which are unable to support sufficiently secure property rights, fail to provide incentives to save, expand, and invest. Deficiencies in the regular observation of the positive law

---

22. D. North, "Institutions," *The Journal of Economic Perspectives* 5.1 (1991), 97.
23. North, *Structure and Change in Economic History*, 3–32.
24. See North, "Institutions"; B. Weingast, "The Economic Role of Political Institutions: Market-Preserving Federalism and Economic Development," *Journal of Law, Economics, and Organization* 11.1 (1995), 1–31.

as well as traditional communal ethos put a community's fundamental freedoms in jeopardy, placing the passages in Chapter 5 in a new, more serious light. When Nehemiah's petitioners bemoaned "We are mortgaging our fields, our vineyards, and our homes to get grain during the famine," "We have had to borrow money to pay the king's tax on our fields and vineyards"; they might have been complaining about an immediate crisis, but Nehemiah's responses indicate an attention to a concern for a broader set of issues, hinting at his belief that these events might have import for the economic and political freedoms of the entire Jewish society in Yehud over time.

In an ideal institutional framework, according to North's view of economic performance, "property rights are protected, contracts are enforced and political authorities do not interfere with the choices made by economic entrepreneurs."[25] When these conditions are in place, assuming stability in other areas, over time the markets can operate efficiently. Even the risk of expropriation due to the violation of one of these principles stunts economic growth. North explains that such stipulations provide incentives to economic and political entrepreneurs when the decision-making power is decentralized and democratized, thus making the market adaptive and nimble.

Therefore, North and Hayek coincide in their conclusion that robust and sustained economic growth requires appropriate institutions. In order to achieve successful economic and political outcomes, the parties involved must agree to cooperate and their commitments must be credible.[26] Citizens and public institutions (and officials) create a synergic relationship whereby a trustful environment contributes toward generating a sustainable development and steady production of goods.[27] In this sense, property rights are best understood principally as social relations—interactions between members of the society—and property and contracts themselves constitute two institutions associated with sustained growth. Credible commitments in the context of Nehemiah 5 are the substrate for a stable and reliable political arrangement whereby community members' property rights are protected and enforced. A socially shared understanding of and commitment to the concept of property reinforces economic efficiency, and the state's support for and enforcement of these commitments provides economic security, ensuring reliable and steady revenue streams. Social capital manifests itself as a credible commitment in the economic, political, or social realms; and it is defined as the "features of social organization such as trust, norms and networks that can improve the efficiency of society by facilitating coordinated action." Here

---

25. J. Faundez, "Douglass North's Theory of Institutions: Lessons for Law and Development," *Hague Journal on the Rule of Law* 8 (2016), 385. Also see North, "Economic Performance through Time," 359–68.

26. D. North, "Institutions and Credible Commitment," *Journal of Institutional and Theoretical Economics* 149.1 (1993), 11–23.

27. R. Nanetti and C. Holguin, *Social Capital in Development Planning: Linking the Actors* (New York: Palgrave Macmillan, 2016), 38.

trust is identified as the most important component.[28] The speakers in this biblical account attest to the absence of shared trust, solidarity norms, and a community vision.

Not only was the situation in the Persian vassal province far from being ideal with respect to the upkeep of the property rights, law enforcement, or a functioning civil society but this account also provides a textbook example of the linkage in which a weakened social identity and sense of virtue clearly manifested themselves in asymmetric division of power and resources. The biblical account evinces the inherent correlation between economic systems and political outcomes. The socioeconomic category to which one is relegated prescribes human behavior and social interaction, and economic interactions between members of the society prescribe the social identity of the parties involved and thus accentuate social differences. Financial opportunism through unavoidable, exorbitant interest rates resulted in effectively persistent politics of oppression. Over time, as measures of virtue were internalized through repeated practice, the elites of Yehud legitimized oppressive behavior and subordination. Among the poor, the resulting asymmetric access to power and resources reinforced a decreased sense of utility in their social ties, as seen in the dramatic declaration of the speakers in v. 5.

The profound economic impact of the political legitimization of relationships of superiority and inferiority found in Nehemiah 5 can be better understood by drawing on the modern conception of "possessive individualism." To be specific, the notion of possessive individualism is particularly helpful in articulating the self-perception and rights of the poor in Yehud. Canadian political theorist C. B. Macpherson wrote in his influential book, *Political Theory of Possessive Individualism*, that "the individual is free inasmuch as he is proprietor of his person and capacities. Society consists of relations of exchange between proprietors. Political society becomes a calculated device for the protection of this property and for the maintenance of an orderly relation of exchange."[29] According to this understanding, the poor of Yehud are barred from exercising the proprietorship of their personhood and capacities. Under such a conception, the essence of humanity becomes freedom from dependence on the wills of others; society is little more than a system of economic relations; and political society becomes a means of safeguarding private property and the system of economic relations rooted in property. Then, what is property? Property is a possessive quality—"its conception of the individual as essentially the proprietor of his own person or capacities, owing nothing to society for them."[30] In other words, infringement on one's right to fundamental human freedoms (right of use, right of possession) signifies dispossession of not only property (patrimony, land), but also one's

---

28. R. Putnam and R. Nanetti, *Making Democracy Work: Civic Traditions in Modern Italy* (Princeton, NJ: Princeton University Press, 1993), 167–71.

29. C. B. Macpherson, *The Political Theory of Possessive Individualism* (Oxford: Clarendon Press, 1962), 3.

30. Ibid.

4. Nehemiah's Socioeconomic Reform

actions (labor). Macpherson explains, "Liberty in regard to actions is equivalent to ownership in regard to property."[31]

Scholars of institutional economics observe that natural resources in a collective setting are managed by the community members' internalized measures of virtue. They assert that a society's attitude toward economic justice and equity bears a close correlation with social identity and integrity, highlighting the associated political issues specific to that society. Hence, the socioeconomic category to which an individual is relegated prescribes human behavior and social interaction. One idea from utility function theory is that "people have identity-related payoffs from others' actions"[32]—identity influences behavior. And since prevailing patterns of behavior over time tend to become accepted as social norms, individual actors' sense of self eventually can come to shape economic outcomes. By the same token, social identity serves as a guideline for individuals as to how they should behave as members of society. The economic interaction between members is linked to the social identity of the parties involved and thus accentuates the social differences.

Thus, in order to understand the economic behavior of the elite and the poor in Yehud, one must factor in adequately each societal group's economic choices and social norms and rules that govern behavior. North and Hayek's respective theories of institutions provide helpful insights in order to explain how the crisis of debt and high interest rates could perpetuate the politics of exclusion and subjection in Yehud. Economic history shows that the competitive market is typically unswayed by moral injunctions, and thus the elite in Yehud are, economically speaking, rational people. The "Law of indifference" proposed by the nineteenth-century English economist and philosopher William Stanley Jevons, often cited by today's political economists, is here illuminating. Jevons correctly observed that "traders focus on the price and quantity of goods but are indifferent to the social characteristics of the people they deal with. So long as the other person's 'money is green,' a rational trader will trade with anyone."[33] This sagacious observation also reflects the fact that communal ethics does not always play an influential role in the practice of a free market economy. It needs to be stressed, however, that anthropologists have observed that in smaller communities in particular, "credit relations were interpreted through an ethos of neighborliness, and framed by a language of moral obligation."[34] The poor farmers in Yehud invoke the same principles. Here we see how the rationality of the market in favor of individual interests comes into a direct collision with the communal ethos.

Thus, a discussion of the rationality of the market economy is helpful in understanding the actions of the nobles and officials in the context of domestic

---

31. Ibid., 49.

32. G. Akerlof and R. Kranton, "Economics and Identity," *Quarterly Journal of Economics* 140.3 (2000), 715–53.

33. W. Jevons, *The Theory of Political Economy* (London: Macmillan and Co., 1888), 22.

34. B. Carruthers, *City of Capital: Politics and Markets in the English Financial Revolution* (Princeton, NJ: Princeton University Press, 1996), 192.

affairs, which in turn helps to elucidate their strategic role within the broader imperial-political landscape. As seen above, classical economic and social theorists recognize that diffuse and decentralized institutions in a society provide a profitable environment particularly for economic actors who pursue self-interest single-mindedly. The marketplace is an unrelentingly rational ground, disconnected from a moral conscience or restraint, and communal ethics does not always play an influential role in the changes that a political economy undergoes. Economic actors make decisions based on the individually held subset of information, and the sum of such actions at a societal level drives an increasingly more efficient market.[35] Naturally, one could make the argument that the pecuniary value is simply one kind of value among the many upon which economic agents base their decisions, and that one's social rules, dynamics, and mechanisms can be of greater consequence in economic action. The notion of market rationality is highly controversial and disputed empirically and theoretically. But what seems clear in this biblical account is that though ethical and legal injunctions pertaining to debt did exist in the cultures and traditions of Persian-era Yehud, the functioning of the market economy as driven by profit-maximizing behaviors trumped the code of kinship and shared humanity. This situation, especially in the absence of formal institutions to uphold property rights, law enforcement, or efficient bureaucracy, led to increasing income inequality and the degradation of the economic and political power held by the poorer strata among the indigenous occupants of Yehud.

The rationality of the market economy that Jevons and others speak of demonstrates that the market aims to maximize profit and social ethos may not always play a significant role. Ethical and legal injunctions pertaining to debt were indeed embedded in the Hebrew tradition: Exod. 21:2-11; 23:10-11; Leviticus 25; Deut. 15:1-3; 15:12-18. Indeed, numerous passages beyond the legal corpus demonstrate that debt was a ubiquitously important and sensitive issue in the history of Israel: 2 Ks 4; Isa. 50:1; Amos 2:6; 8:6; 1 Sam. 22:2; Prov. 22:7; 22:26-27. During Nehemiah's time, the nobles and officials of Yehud extended credits to the farmers at stiff interest rates, not because Yehud lacked a language of moral obligation,[36] but because, as Jevons observed, economic gains wield a greater force than social conscience. In fact, in transgressing social boundaries and ignoring the ethics of credit and community relations, the elite of Yehud behaved as have all rational entrepreneurs in history, pursuing profit and the expansion of their own economic power.

Countering such rational yet pessimistic assessment of classical economic and social theorists, North contends that social factors indeed have a powerful effect on economic growth. He stresses the impact of cultural factors when he observes that throughout history, informal social rules have shown to defeat the efforts of even the most zealous revolutionaries. In his work, North consistently points out

---

35. See Hayek, "The Use of Knowledge in Society."
36. Ibid.

how reformers tend to fail in their efforts to bring about societal transformation because they typically focus on changing the formal rules, and underestimate the fundamental importance of informal conventions and norms of behavior. He points out that formal "rules may be changed overnight, the informal norms usually change only gradually."[37] However, it is the norms that lend legitimacy since they are undergirded by communal values, conventions, and codes of conduct.

In Neh. 5:9 Nehemiah exhorts the elites of Yehud, "What you are doing is not right. Shouldn't you walk in the fear of our God to avoid the reproach of our Gentile enemies?" Nehemiah's speech invokes religious ideology and ethical principles in his aim to bring about transformation in Yehud. Just as North regularly stresses in his work on economic structure and performance, and unlike some reformers in history, Nehemiah seems to understand that successful attempts to bring about economic or political change must incorporate community's beliefs, morality, and culture.[38] North asserts that "successful institutional change requires changing collective belief systems."[39] Precisely, in this account Nehemiah does not attempt to propose or promulgate a set of laws on a right lending system. As a temporary governor and given the lack of reliable enforcement mechanisms in Yehud, Nehemiah seeks to shift cultural values collectively and individually. His approach is to resort to the hearts and minds, which have the real ability to effect change on the credit practices being criticized here. One may observe that North and Nehemiah coincide in their understanding that "ideology is an external force that plays a role in changing behavior."[40] In the case of the nobles and officials of Yehud, their proclivity to maximize wealth eventually yielded to their sense of religious and ethical conscience, at least in their public pledge to change their course of action. Among the informal institutions North includes ideas, ideologies, myths, dogmas, prejudices, and superstitions.[41] In the Persian-era Yehud, the notion of "the fear of God" was effectively deployed by the Persian governor, and it held a powerful sway over his audience.[42]

> "We will give it back," [the nobles and officials] said. "And we will not demand anything more from them. We will do as you say." Then I summoned the priests and made the nobles and officials take an oath to do what they had

---

37. D. North, "Epilogue: Economic Performance through Time," in *Empirical Studies in Institutional Change*, eds. L. Alston, T. Eggertsson, and D. North (Cambridge: Cambridge University Press, 1996), 353.

38. North, *Structure and Change in Economic History*.

39. North, "Epilogue: Economic Performance through Time," 353–54.

40. North, *Institutions, Institutional Change, and Economic Performance*, 140.

41. North, *Understanding the Process of Economic Change* (Princeton, NJ: Princeton University Press, 2005), 72, 83, 156; North, "Economic Performance through Time," 363.

42. Regarding the denouement of this account, commentator J. Myers also concludes, "The prime motive for consideration was the fear of God," (*The Anchor Bible: Ezra—Nehemiah* [Garden City, NY: Doubleday & Company, Inc., 1965], 131).

promised. I also shook out the folds of my robe and said, "In this way may God shake out of their house and possessions anyone who does not keep this promise. So may such a person be shaken out and emptied!" At this the whole assembly said, "Amen," and praised the LORD. And the people did as they had promised. (Neh. 5:12-13)

Nehemiah is a good example of what North calls a "would-be reformer," who does not ignore cultural heritage. Still, North does not accept the notion that a single individual may be the source of informal institutions. He explains that innovation and imitation, encapsulated in informal institutions, are spread diachronically and synchronically in a social group that is learning collectively. Put otherwise, what North calls the "cultural transmission of values" can potentially change people's behavior, even a society's economic performance and political process.[43] Nehemiah, as a temporary governor of Yehud, might have been conscientious of the fact that legislative injunctions or any other formal action in a diffusive and decentralized society such as Yehud could not effect a long-lasting structural change to the unjust and abusive lending system. However, with the collective and voluntary adjuration of the elites of Yehud ensuing Nehemiah's authoritative and persuasive discourse, one may argue that Nehemiah 5 signals the dawn of a new economic and possibly political order. With the aid of North and Hayek's theories, one may suggest that although the full intent and objectives of the biblical author are unknown to the modern reader, it can be inferred that one impact of Nehemiah 5—whether intended by the author or simply a beneficial byproduct—would have been to bolster the legitimacy of Nehemiah's leadership in the eyes of both Persians and Jews alike. On the one hand, the Jewish community would see Nehemiah's reform as proof of his deep concern for his ancestral kin and land's political and economic welfare. On the other hand, the imperial administration would see in Nehemiah a savvy diplomat who uses his knowledge of the province's informal social institutions, its slow-moving institutions, to promote local security and stability as desired by the *Pax Persica*.

---

43. North, *Institutions, Institutional Change, and Economic Performance*, 138–40.

Chapter 5

VEILED RESISTANCE: THE COGNITIVE DISSONANCE OF VISION IN GENESIS 38

Carolyn Alsen

Introduction

In the ancestral narratives of Genesis, many risky trickster escapades explore the theme of Israelite identity, in conversation with other competing views on Israelite ethnic and religious identity in the wider Hebrew Bible. In particular, Genesis tricksters often evoke revolutionary or radical dissension within the conventional religious world of the Judean returnee community.[1] One of these narrative dissentions involves the conundrum surrounding the use of a veil by Tamar in Genesis 38. Scholarly discussions on Genesis 38 and veiling can range from historical analyses of the legal and social standing of the user of veils[2] to more complex questions about the overall narrative logic of apology or polemic represented by characters and the narrator.[3] While marriage politics continues

---

1. The trickster who breaks social or legal rules in the ancestral stories of Genesis is quite often an insider, from the perspective of an Israelite tribal and political tradition. Yet, they can also be an outsider, yet to be enveloped or expelled from a story. See, for example, S. Niditch, *Underdogs and Tricksters: A Prelude to Biblical Folklore* (New Voices in Biblical Studies; San Francisco, CA: Harper & Row, 1987). Feminist criticism of the Bible uses trickster tales as an awareness raising enterprise of the theme of otherness. See M. Jackson, *Comedy and Feminist Interpretation of the Hebrew Bible: A Subversive Collaboration* (Oxford: Oxford University Press, 2012), 41–66.

2. K. van der Toorn, "The Significance of the Veil in the Ancient Near East," in *Pomegranates and Golden Bells: Studies in Biblical, Jewish, and near Eastern Ritual, Law, and Literature in Honor of Jacob Milgrom*, eds. J. Milgrom, D. P. Wright, D. N. Freedman, and A. Hurvitz (Winona Lake, IN: Eisenbrauns, 1995), 327–40.

3. Y. Amit, "Hidden Polemics in the Story of Judah and Tamar (Genesis 38:1–30)," *Shnaton: An Annual for Biblical and Ancient Near Eastern Studies* 20 (2010), 11–25. (Hebrew)

to be a feature of the scholarship of Genesis,[4] a study is yet to emerge that seeks to address a postcolonial and feminist reading of the dissonance between the historical and narrative worlds of Tamar, in and out of her veil.[5] In response to this, I suggest that interpreters read the veil through the lens of the sociology of public visibility, as a postcolonial feminist symbol of the irreducible identity of Tamar and therefore Israelite/Judahite identity. The ideas of social conformity and deviance are here specifically investigated in terms of revealing or covering through garments or body coverings to create perceptions in public space.[6] In that sense, this study shares similar themes to Anderson's view on imagined identity: the veil marks aspects of public identity and space, in which all members recognize they are part of a larger sociopolitical body, and deviance is a response to an imposed subordination in a dominant androcentric-imaginary sociopolitical identity.[7] The deviance is illustrated between the postcolonial condition and official writing of historiography that creates a trace of the subaltern. The publicly veiled woman in Genesis 38 is an illustration of the struggle of an official nationalism anticipating possible threat or exclusion from a community of imagined nationalism.[8]

To offer its endpoint here, for the purpose of logical strategy, this study concludes that head veiling constitutes a dual sign: resistance to colonization, and acquiescence to gender domination. The veiled woman, in a postcolonial feminist sense, is under *double colonization*. That is, she operates under a double layer of subordination by both imperial and androcentric ideologies.[9] Groups that are culturally dominated by an imperial power have also within them an internal gender domination, so that the two kinds of subordination layer on those

---

4. M. Warner, "'Therefore a Man Leaves His Father and His Mother and Clings to His Wife': Marriage and Intermarriage in Genesis 2:24," *JBL* 136.2 (2017), 269–88.

5. I acknowledge the excellent studies on the social position of Tamar in relation to the "harlot" as described by S. Niditch and P. A. Bird. S. Niditch, "The Wronged Woman Righted: An Analysis of Genesis 38," *HTR* 72.1-2 (1979), 147, n. 13; P. A. Bird, "The Harlot as Heroine: Narrative Art and Social Presupposition in Three Old Testament Texts," *Semeia: An Experimental Journal for Biblical Criticism* 46 (1989), 119–39 and P. A. Bird, *Missing Persons and Mistaken Identities: Women and Gender in Ancient Israel* (Overtures to Biblical Theology; Minneapolis, MN; Fortress, 1997), 206, n. 20.

6. S. Watson and A. Saha, "Suburban Drifts: Mundane Multiculturalism in Outer London," *Ethnic and Racial Studies* 36.12 (2013), 2016–34; J. Lim and A. Fanghanel, "'Hijabs, Hoodies and Hotpants'; Negotiating the 'Slut' in Slutwalk," *Geoforum* 48 (2013), 207–15.

7. Anderson, *Imagined Communities*, 101.

8. Ibid.

9. First coined in K. H. Petersen and A. Rutherford, *A Double Colonization: Colonial and Post-Colonial Women's Writing* (Mundelstrup, Denmark: Dangaroo Press, 1986). See also R. S. Sugirtharajah, *Exploring Postcolonial Biblical Criticism: History, Method, Practice* (Oxford: Wiley-Blackwell, 2012), 14–16; M. W. Dube, "Toward a Post-Colonial Feminist Interpretation of the Bible," in *Hope Abundant*, ed. K. Pui-lan (Maryknoll, NY: Orbis Books, 2010), 98.

in the dominated group that identify as female. Those in this situation remain in the tension between nationalistic struggle against imperialism or the struggle against gender domination. Tamar operates within the androcentric-nationalistic symbolic world of the text, under the social and legal expectations of the ideal (Israelite elite male) readerly gaze, while being incorporated into a Judahite line represented to the view of the reader in a spectacle of nationalistic struggle. In this way, her public visibility occurs not only through the gaze of the characters, but also as a result of the gaze of the reader, who translates his or her reading strategy to the social world. This is because the binary of seer and seen can result in domination when a reading has social meaning, as the object of the gaze is categorized, named, or controlled. However, the process of reading that analyzes and uncovers multiple gazes in reading Genesis 38 can transcend and deconstruct this relationship. In the narrative, Tamar has a visible presence, which when seen from particular perspectives can lay bare postcolonial and feminist concerns and can thereby challenge a dominant optic of an ideal reader.[10]

There are two key sociological questions in this study. First, what is the symbolism in the use of the veils of Tamar (and Rebekah) in Genesis as carriers of knowledge and/or (non)recognition? Second, how does this polyvisual symbol illustrate the polyvalent nature of Israelite identity in Genesis 38? The exploration of these questions includes the ideological frame (or social world) of the religious and ethnic role of the קָדֵשׁ/קְדֵשָׁה in the Hebrew Bible, and the way in which this informs a visual reading through multiple character and narrator gazes. As the historical data on the קְדֵשָׁה is limited, sociological and postcolonial feminist theories are employed to understand gender and ethnic recognition in Genesis 38. Similarly, as the use of the veil (הַצָּעִיף) itself in Genesis is not sufficiently understood through historical data, the veil itself will be examined through the above sociological questions. These questions are concerned with complexes of seeing and the resulting sociological imposition of conformity or deviancy that occur in studies of women's head-covering garments in postcolonial literature and contemporary sociology.[11]

This chapter uses narratology—the functions of narrative art—to understand the symbolism and language choices in the narrative. More specifically, this study uses narratology for a sociological and postcolonial reading, by examining characters' perception and understanding of the social use and control of

---

10. One of the transformations of the Hegelian master-slave dialectic in postcolonial thought is mutual recognition. F. Fanon, *Black Skin White Masks*, trans. Charles Lam Markmann (London: Pluto, 2008), 169.

11. "The veil is a 'double shield,' protecting women against society and protecting society against the 'inherent evil' of woman." D. Grace, *The Woman in the Muslim Mask: Veiling and Identity in Postcolonial Literature* (Sterling, VA: Pluto Press, 2004), 21; "People resort to cultural references like the veil [in the Palestinian community], especially when they perceive their whole national existence is threatened." V. M. Moghadam, *Modernising Women: Gender and Social Change in the Middle East* (London: Lynne Reiner, 1993), 163.

covering or uncovering bodies with garments. In order to understand some of the ambiguities in ancient references to the veil, and being aware of possible anachronism, the modern sociology of the veil is suggested as a tool to read the veil of Tamar as a polyvalent index of social deviance or conformity which represents an identity in public space. The gaze of a particular character or reader on the veil wearer renders the one in the garment as either a risky outsider or an insider who belongs. In response to this gaze through her actions in the text, Tamar both conforms and deviates to resist her categorization. In this way, a postcolonial view of the veil renders it as a dual visual sign of gender or cultural domination.

Visuality, veils, and variation

From the late Bronze Age (thirteenth century BCE) to the Sassanid dynasties (third–seventh centuries CE), women, particularly those in the upper classes, were increasingly restricted through urbanization, which resulted also in a decline in social standing. During that long period in ancient West Asia, veiling became a complex symbol of status in successive religious and political eras.[12] Likewise, modern veils have differing social functions as an indexation of social categories such as religion, status, gender, and race. The meaning of the veil as a visual symbol of status is partly generated inside the social group which uses the veil, and partly by views from outside the group. Different social mores can frame the use of veils to yield particular meanings. These optics of the veil are through not only the garment itself but also the age, gender, ethnic, spatial and social positioning of the wearer.

To Frantz Fanon, the veil is a symbol of belonging that held women to the faithful appropriation of their culture against outsiders. One area in which the struggle is illustrated is in the photographic medium. Early colonial-era postcards from Algeria, intended for French or European consumption in the early twentieth century showed women veiled in terms of their faces, but exposing many other body parts. These models were not considered by their own Algerian communities to be "respectable" Muslim women but women who lived in poverty to the point that they would accept payment to be photographed. They were, to their own communities, discarded for their misuse of the veil and appropriating the visual symbol for the sake of colonial fantasies of control. This control spread to include all veiled women. Indeed, French authorities in the 1960s would force Algerian women to be photographed without veils, using the excuse of the production of identity cards.[13] In regard to this and other social instances, the projection of

---

12. S. Amer, *What Is Veiling?* Islamic Civilization and Muslim Networks (Chapel Hill, NC: The University of North Carolina Press, 2014), 5–6.

13. Ibid., 213, n. 6.

colonial fantasies on these and other veiled women is a topic taken up by Fanon to encourage resistance.[14]

Understanding visual recognition is a crucial part of negotiating identity in postcolonial and race discussions. However, the project to recognize another must first acknowledge the social contracts and layers of assumptions that surround those others. To recognize ethnicity or gender, the process demands the use of comparison. For example, the colonial project to Frantz Fanon means that in order to be black, the black man must be compared to the white.[15] In this encounter, the white subject considers his or her own self in comparison to the other which only has an identity because of the white normative center. To make up this black identity, an assemblage of characteristics according to ethnicity and gender is constructed on a quasi-biological, visual basis. This categorization remains in the spaces between visual biology and social ways of being, for the benefit of some and the detriment of others.[16] Legal recognition alone is not the hinge on which this discussion turns, because both gender and ethnic/racial categories are already legal assumptions.[17]

The various meanings of this identity often depend on the viewpoint of those viewing the person(s) in the veil. In the biblical text, I suggest that a postcolonial negotiation of this optic lies in considering the veil as mimicry of colonial representations of the veiled woman. The veil in modern and premodern social worlds are different in function, but the issues of the visual nature of representation and the desire to see or hide beneath coverings over bodies provide sociological links to the social worlds of the Hebrew Bible. As the historical data on veils in the ancient world is often divergent from the various uses of the veil in the Hebrew Bible, I suggest that this study of public space and veiling exists within a textual social world that reflects the ideology of Israelite identity in tension with other kinds of identity. That is, the world of the text itself is where social signs such as the head veil are to be viewed. Cultic, theistic, and legal aspects of Israelite identity emerge from comparisons and recognition of others as different or similar.[18] In Genesis 38, these aspects are negotiated by way of viewing in public space as a place of negotiation of identity, commenting on topics such as public and private religion, orthodoxy

---

14. F. Fanon, "Algeria Unveiled," in *The New Left Reader*, ed. Carl Oglesby (New York: Grove, 1969), 69-70.

15. Fanon, *Black Skin White Masks*, 82-83.

16. A. G. Weheliye, *Habeas Viscus: Racializing Assemblages, Biopolitics, and Black Feminist Theories of the Human* (Durham, NC: Duke University Press, 2014), 77.

17. Ibid., 77.

18. Discourses of resistance, strict ideological boundaries, and ritualizing divine authority over all creates this identity in such texts as Ezra-Nehemiah. J. W. Cataldo, *Breaking Monotheism: Yehud and the Material Formation of Monotheistic Identity* (London: Bloomsbury, 2009), 187. The boundaries of these areas are often renegotiated in Genesis. See M. G. Brett, *Genesis: Procreation and the Politics of Identity* (London; New York: Routledge, 2000).

and heterodoxy, and Ezraic marriage politics. Tamar is enculturated into the line of Judah, but then rendered socially invisible. She then dons the veil to illustrate her ethnic Israelite ambiguous characterization. This is interpreted differently by Judah and Hirah, and the anonymous crowds that represent the androcentric gaze from Israelite and Canaanite groups. Ultimately held to Israelite legal and social norms, she is recognized as both Israelite, Canaanite, and dominated female. By her overconformity to Israelite male expectations, she questions her gender domination. Through deviancy to Israelite cultic expectations, she questions the nationalistic struggle. In terms of a postcolonial feminist analysis of the head veil in public, Tamar's social identity lies in the unstable intersectional space between gender domination and political or religious solidarity.

Social worlds of the text: A postcolony of gazes

When making links to the ancient world from modern sociology, I take some cues from David Chalcraft, who has used the sociology of risk to study the issue of trauma and disaster in Chronicles.[19] Chalcraft notes that historical questions arising from biblical texts can be usefully examined through sociology. However, he also concedes that modern methods and data can interfere with the study of ancient historical contexts, often called the "world behind the text." To clarify this, Chalcraft separates studies that seek the historical social world behind the text from those that "regard the text as constructing the [biblical] social worlds themselves."[20] The narrative world of Genesis 38 is constructed by familiarity with biblical texts that inform the use of the veil and the practice of selling sex, quite differently to much of the historical evidence for such issues outside the biblical text. Anderson's thesis that official nationalism is an imperialist-based reactionary stance modelled on popular nationalisms representing indigeneity begs the question:[21] Is this imagined community an organic popular nationalism or a result of policies as reactionary ideas from colonized Judean returnee ideology, particularly those interested in marriage and ethnic exclusion? The biblical text is certainly a linguistic product for the nationalistic imagination of those audiences of Genesis 38 familiar with the symbolism of Davidic power. Part of the narrative analysis here seeks to explore how much the world of the text is a drama of a community seeking a nationalistic identity apart from the colonial, narrowed

---

19. D. J. Chalcraft, "Sociology and the Book of Chronicles: Risk, Ontological Security, Moral Panics, and Types of Narrative," in *What Was Authoritative for Chronicles?*, eds. E. ben Zvi and D. V. Edelman (Winona Lake, IN: Eisenbrauns, 2011), 201-27.

20. D. J. Chalcraft, "Biblical Studies and the Social Sciences: Whence and Wither?," in *Methods, Theories, Imagination: Social Scientific Approaches in Biblical Studies*, eds. D. J. Chalcraft, F. Uhlenbruch, and R. S. Watson (The Bible in the Modern World 60; Sheffield: Sheffield Phoenix, 2014), xxii.

21. Anderson, *Imagined Communities*, 110.

political situation of history and how much is a resistance against this very identity because of its association with ethnic and gender limitations.

Susan Niditch, in *The Responsive Self: Personal Religion in Biblical Literature of the Neo-Babylonian and Persian Periods*, considers Tamar to be a trickster who becomes a helper, never reaching the interiority of the fully constructed narrative self. Niditch notes that in this type of narrative, "cultural cues supply a sense of characters' interiority, thus making the medium exquisitely communicative to its intended audience."[22] This lack of interiority in the narrative social world created in Genesis 38 is a frame in which postcolonial hybridity and mimicry occur through veiling and unveiling. Therefore, I suggest that this text about a woman's ambiguous identity as a Davidic ancestor, assuming a broad Persian-era readership and formation of Genesis, functions as a way in which the intersection between colonial and androcentric power can be read. Therefore, the veil of Tamar is a tool for the negotiation of her ambiguous ethnicity, via the implied male, elite, Israelite readerly gaze, to the visual function of the text as a resistant tool to categorization. This intersection of ethnicity and gender in the semiotic symbol of the veil illustrates the challenge of readers to understand Tamar, not as a woman who fights for her "rights" in an androcentric schema, nor as a dangerous woman who brings death, but as resistant reading to her fetishization as "foreign woman" versus "Mother in Israel." This resistance is achieved by examining who sees her in her veil, who does not see and what Tamar does to negotiate her (in)visibility.

Achille Mbembe describes the postcolonial condition as a combination of both collaboration and resistance, forming a new type of existence in the "postcolony," a political way of being "post" domination and subjection.[23] In this situation, where a society is emerging from violence within the colonial relationship, the postcolonial subject exists in "illicit cohabitation"[24] with the social performance created by this postcolony. Various types of public space determine the kinds of behavior carried out in each. For example, the official designated visual symbols are used publicly to assume conformity, but then in another space, they are used contrary to the official sense.[25] In fact, the social world that Mbembe describes is itself an unreality, a simulacrum, which only becomes real by institutionalizing meaning.[26]

For example, during colonial occupation by France, Algerian women could employ violence under the cover of the veil. This was unexpected, due to the way the veiled woman was viewed in Algeria by the French as either a tool of Algerian male oppression, or a suspicious way of hiding "imperfections," or misleading

---

22. S. Niditch, *The Responsive Self: Personal Religion in Biblical Literature of the Neo-Babylonian and Persian Periods* (Anchor Yale Bible Reference Library; New Haven, CT: Yale University Press, 2015), 123.

23. A. Mbembe, *On the Postcolony* (Studies on the History of Society and Culture 41) (Berkeley: University of California Press, 2001), 102.

24. A. Mbembe, "Provisional Notes on the Postcolony," *Africa* 62.1 (1992), 4.

25. Mbembe, *On the Postcolony*, 104.

26. Mbembe, "Provisional Notes on the Postcolony," 3, 8.

others.²⁷ Frantz Fanon concludes that the phenomenon of the veil in Algeria is an obscuring tool which facilitates the struggle against colonial control while uncovering orientalism. However, Drucia Cornell makes it clear that by doing this, Fanon also contributes to the "fetishization" of women's bodies. That is, Fanon implies that women are more likely to be able to conduct mimicry than men and therefore are more easily romanticized or orientalized as political figures.²⁸ Similarly, the ethnic and gender identity of the different characters in Genesis 38 can engender diverse responses to the public spectacle of veil wearing, to consider not only the Judahite nationalistic polemic but also the positioning of Israelite women. Israelite identity is thus constructed in the light of a "postcolony" world behind the text and the storyworld of the text.

The imperial realities of power hover over the ethnic conflict and collaborations between dominated groups. These groups are diverse within themselves and in relation to each other: unable to address the power of continuing hegemonic imperial control in the postcolony, they may emphasize their own traditions and culture above others, and/or seek their own infiltration of colonial hegemony into an (often androcentric) anti-colonial project.²⁹ The social space of Genesis is the place in which striving for recognition in an imperially controlled postcolony is worked out: tribal conventions are set up and assumed which power the general narrative motion. The power of cultural ties and expectations, ethnic separation and mixing, and an androcentric symbolic order tug at the characters' lives, in their intimate and public space, which drives their personal actions. Readings of Genesis ancestors can feature this dynamic process in narrative action and characterizations to discuss conflict and diversity of identity between dominated groups (Israelite/non-Israelite). The interpretation of these kinds of biblical texts can include allusions to "ethnicities" such as "Canaanite" and other terminologies. However, embodiment in the narrative provides self-determination to ethnic and gendered others, away from the implied narratorial or readerly gaze that creates nationalistic/androcentric profiling.³⁰ This method of reading requires a stance that considers the use of visual processes as a reading tool, particularly embodiment and body coverings such as the veil.

27. "There is not a European worker who does not sooner or later . . . ask the Algerian the ritual questions: 'Does your wife wear the veil? Why don't you take your wife to the movies, to the fights, to the café?' . . . The European women . . . proceed to compare the strategy to correct, to embellish . . . with that of the Algerian woman who prefers to veil, to conceal, to cultivate the man's doubt and desire" (Fanon, "Algeria Unveiled," 69–70).

28. D. Cornell, "The Secret Behind the Veil: A Reinterpretation of 'Algeria Unveiled,'" *Philosophia Africana* 4.2 (2001), 28–29.

29. L. Gandhi, *Affective Communities: Anticolonial Thought, Fin-de-Siècle Radicalism, and the Politics of Friendship* (Durham, NC: Durham University Press, 2006), 1–2.

30. D. Callender, Jr., "Fear and Foreign Bodies: The Bible and 'Post-Racial' American Identity," *Political Theology* 13.5 (2012), 544.

Marriage and veiling in ancient West Asia and the Hebrew Bible

Ancient texts featuring the use of the veil in marriage customs describe the covering or uncovering of a woman in response to a certain social gaze. In texts from Mari, obscuring the face is a symbolic demonstration of the convention of female dignified behavior and legal marriage. An important part of the act of veiling is that the woman is covered by a male member of the family, or the groom. For example, the veiled daughter of Zimri-Lim is sent to her new family with gifts that identify her, as she is continually covered from her betrothal until the marriage ceremony.[31] Covering a woman was part of the liminal experience of being promised in marriage but not yet married, and to identify particular high-status married women. For example, the public veiling (*pussumu*) of a woman, to promote her from *esirtu* (domestic "captured" concubine) to legal wife, was a performative declaration of that change in legal status.[32] This veiling act done by a male was the basis of a claim to marriage: as seen in the earlier Sumerian and Hittite customs of covering the head of a woman to either marry, remarry, or pardon her from adultery.[33] Inversely, the Babylonian Law of Hammurabi, for close comparison, denotes divorce as uncovering the woman to "cut the fringe of her garment" to symbolize breaking the relationship.[34] For one of the daughters of Zimri-Lim, her husband "cut the cord" in public.[35] Middle Assyrian Laws require the concubine of a high status man, when publicly seen with his legal wife, to wear a veil only because of their association.[36] It is disputed as to whether an unmarried upper-class Assyrian woman would still be required to veil, due to the incomplete

---

31. Archives royales de Mari 26.10; 26.11 "We made haste to have the *biblum* (gifts/dowry) . . . (entered into the palace grounds). Moreover, we draped veils over the young woman." As cited in Jean-Marie Durand, *Archives Épistolaires du Palais de Mari*, ed. J. Durand (Littératures Anciennes du Proche-Orient 18; Paris: Cerf, 2000), 165–84.

32. T. J. Meek, "Middle Assyrian Laws," in *Ancient Near Eastern texts relating to the Old Testament*, ed. James Bennett Pritchard (Princeton, NJ: Princeton University Press, 1969), 183, n. 41.

33. See note 29.

34. Hammurabi, *The Babylonian Laws*, trans. G. R. Driver and J. C. Miles (Oxford: Clarendon, 1952), 291. See also Ruth who asks Boaz to cover her with the hem of a garment in Ruth 3:9. The action of taking on another wife is the most common way to "release" the first wife in Babylonian marriage agreement provisions. M. T. Roth, *Babylonian Marriage Agreements: 7th-3rd Centuries B.C.* (Alter Orient und Altes Testament 222; Neukirchen-Vluyn: Neukirchener Verlag, 1989), 13.

35. B. Lafont, "The Women of the Palace at Mari," in *Everyday Life in Ancient Mesopotamia*, ed. J. Bottéro (Hathi Trust Digital Library; Edinburgh: Edinburgh University Press, 2001), 133–34.

36. A concubine is literally a "captive woman." Meek, "Middle Assyrian Laws," 40, 183.

lines in the laws.³⁷ The veil seems to have been the realm of wealthy and higher-status women.

The layers of social and gender categories of female marriage veiling are just as complex and contrastive in the Hebrew Bible. The invisibility of the bride because of the veil is not only a symbol of chastity or legal status. It also renders the personal, particular appearance of the woman opaque (such as the deception of Jacob in Gen. 29:21-25). The social meaning of the veil as a marriage rite can also be extended to spreading the hem of a garment (Ruth 3:9) which indicates the social acceptance of being covered by clothing. This is in contrast with the rejection symbolized through uncovering clothing from the body (Isa. 47:1-3).³⁸ References to a veil, including the hapax legomenon רְעָלָה in Isa. 3:19, are used in Isaiah (3:18-23) to illustrate the removal of garments to posit an androcentric voyeur on sexual violence against women, partly because they have been demoted in status.³⁹ The mention of צַמָּה in Isa. 47:2 similarly assumes that the dignity of a veil is to be taken from women in order for them to work on lower-class tasks. Both of these words for veil are feminine nouns. But the word for this kind of garment in Genesis 24 and 38 (צָעִיף) is masculine; it is employed semantically in deconstructing the social expectations of the viewer and the wearer.

Tamar and Rebekah can be compared and contrasted in the vocabulary of veiling itself.⁴⁰ Rebekah is of high status, according to Jack Sasson, indicated by her use of the צָעִיף (24:65).⁴¹ Van der Toorn cites Babylonian influence as an influence on words such as רְעָלָה, in Isa. 3:19, which is often considered to mean a "veil" of the elite.⁴² Tamar does the same action as Rebekah with the same garment (צָעִיף), but is considered lower in status by Judah through narratorial visual descriptions of his thoughts. Moreover, Rebekah does not veil until she sees her groom, to identify herself as his bride, while Tamar veils, when she hears Judah is coming, to be incognito. Within this social world of the text, Tamar and Rebekah use the veil as illustrations of the diverse ways in which this action can create a visual dissonance in regard to resisting gender domination and social expectations. When Rebekah veils herself in Gen. 24:65, she fills the role of a male family member. Her action, unusual in ancient contexts, is to leave herself uncovered until she sees Isaac in

---

37. The text simply says, "Whether . . . or . . . or . . . when they go out in the street alone, they must veil themselves." Meek, "Middle Assyrian Laws," 183.

38. van der Toorn, "The Significance of the Veil in the Ancient Near East," 335.

39. It is an aurally unique construction seeking to satirize rather than accurately describe women's garments. The daughters of Zion are caricatured by their garments, rather than given a voice, to use mockery of vanity as an excuse for sexual violence against women. See J. Miles, "Re-reading the Power of Satire: Isaiah's 'Daughters of Zion', Pope's 'Belinda', and the Rhetoric of Rape," *JSOT* 31.2 (2006), 209.

40. Tamar and Rebekah both have male twins, wear a veil and trick their "husband."

41. J. M. Sasson, "The Servant's Tale: How Rebekah Found a Spouse," *JNES* 65.4 (2006), 262.

42. van der Toorn, "The Significance of the Veil in the Ancient Near East," 330.

the distance.⁴³ Tamar makes sure that she is completely opaque in order to control the situation. Rebekah also uses coverings as a hiding strategy of false recognition (Gen. 27:15-16) while Tamar is eventually brought out to demand that Judah truly recognize her. Recognition and control is therefore a negotiated process of covering or uncovering when reading the characters Rebekah and Tamar.

The biblical sexual politics of the veil for the קְדֵשָׁה and זֹנָה

As cultural meaning is associated with the veil, religious and social location can determine or obscure identity, particularly characters designated as a קְדֵשָׁה. Much of the scholarly quest for cultural meaning of this role has been through ancient West Asian evidence, with limited results. In Akkadian poetic literature, the *qadištu*-woman has a kind of special religious status, being often located in the street.⁴⁴ This street location can be a social indicator of the offer of sex, but a *qadištu*-woman maintains a status defined outside of physical location.⁴⁵ A *qadištu* was also to wear the veil when married to an upper-class man.⁴⁶ Babylonian law contains several terms but scant descriptions of female religious orders. These are the "high-priestess" (*entum*), the "priestess" (*nadîtum*), the "epicene" (Sumerian *SAL-ZIKRUM*), the "hierodule" (*qadištum*), the "votaress" (*kulmašitum*), and the "lay sister" (*šugê/itum*). Babylonian categorization grants the *qadištum* a particular status to carry out special tasks and functions in relation to a male deity. These *qadištum* were regulated in their sexuality. This is in contrast with other classes of religious orders dedicated to a female deity who were not regulated.⁴⁷ The *qadištum* could marry and have children, nurse other's children and receive inheritance.⁴⁸ However, she could not pass on property to her sons.⁴⁹ Little other evidence can be found for the specific tasks carried out by the *qadištum*. As for the veil, the Assyrian Laws mentioned above stipulate that a married *qadištu* must wear a veil in public,

---

43. "Why is Rebekah not veiled in Haran by the servant? . . . by veiling herself, [Rebekah] takes control of the stories that will be told about her." Sasson, "The Servant's Tale," 265.

44. J. G. Westenholz, "Tamar, Qědēšā, Qadištu, and Sacred Prostitution in Mesopotamia," *HTR* 82.3 (1989), 251.

45. "In the myth of Enlil and Sud, Enlil mistakes her for a prostitute since she is standing in the street" (ibid.). See also Miguel Civil, "Enlil and Ninlil: The Marriage of Sud," *JAOS* 103.1 (1983), 46.

46. "A sacred prostitute whom a man married must veil herself on the street, but one whom a man did not marry must have her head uncovered on the street; she must not veil herself." Meek, "Middle Assyrian Laws," 183.

47. Westenholz, "Tamar, Qědēšā, Qadištu, and Sacred Prostitution," 251.

48. Lipit-Ishtar 22. M. T. Roth, H. A. Hoffner, and P. Michalowski, *Law Collections from Mesopotamia and Asia Minor* (Writings from the Ancient World 6; Atlanta, GA: Scholars Press, 1995), 30.

49. Hammurabi, *The Babylonian Laws*, 370.

contrasting with the female who offers sex for money and the slave, identified by being uncovered in the street. To ignore this difference was illegal and punishable corporally.⁵⁰ In earlier eras, Mesopotamian *entu* priestesses were kings' daughters, symbolically married to the Storm-God which included both wearing a red turban and a marriage veil.⁵¹

In the Hebrew Bible, this word is generally considered a term for a religious server or worker set apart for a cultic context, male or female. The prohibition against "cult prostitution" is evidence of the social standing of these persons (Deut. 23:18; Hos. 4:14; Job 36:14). Male practices of Canaanite religious practices are described in terms of male "prostitution" or illicit sexual activity (קָדֵשׁ) in 1 Kgs 14:24 and groups within the temple in 2 Kgs 23:7 (קְדֵשִׁים). However, there is no evidence of a cultic use of sex in other witnesses. Moreover, descriptions of female cultic functions are scant in the Hebrew Bible.⁵² It is not persuasive to describe this role in terms of sex merely because קְדֵשָׁה seems to be considered a synonym of זֹנָה in Genesis 38.⁵³ Biblical interpreters of this view usually begin not with ancient texts contemporaneous with the Bible, but Herodotus.⁵⁴ Thankfully, the necessary revisions of this interpretation are now much more widespread in biblical scholarship.⁵⁵

Because of a lack of contemporary evidence for ritual or priestess "prostitution" in ancient Mesopotamia,⁵⁶ interpretations of Genesis 38 rely mostly on an argument from silence. The symbolic world of the Hebrew Bible creates the קְדֵשָׁה as transgressive for legal and cultic reasons. Therefore, in this study, while it is important to note the biblical and historical evidence, the interpretation centers

---

50. Meek, "Middle Assyrian Laws," 183.

51. Jo-Ann Scurlock, "Religious Participation: Ancient Near East—Sacred Prostitution," in *The Oxford Encyclopaedia of the Bible and Gender Studies*, vol. 2, ed. J. M. O'Brien (Oxford: Oxford University Press, 2014), 205.

52. "To the Hebrew author, the pagan priestess must be a harlot, and vice versa, the harlot must have been a pagan priestess." Westenholz, "Tamar, Qĕdēšā, Qadištu, and Sacred Prostitution," 248.

53. M. I. Gruber, "Hebrew Qĕdēšāh and Her Canaanite and Akkadian Cognates," *UF* 18 (1986), 133–48.

54. Herodotus, *The Histories*. I: 199 (A. D. Godley, LCL). T. S. Frymer-Kensky, *In the Wake of the Goddesses: Women, Culture, and the Biblical Transformation of Pagan Myth* (New York: Maxwell Macmillan, 1992), 200.

55. See also K. Adams, "Metaphor and Dissonance: A Reinterpretation of Hosea 4:13–14," *JBL* 127 (2008), 291–305; Scurlock, "Sacred Prostitution," 205–11.

56. Former interpreters have suggested organized "sacred prostitution" outside Israel. Within Israel, it could be misguided festival-based orgies or heterodox Temple practice. "Prostitution as a source of profits for the Temple? Yes. Prostitution as an integrating part of fertility rituals? No." K. van der Toorn, "Female Prostitution in Payment Vows in Ancient Israel," *JBL* 108.2 (1989), 203.

5. Veiled Resistance

on the metaphoric narrative strategy of visual dissonance between the veiled and unveiled. Prophetic literature commonly pairs metaphors of "adultery" (נָאַף) and "prostitution" (זָנָה), particularly in their relationship to veils (Hos. 4:13-14; Ezek. 16:24). A metaphor is not the comparison of two similar things, but two or more dissimilar things that connect new meaning in the minds of an assumed audience. This process illustrates the idea that metaphor is artistic, but only contextually meaningful between human subjects through a social contract.[57] For example, in Ezekiel 16 and 23, the handling of sexual deviancy in the dissonance between semantics of metaphor and social worlds of the Hebrew Bible can result in the mismanagement of a metaphor.[58] In prophetic texts such as Ezekiel, this is illustrated by the use of sex metaphors interacting with covenant breaking. In Genesis 38, the conflation of זָנָה and קְדֵשָׁה should be read within the wider use of this in the Bible as a dissonance of illicit or covenant-breaking activity juxtaposed alongside cultic activity.

Prophetic and Deuteronomistic traditions create the category of the קְדֵשָׁה to compare and define Israel alongside others, particularly those others who engage in cultic (non-Yahwistic) apostasy, notwithstanding that it can also illustrate heterodox religious practices.[59] Another example of the metaphoric comparison to describe social deviancy, which is also licit (a vice, but socially acceptable), is the social position of women (or subordinated men) who sell sex (זָנָה).[60] Tamar uses her veil to create a trick that is both socially deviant and licit. Some biblical commentators find it difficult to hold the dissonance between the pairing of social deviancy and licit behavior. But the narrative of Tamar and Judah plays with the idea of a licit social contract between language of conformity and deviancy, perhaps influenced by prophetic genres mentioned above that also create this cognitive dissonance. This dissonance is shown in the idea that, if the צָעִיף is socially and

---

57. Plato denigrated art as it does not have a direct correspondence with knowledge, and Aristotle would reply that only worthwhile, real art carries knowledge. But is access to knowledge the point? Or rather is it a communication event showing the interaction of a community? See T. Cohen, "Metaphor and the Cultivation of Intimacy," *Critical Inquiry* 5.1 (1978), 7-8.

58. P. L. Day, "Adulterous Jerusalem's Imagined Demise: Death of a Metaphor in Ezekiel XVI," *VT* 50.3 (2000), 285-309.

59. From Herodotus to modern states, categories such as "cannibal," "sexual deviant," or other cultural practices are accusations raised to intensify emic views of themselves against others. R. A. Oden, *The Bible without Theology: The Theological Tradition and Alternatives to It* (New Voices in Biblical Studies; San Francisco, CA: Harper & Row, 1987), 132-34.

60. The זָנָה is "an outcast, though not an outlaw, a tolerated but dishonored member of society." Bird, *Missing Persons and Mistaken Identities*, 199. Inspired by Niditch, "Prostitutes seem to have an accepted, outcast place in society." S. Niditch, "The Wronged Woman Righted," 147.

politically the sign of conformity for women in Genesis, this is not the case for Rebekah, and certainly not for Tamar.⁶¹

These two narrative occurrences of the veil in Genesis can illustrate resistance to the construction of deviance by using an alternative method. Rather than a normative use of the veil, something else is occurring in the narrative. Moreover, the Bible creates a קָדֵשׁ/קְדֵשָׁה as deviant and connected with the זֹנָה, both female and male (Deut. 23:17-18; 1 Kgs 14:24; 15:12; 22:46; 2 Kgs 23:7; Hos. 4:14; Job 36:14), but with no explicit evidence that they engage in selling sex.⁶² The confusion of this status is clear in later traditions, from the LXX translators' ambiguity between "prostitutes" and "initiates" into a holy order.⁶³ It is perhaps because the Hebrew Bible prohibits a status in the cult similar to the קְדֵשָׁה that it is described as "Canaanite" and therefore apostate or non-Yahwistic.

Genesis 38 and Tamar's visibility

Genesis 38 uses visual covering and perception in public and private space, through motifs of moving out and returning in. The spaces are the scenic locations for the framing of the actions of characters. In v. 1, Judah "goes down" (יָרַד) and "stretches" (נָטָה) himself to a different public sphere in his male homosocial association with an Adullamite named Hirah. Like his descendant David,⁶⁴ Judah seems to befriend this Canaanite to both rule over and escape the non-Israelite. An exogamous marriage is conducted with a Canaanite woman, after he sees (רָאָה) her (v. 2). In a similar fashion to David in 2 Sam. 11:4-5, Judah's action is described in a quick succession of verbs: see, take, go into, and conceive. The two eldest sons produced are named Er, a reversal of "evil," perhaps meaning "laid bare" or "blind,"⁶⁵ contrasting with the sight of YHWH (v. 3, 7), and Onan, "vigorous"⁶⁶ (v. 4). Ironically, Onan hardly shows this quality to Tamar in the narrative ahead.

---

61. Is Judah seeing Tamar this way as he is drunk or sex-starved? T. J. Schneider, *Mothers of Promise: Women in the Book of Genesis* (Grand Rapids, MI: Baker Academic, 2008), 129–30. Or does Abraham's servant/narrator see Rebekah as a liminal bride or vain? Schneider, 42–43. These everyday concerns are somewhat relevant, but the wider social and religious world specifically constructed in the Hebrew Bible concerning veils should be the first place to consider these questions.

62. See the discussion on Mesopotamian texts regarding the description of the cultic activity of female and male priests by way of sexual penetration, and how this is mistakenly described as "prostitution" in scholarship. I. Peled, *Masculinities and Third Gender: The Origins and Nature of an Institutionalized Gender Otherness in the Ancient Near East* (Alter Orient und Altes Testament 435; Münster: Ugarit-Verlag, 2016), 157.

63. Westenholz, "Tamar, Qĕdēšā, Qadištu, and Sacred Prostitution," 248.

64. 1 Sam. 22:1-2; 2 Sam. 23:13.

65. "עוּר," F. Brown, C. A. Briggs, and S. R. Driver, eds. *BDB* (Peabody, MA: Hendrickson, 1997), 734.

66. Brown et al., "אוֹנָן," *BDB*, 20.

After the deaths of the two eldest brothers, married consecutively to Tamar, Judah sends her to her father's house: a private space where she is no longer seen. After his wife dies, perhaps from grief, Judah "goes up" again and returns to see a new woman at Timnah, like Sampson.[67] Tamar is informed by an unnamed informant that Judah is coming, and assuming she is living near Timnah (Edom: see Gen. 36:40), decides to go out. Instead of sitting in her father's house, Tamar sits in the public space, at the "eye-gate" (בְּפֶתַח עֵינַיִם). Like Dinah, she goes out (34:1). However, rather than to see others, Tamar goes out specifically to be seen. Unlike Sarah, she opens others' eyes to her plans rather than hiding them.[68] She takes off her widow's clothes and puts on a veil, wrapping herself in it (38:14). The moral and functional double meaning of the veil are in the vocabulary of covering. In this verse, using "take off" סור, "wrap up" עלף, and the priestly language of "cover" כסה to illustrate the two dimensions of objective and moral visibility in the veil and its possible licit or deviant nature.[69] After the encounter in v. 19 she "takes off" (סור) and "puts on" (לבש),[70] the widow's garments, signifying this fabric as of pragmatic conformative use, such as when the deity, Pharaoh or a parent such as Rebekah place garments on others for social conformity (e.g., Gen. 3:21; 27:15; 41:42). This is rather than the moral language of גלה "uncover" or again כסה. On the one hand, a risk to Tamar is possible punishment for the "wrong" use of the veil, contrary to the expectations of the implied reader. On the other hand, it is a perfectly normative and functional action. The risk to Judah is tacit to himself and the implied reader but comes to fruition when the reader steps away from singular empathy with the Judahite gaze and takes in an overview of the polyvisual political situation represented by the garments.

Judah understands Tamar's clothing as a kind of identity which involves covering the face. As with his non-Israelite friend, Judah "stretches" (נָטָה) again over to her on the side of the road (v. 16), as a clue to the difference, if not clearly foreignness, of Tamar. In his mind, her head covering implies זְנָה. Due to her self-concealment, the future of Judah as a tribe is transferred temporarily from male to female control. Just as Onan should have "stood up" (קוּם) to give her a child in v. 8, Tamar herself "sits down" (יָשַׁב) (v. 14). Tamar is eventually brought back out (יָצָא) to the public sphere to vindicate herself (vv. 24-25), as in due course her sons come out (יָצָא) (vv. 28-30). Tamar returns to the private sphere for three months (v. 24), then the nameless crowd, stirring panic, use Judah's word in v. 24 and calls her a זְנָה, making a report of their Israelite male voyeurism using הִנֵּה "see." Her question as to the owner of the staff, cord, and seal is the *anagnorisis* moment for Judah[71] and returns to the narrator's ideology of Israelite social expectation.

---

67. Judg. 14:1, 5.
68. I. Robinson, "Bepetah Enayim in Genesis 38:14," *JBL* 96.4 (1977), 569.
69. See Deut. 13:9 and the use of this moral vocabulary.
70. Cf. Gen. 3:21.
71. Judah realizes he has been "acting like a Canaanite." A. J. Lambe, "Judah's Development: The Pattern of Departure—Transition—Return," *JSOT* 24.83 (1999), 57.

When Tamar demands recognition as a person of status, including a mother and wife, she is not removed from the androcentric legal world which overarches her struggle. Levirate law (Deut. 25:5-10), and to a lesser extent primogeniture, are parts of a biblical textual culture which is key to the recognition of characters as important to Judahite legal identity. This hermeneutical assumption also remains in legal force over the ethnicity and gender of characters such as Tamar, Judah's wife (daughter of Shua), and Hirah. These characters do not benefit directly from Levirate law but play the gaps and layers in between the law to find a visual place somewhere within it. For example, although the recognition scene in vv. 25-26 seems to mimic a judicial process that implies public witnesses, we do not know if Judah's friend Hirah actually saw Judah with Tamar, or if בְּפֶתַח עֵינַיִם in v. 14 means that Judah and Tamar were in the public eye the whole time. It requires a suspension of strict legal and social codification and gaps in the visual story to come to the decision that Judah is guilty and Tamar is telling the truth. Judah is characterized as non-observant of the law; however, his arbitrary suspension of legal responsibility is his androcentric prerogative and he is finally restored. However, the ambiguity lingers: seeing a veiled person in public creates either solidarity (Hirah) or othering (Judah).

Visualizing fellow friends or foreign foes?

We do not know why Tamar is incorporated into the family of Judah at the beginning of the story, but we can look at the theme of the recognition of foreignness as a clue as to her later incorporation. The recognition of Tamar is through a veil, a gate, her body, and presented objects. Is Judah's recognition of Tamar's identity as a woman integrated into the Israelite system, or is it of his own dislocation from the kinship and covenant system? Many interpretations use the former, with many asserting that Judah is ultimately integrating Tamar. But the lack of punishment for Judah for his actions is a problem for integrating Tamar into the Davidic line and the accompanying ethnic requirements. If this argument is followed, then Tamar is a visual scandal of being both a foreigner and also subject to the law.[72] This does not make her origin irrelevant, as it is her origin that might solve the puzzle of recognition.[73] However, as this is not clear, and the veil

---

72. Y. Amit, "Narrative Analysis: Meaning, Context and Origins of Genesis 38." Pages 271–92 in *Method Matters: Essays on the Interpretation of the Hebrew Bible in Honor of David L. Petersen*, eds. J. M. LeMon and K. Harold Richards (Atlanta, GA: Society of Biblical Literature, 2009), 283.

73. Y. Amit assumes that Tamar is Canaanite because she comes from Timnah or Adullam, and in juxtaposition with Ruth and therefore the justification of intermarriage. This connects with Hirah's vision (*Hidden Polemics in Biblical Narrative* [Biblical Interpretation Series 25; Leiden; Boston, MA: Brill, 2000], 83). The matter of guilt or innocence, to the Rabbis, is predicated on placing Tamar in an Israelite ethnic category, influenced by other

covers from initial recognition, it is the dialectic of gazes which builds an Israelite identity. But the relationship of the gazes involved can provide literary illustrations of this hybrid state.

Tamar's visual place in the social and tribal world is compared to the differing powers of others' covering from danger. Tamar's genealogy is not mentioned by the narrator; she initially appears outside the Mother in Israel traditions and yet is received into them by the conclusion of the story. Judah is responding to events occurring within the storyworld of family and tribal expectations, and yet ultimately declares Tamar as the one who is observing law "correctly." Judah perceives dimly what is occurring throughout the story, until the last revelation of the truth. Shelah foreshadows the protection around the beloved Benjamin (42:38). Because of the masculine pronominal in the verb in v. 5, the Masoretic text suggests[74] that the referent for "he was in Chezib" (כְּזִיב) could mean birth with a caul: a layer of membrane over the baby's head.[75] Shelah is veiled (Chezib can be semantically linked to אַכְזָב "deceptive, disappointing")[76] because of the possible risk his death plays as the last living son of Judah. He is protected by a force outside himself even from birth. The birth with a veil/caul could be a foreshadowing of Tamar's twins, as in many cultures, a caul is a prediction for twins.[77] It could also foreshadow the scarlet thread (שָׁנִי "red") on the hand of the first of Tamar's twins, Zerah, so as to protect him from envious evil eyes as the true firstborn.[78]

The verb form from נָכַר "to recognize, regard" does not appear in the common *qal* stem in the Hebrew Bible.[79] The transitive nature of the verb means that it does not refer to the typical *qal* themes such as stative (being described with an adjective) or ditransitive action (e.g., to give or take). In many cases, the semantic field consists of visual or psychological processes from one subject to another subject or object. Pointing out objects to identify the correct owner occurs in Gen. 31:32, 37:32-33, and 38:25-26,[80] which involve careful visual examination.

---

narratives in Genesis. Leviticus 21:9 declares the punishment of the sexual activity of the daughter of a priest to be death by fire. She is the cause of "profane" (חָלַל) effect on the honor of the priestly father. *Gen. Rab.*, 2, 85, 10. *Tg. Ps.-J.*, 1, vv. 6 and 24, n. 9.

74. LXX αὐτὴ δὲ ἦν (וְהִיא) Elliger and Rudolph, eds. *Biblia Hebraica Stuttgartensia*, 61.

75. C.A. Ben-Mordecai, "Chezib," *JBL* 58.3 (1939), 283–86.

76. Brown et al., "אַכְזָב," *BDB*, 469.

77. S. Diduk, "Twinship and Juvenile Power: The Ordinariness of the Extraordinary," *Ethnology* 40.1 (2001), 29–43. M. Houlberg, "Two Equals Three: Twins and the Trickster in Haitian Vodou," in *Twins in African and Diaspora Cultures: Double Trouble, Twice Blessed*, ed. P. M. Peek (Bloomington: Indiana University Press, 2011), 271–89.

78. The visceral physical and spiritual quality of the use of the evil eye in the biblical text can be an expression of the anxieties of precarious or dangerous living conditions. J. H. Elliott, *Beware the Evil Eye: The Evil Eye in the Bible and the Ancient World* (Cambridge: James Clarke & Co., 2016), 59.

79. Brown et al., "נכר," *BDB*, 647–48.

80. In the causative *hiphil*.

It distinguishes between at least two states or identities by sight (Gen. 27:23; 42:8; Judg. 18:3; Job 34:19). Disguise used by characters can be part of a ruse or change the status of an Israelite to foreigner through location (1 Sam. 23:7; 1 Kgs 14:5-6). Cultural activity or appearance can be an indicator of foreignness (Neh. 13:24; Isa. 61:9; 63:16; Jer. 19:4; 24:5; Lam. 4:8; Obad. 1:12). The noun הַכָּרַת refers to the facial expression which betrays inner motivations (Isa. 3:9).[81] The adjective evolved to נָכְרִי to indicate social groups such as gentiles or distant foreigners.[82]

Genres such as wisdom stretch this meaning to moral actions (Prov. 2:16; 5:20; 7:5; 23:27; נָכְרִיָּה). In discussions on the "strange" woman in Proverbs and why she acts in this way, the semantics of this noun indicate comparison of a type with another type.[83] Whether in terms of marriage or nationalistic boundaries, a foreign person is only recognized when compared with an Israelite or another type of foreign person.[84] This type of comparison in Proverbs is well known for the cognitive (and psychological) dissonance for female readers as the foreignness is a trait which they must identify with a subject against the self.[85] In any case, Exodus uses the noun for positive characters such as Moses (2:22; 18:3); and it is used for Ruth (22:10) and YHWH (Isa. 28:21). נָכְרִיָּה is paired with הָשַׁב, "to reckon" as a decision to see in a certain way in Gen. 31:15, alluding to the way YHWH sees Abraham in covenant (15:6) and Joseph compares YHWH and his brothers (50:20).

The comparison is a result of a decision to see in a certain way. How does the use of נָכַר in Genesis 38 play with this idea of looking, comparison, and decision, based on covering and uncovering? With what does the narrator compare the garments/objects of Judah in Gen. 38:25?[86] The clue may be in v. 26, where there is a comparison between Judah and Tamar. Judah is recognizing and acknowledging (נָכְרִיָּה) one type of object with any other type. Is it the objects or Tamar which is an example of a visible identity which defies the categorization of another's ethnic or gendered gaze? This is in contrast with the more straightforward comparison of Judah with Hirah in his nationalistic struggle alongside a foreign "friend" רֵעַ in 38:12, 20 (alluding to David's Adullamite man-cave) and Judah with his sons as evil (רַע) (38:7) in the eyes of YHWH.

---

81. "נכר," BDB.

82. The other categories in the Holiness School vocabulary are תּוֹשָׁב "rent paying tenant" (paired with גֵּר in Gen. 23:4) and שָׂכִיר "hireling." See J. Mayshar, "Who Was the Toshav?," JBL 133.2 (2014), 226.

83. Van der Toorn, "Female Prostitution in Payment Vows in Ancient Israel," 199.

84. Nehemiah 6:12; 13:24.

85. G. A. Yee, "'I Have Perfumed My Bed with Myrrh': The Foreign Woman ('Iššâ Zārâ) in Proverbs 1–9," JSOT, no. 43 (1989), 67.

86. Robert Alter's famous illustration from Rabbinical sources: "The Holy One praised be He said to Judah, 'You said to your father haker-na. By your life, Tamar will say to you, haker-na.'" Gen. Rab., 1, 85.11, 214. "The spectator knows something which the protagonist doesn't and should know" (see The Art of Biblical Narrative [New York: Basic Books, 1981], 11).

Rachel Adelman points out that the key verbs "to know" and "recognize" play a part in understanding the way in which biblical narratives stretch legal categories. The three stories of Lot's daughters (Gen. 19:30-38), Ruth (2:10; 3:3), and Tamar in Genesis relate to each other in terms of the use of knowledge and recognition.[87] These themes of knowledge and recognition are also illustrated through covering and uncovering, particularly with garments. The recognition of foreign persons in Ruth is also linked by Edward Greenstein to the root נָכַר.[88] The way in which Tamar fits into the Davidic line is as a direct link to the idea of the origin of Moab by the daughters of Lot and the adoption of Moab into the line through Ruth. Lot's daughters are half Israelite, who produce the line of Ruth, which coalesce with the line of Tamar, ambiguously or double-sidedly "foreign." Recognition נָכַר through sight and knowledge is a link between representation and foreignness in the three narratives, creating David's line through both Israelite and Moab/Ammon incorporation.[89]

However, what does the idea of recognition have to do with foreignness or non-Israelite identity, since the verb for recognition is used as a key term in recognizing others ethnically? Interpreters differ as to the ethnocentric or imperial vision of David's dynasty and the way these narratives are constructed.[90] The juxtaposition of recognition with risk, both of detecting deviancy or foreignness, in these stories heightens the importance of visual recognition. The link of risk with vision relates to these stories of Israelite covenant and that of postcolonial concerns of the veil as the meaning of conformity/deviancy or insider/outsider status is through wearing or not wearing a veil rather than law, postcolonial theories on the veil posit a set of challenges to political resistance, including gender domination through wearing a veil publicly. What difference does the use of the veil make to the idea of possible redemption? The "line of the law" inspired by Talmudic tradition is used by Adelman to make the point that there exists a way of interpretation and observance of the law that sees a space, or liminal reality, between the lines of the law itself.[91] For Tamar, the promise of Shelah is never fulfilled, so she works within this layer in between the law.

Tamar sees everything clearly throughout the narrative of Genesis 38, as evidenced by her actions, although her inner vision of herself is not described.[92] Moreover, her covering, rather than hindering her, is the way to question her

---

87. R. Adelman, "Seduction and Recognition in the Story of Judah and Tamar and the Book of Ruth," in *Nashim: A Journal of Jewish Women's Studies and Gender Issues*, no. 23 (2012), 87–109.

88. E. Greenstein, "Reading Strategies in the Book of Ruth," in *Women in the Hebrew Bible: A Reader*, ed. A. Bach (London; New York: Routledge, 1999), 211–31.

89. Adelman, "Seduction and Recognition," 102.

90. Greenstein, "Reading Strategies in the Book of Ruth," 216.

91. Adelman, "Seduction and Recognition," 102.

92. The only time Tamar "sees" is to understand that Shelah is not to be her husband (38:14).

orientalization precisely because she is *not* seen. This dissonance is in the polyvisual and opaque nature of many of the visual tropes and positions in and out of this storyworld. Judah sees her as an Israelite male, and Hirah as a Canaanite male. The anonymous crowd in v. 21 sees Canaanite judiciaries and the whistleblower group in v. 24 as Israelite judiciaries. The narrator negotiates between these gazes. Tamar creates her own outer visual identity through mimicry, using the visual props of the structures around her by appropriating their symbolism. This keeps her identity changing in order to move within worlds.

Negotiating through gazes

Veils worn by certain persons can expose the dominance of others. For Judah's gaze, the desire is simply for sex without observing visible social boundaries, through the licit use of what is perceived to be no more than a veiled woman. This is despite the misrecognition of the risk of exposure as a participant in a fantasy of androcentric dominance within a postcolony that seeks to maintain Israelite legal and religious exclusivity against outsiders. The danger of being caught as illicit is present for both Judah and Tamar, but the tacit "doxa" of the ideology of gender and ethnicity veils this danger to Judah. Indeed, he seems to be in contempt of granting any status for a woman wearing a veil in public, if he considers her to be "just" a Canaanite. His position of gender domination over those lower in status because of gender and ethnicity must not be questioned (38:23), "lest we be laughed at," or "despised" (לָבוּז) in the eyes of the Israelite audience. Judah has a glimpse of the edge of the *anagnorisis* that will come soon, as the recognition (נָכַר) is of what he knows from silence and vision but does not know that he knows.[93] Ethnicity and gender norms are uncovered and recognized through the viewpoint of Judah. The exposure of the Israelite dominant fantasy is a feature of broader Genesis narratives, that deal with the position of foreigners (12:3; 17:12, 16), widows (38:11; 19:31), and orphans (21:16-18; 22:8).

Putting on a veil is fraught, depending on identity. If an at-risk person because of racial or gender othering, like Tamar as a יָבָם widow, puts on her veil, it can create a simultaneously licit and conformative public spectacle. The veil is worn by a particular member of an ethnic group for the sake of solidarity with that group. This is despite the fact that the person already "looks" part of this group, while the

---

93. The political aspect to this is in Bourdieu's application of *doxa* to a state which legitimizes a dominant group by requiring invisible and unconscious assent. "Doxa is a particular point of view, the point of view of the dominant, which presents and imposes itself as a universal point of view—the point of view of those who dominate by dominating the state and who have constituted their point of view as universal by constituting the state" (P. Bourdieu, *Practical Reason: On the Theory of Action* [Stanford, CA: Stanford University Press, 1998], 57). See also J. Berlinerblau, "Ideology, Pierre Bourdieu's Doxa, and the Hebrew Bible," *Semeia* 87 (1999), 202.

covering intensifies this sign of othering. The person who identifies with a dominant power does not join in this solidarity but interprets the covering differently. Judah, the father-in-law in charge of levirate marriage, maintains androcentric gaze in dominance. But as Judah occupies a culturally dominated position, when seeing a woman in a veil, Judah does not see a risk to safety, but unconsciously opens a threat to his own status. He is drawn sexually, but the veiled woman is tinged with a licit/illicit danger for the narrator and other readers/viewers. The real risk to which Judah is exposed is through the possibility that he and others will reveal the knowledge of his identity as a culturally dominated man, not able to "control the women" in his world. This illustrates Tamar's position beneath colonial and gender domination. Dominance works best when not detected for what it is. Judah does not fear censure for his actions, but his possible demotion in status by exposure.

Although he recognized the veil as a political symbol of resistance to colonization, Fanon missed the important gender dominance symbolism of the veil, or the reality of the Algerian woman's double colonization. Fanon only expects women to wear the veil to participate in the resistance to colonial vision and power. When women participate in resistance, they choose the universal nationalistic struggle to the internal, particular gender struggle. The women who veiled in Algerian decolonial struggle were seeking to uncover the mask of the colonial master-slave identity to expose the dominant status of the French. They must choose solidarity with the Algerian men in spite of gender dominance, as illustrated in other colonized cultures.[94]

Tamar already possesses a complex status in the narrative, placed on her by both Israelite and gender expectations. To complicate this and create a visual dissonance, she employs the veil not as a "Bedtrick" or active obfuscation of identity. Rather than swapping one person for another (as Leah for Rachel in Gen. 29:23), Tamar creates this cognitive dissonance within herself through

---

94. "Not that long ago, Black Panther Woman—a documentary about Marlene Cummins—came out speaking of the sorts of abuses she and other Aboriginal women experienced within the Australian Black Panther movement during the early 1970s. There is one scene in particular which has continued to stick in my head ever since I first saw the film nearly two years ago. It's a piece of archival footage in which a group of Aboriginal women are having an argument with white feminists who are trying to engage the Black Panther women in their struggle. In one part Aunty Isobel Coe, I believe, points out to the feminists that splitting the Indigenous rights movement was not an option on the basis of gender because there was a need to walk together, and while women had experienced issues within this movement, the feminist movement was not a safe space either because it erased Aboriginal experience. Another Aboriginal woman in the group said that she believed that the place of Aboriginal women was behind their men, supporting them. Yet while women are supporting men and children and community, who ends up looking out for the women?" C. Liddle, "Molly Hadfield Social Justice Oration" (paper presented at the City of Darebin Molly Hadfield Oration, Preston, Victoria, Australia, March 10, 2016).

(in)visibility.⁹⁵ For visible female embodiment, a head covering both in an ancient and modern context is publicly acknowledging subordination to the androcentric symbolic order. At the same time, it can be a symbol of overarching resistance to other dominating structures, such as colonial power. Those that see from outside these power structures can analyze this cognitive dissonance. For those within these structures, the veil reveals their own assumptions, but any knowledge and recognition of this dominance remains tacit. When the veil is used by the narrator to characterize, there is a possibility that it will reveal feelings of mimetic resistance, threat, panic, or sexual invitation from a woman who seems to bring death, even to herself.⁹⁶ Judah, through the narrator, sees Tamar's veil as a public display of sex vending, a licit activity. Hirah and the male crowd saw a fellow Canaanite religious practitioner, therefore assuming the presence of a fraught relationship with Israelite ideology. However, a postcolonial feminist gaze on Tamar sees both an ambivalent and mimetic visual negotiation of an androcentric symbolic order through a doubly colonized woman.⁹⁷

Who is the crowd that condemns Tamar to Judah, except that of the implied Israelite audience? This audience, amid their own colonized experience, is informed that "Israelite" is a term that is examined on the borders, the edges of the identity, and the "line of the law": it is separate, but not dominant. The crowd spectates on this scene, but we do not know if they accept responsibility for their spectatorship. The task remains; how does the reader then respond to Tamar? Do we see her as she represents herself or as we would like to see her, to rescue her or

---

95. The Bedtrick has been noted as a narrative strategy in biblical texts where "women are often able to subvert the powers of men precisely because men regard women as indistinguishable or not worthy of distinction ... because men think women are alike, they do not notice them, and that invisibility can be used as a weapon of the weak." W. Doniger, *The Bedtrick: Tales of Sex and Masquerade* (Chicago, IL: Chicago University Press, 2000), 179–80. Rachel Adelman uses the Bedtrick to illustrate the false identity of Tamar in "Seduction and Recognition." But Doniger also considers multiple changing identities within one person in contrast to the Bedtrick in *The Woman Who Pretended to Be Who She Was: Myths of Self-Imitation* (Oxford: Oxford University Press, 2005), 26.

96. This folk motif in Succession History and other narratives was coined by J. Blenkinsopp. "The woman that brings death" is a motif of a woman that potentially leads to the personal deprivation and danger of men through chaos and or death ("Theme and Motif in the Succession History [2 Sam. xi 2ff.] and the Yahwist Corpus," in *Volume du Congres: Geneve, 1965*, ed. P. A. H. de Boer [Vetus Testamentum Supplement 15; Leiden: E.J. Brill, 1966], 52).

97. When speaking of the contemporary Dutch political situation toward public veils, Annelies Moors notes, "It is the dissonance between framing face-veiling women as victims and the perception of their public presence as challenging Dutch sociabilities that evokes resentment." A. Moors, "The Affective Power of the Face Veil: Between Disgust and Fascination," in *Things: Religion and the Question of Materiality*, eds. D. Houtman and B. Meyer (New York: Fordham University Press, 2012), 294.

vilify her actions? The way that we as readers see her informing Israelite identity itself is the task of viewing Genesis 38.

Concluding remarks

The lack of determinate historical data on the social and religious function of the veil in Mesopotamia leads us to ask instead sociological, feminist, and postcolonial questions of this biblical text. If readers are not attentive to polemics against the קְדֵשָׁה/קָדֵשׁ throughout the Hebrew Bible, it can create a narrow lens for reading the veil of Tamar. Modern postcolonial views of the women's veil suggest that it is a double sign, or a choice between ethnic or gender solidarity. Women can wear veils to identify with their group and their history of colonization or domination by others. On the other hand, veil wearing can be fetishized Fanonian-style or render the wearer subject to gender domination. Androcentric views of biblical women are problematic, but "white/Western" feminisms can also create a problem by not attending to double colonization. If this is missed in the broader feminist discussion, specific cultural domination can continue to create the tension and choice of such issues as the veil. In the Hebrew Bible, particularly in the dense narrative world of the political messages in Genesis, we see in narratives these nationalistic ambiguities and emptiness, a characteristic which Anderson considers inherent to nationalistic philosophy.[98] Nationalism is ultimately not political or legal but social in that it lacks the strength of ideology and falls back onto human relationships. Thus, Tamar's veil works on ambiguous intersections, begging questions such as, is she Canaanite or Israelite? Is she law-keeping or law-breaking, and which law? Why is the narrator creating her as a קְדֵשָׁה or a זֹנָה? The ethnic religious identity of "foreign women" is illustrated here as unresolvable. Tamar veiled and unveiled is a figure left in the tension between, for example, Ezraic traditions of marriage purity and challenges to this endogamous Israelite identity or the religious practitioner of non-Yahwistic heterodoxy. This dissonance of vision and ambiguity in Israelite identity is expressed through multiple seeing perspectives of characters contrasting with the signifier of Tamar's own public visibility.

98. Anderson, *Imagined Communities*, 5.

Chapter 6

THOSE AT EASE HAVE CONTEMPT FOR MISFORTUNE: BIBLICAL APPROACHES TO CHALLENGING ANTI-POOR SENTIMENT

Matthew J. M. Coomber

Many aspects of a person's reality are thrust upon them, such as the death of a loved one or an unexpected encounter that results in love. But as the chapters of this volume highlight, there are also aspects of our realities that we create for ourselves, as attested to by such catchphrases as "turning lemons into lemonade" or "fake it 'till you make it." While humans have an incredible ability to construct their perceptions of reality so as to match their hopes, desires, and preconceptions, what I find especially fascinating are those unconscious ways in which people alter their realities to fit their learned expectations. It is difficult to discern how much of what we perceive—from the nature of a comment by a loved one to whether or not a stranger walking toward us is a threat—aligns with what is real.

Recent psychological research has found that our perceptions of people are greatly impacted by how we view another's economic and class status in relation to our own. This chapter examines two ways in which studies into the psychological effects of status and privilege may be of benefit to the field of biblical studies. First, discoveries on how privilege effects the human mind might reveal the psychological underpinnings of numerous biblical laws, stories, and oracles, enabling these texts to be read and understood in new and useful ways. What results is a heuristic tool that not only has the potential to shed new light on biblical texts that address privileged contempt but can also help to gain new insights into their histories of interpretation. Second, numerous biblical stories address the dangers of privileged contempt toward those of lower status, from the story of David and Bathsheba to the parable of the rich man and Lazarus.[1] Through gaining a deeper understanding of how such contempt arises and affects both its subjects and also its objects, readers may be better able to connect these stories to anti-poor sentiment in their own time.

---

1. This chapter focuses on texts for the First Testament, but its thesis can be applied to the Second Testament, just as easily.

The story of Job and the psyche of contempt for misfortune

My primary area of research is in exploring the connections and contrasts that exist between systems of economic exploitation in the First Testament[2] and those found in our time. It was not until I encountered a student who made me take a second look at Job 12:5, "Those at ease have contempt for misfortune,"[3] that I considered the psychological state of those who abuse people of lower status for their own gain. Offering several modern examples—including seeing a food-stamp recipient being poor-shamed at a grocery store—the student drew our class into a fruitful discussion on how those with so much can be callous toward those with so little. My students raised several hypotheses, ranging from sociopathy to an unintended side-effect of the *American Dream*, which proposes that anyone willing to work can be financially stable. Nevertheless, my students did not think that they had satisfactorily answered such questions as "how can CEOs sleep after further enriching themselves by exporting their workers' jobs?" or "how can people live in total luxury, yet demand even more at the expense of the poor?" Realizing that these are fundamental questions for effectively confronting systemic injustice, my research was led in new directions. For me, it began to appear that it all comes back, somehow, to Job's lament: "Those at ease have contempt for misfortune."

The contempt of Job's friends

The lament found in Job 12:5 is the result of Job, who had been left entirely destitute by no fault of his own, being forced to suffer the condescension of his closest friends. Job was a blameless and upright man who enjoyed great wealth—in the form of vast amounts of land, livestock, and numerous children—due to the favors he had earned from YHWH. But Job's fortunes came to a cataclysmic end when YHWH and the Satan enter into a wager as to how loyal Job really was. When the Satan suggests that Job only fears YHWH[4] because he desires the deity's blessings and fears YHWH's wrath, the deity sets out to prove the Satan wrong, allowing him to take Job's possessions, kill his children, and eventually inflict great physical torment upon his person. While this divine wager results in a living hell and existential crisis for the innocent Job, the situation forces his friends to confront a paradigm-shaking dissonance that they prove unable to resolve.

The three friends that first come to comfort Job, Eliphaz, Bildad, and Zophar, know Job to be a righteous man. However, when Job refuses to confess that he committed some sin to bring his plight upon himself, his friends are forced to confront a flaw in their understanding of evil and suffering. The friends maintained a common view that the righteous would enjoy success and wealth in this life and, conversely, the wicked would suffer: ideas reflected in Deut. 28, Prov. 12:13, and in

---

2. The terms *First Testament* and *Second Testament* will be used in place of *Old Testament* and *New Testament*, respectively
3. לפיד בוז לעשתות שאנן
4. "Worships YHWH," in the Septuagint.

Sir. 15. Simple observation of the human condition, however, threatens an absolutist take on this worldview; good people suffer needlessly all the time, and often at the hands of wicked people who profit from their anguish. But worldviews do not easily change, and rather than challenge their own, the three friends take turns at easing their own cognitive dissonance by attacking Job's character (Job 4–11). Whereas Job continually maintains his innocence from any evil that might have brought such suffering, the friends assert that he *must* have sinned and was getting what he deserved. It is under the crushing weight of Satan's torments and Zophar's faulty accusations that Job unleashes his cry, "Those at ease have contempt for misfortune."

The psychology of privilege and contempt

A few years after my students' discussion on Job 12:5, I came upon the work of psychologists and social behaviorists who study the effects of privilege on the human mind. Paul Piff, Stéphane Côté, Michèle Lemont, and Michael Kraus are among those who investigate how social-class standing—and its relation to others—uniquely shapes people's feelings, actions, and even unconscious thought patterns. While a casual observer can find countless examples of people using power or wealth to take advantage of others, this area of study reveals a deeper mechanism at work: how privilege alters thought patterns and shapes our perceptions of others.

The idea that there are disparities in behavior between the wealthy and the less affluent is neither new nor surprising. Simple observations, such as a person's gait, accent, vocabulary use, and dress are often used to distinguish people's social or financial standing. As early as the first half of the nineteenth century, Émile Durkheim and Karl Marx observed connections between social class and how people interact.[5] Later psychological studies revealed that a number of these behaviors were influenced by income. What Piff and other researchers are now bringing to the conversation is a theory for understanding how social class shapes our basic psychological processes.[6]

According to his research, Piff finds that two of the primary influential markers of those who live at the higher end of the class spectrum are of elevated rank and access ample resources. These markers tend to result in the following advantages:

1. More control over one's own life
2. Greater protection from such external financial influences such as unexpected shifts in the economy or loss of employment
3. Lower anxiety attributed to long-term concerns like saving for retirement or educational expenses

---

5. E. Durkheim, *The Division of Labor in Society* (New York: Free Press, 1802); K. Marx and F. Engels, *The Communist Manifesto* (New York: Penguin Classics, 1848/1967).

6. M. Kraus and P. Piff, "Social Class, Solipsism, and Contextualism: How the Rich Are Different from the Poor," *Psychological Review* 119.3 (2012), 546.

All of these factors lead to greater personal choice for people of elevated rank, causing them to exhibit greater independence, heightened self-focus, and higher levels of narcissism due to an increased sense of entitlement.[7] The results can be broken down into five primary characteristics that tend to separate those of privilege from their lower-class peers:

1. Self-focused patterns of thought and behavior
2. Lowered awareness of others
3. A disregard for the consequences of one's actions toward others
4. Feelings of entitlement
5. A decreased ability to identify others' emotions.[8]

Furthermore, people from society's upper echelons tend to turn to the accumulation of material wealth, over the development and maintenance of social connections, as a primary coping mechanism for dealing with social chaos and perceived threats to their social environments.[9]

At the other end of the spectrum, those of lower-class standing tend to exhibit more interdependent and other-focused behavior; this is due to numerous factors. First, a lower-class person's subordinate rank, coupled with limited available resources, translates into fewer opportunities. Consequently, people of lower-class status tend to be far more vulnerable to economic uncertainties and external influences, such as unforeseen health costs, loss of employment, and economic downturns. All of this leads to a person's psychological development being set in an environment of highly limited personal choice. While those at the low end of the class spectrum may engage in material accumulation as a means for coping with chaos,[10] the preferred coping mechanism is a greater orientation toward engaging in community structures.[11]

It is interesting to note that some of these processes are not only evidenced in humans, but also in non-human primates. Kraus and Piff write,

> In stable hierarchies within non-human species, low ranking individuals tend to show higher chronic levels of cortisol, increased aggression, and reduced access

---

7. P. Piff, "Wealth and the Inflated Self: Class, Entitlement, and Narcissism," *Personality and Social Psychology Bulletin* 40.1 (2014), 34–43.

8. P. Piff, Daniel M. Stancatoa, Stéphane Côtéb, Rodolfo Mendoza-Dentona, and Dacher Keltner, "Higher Social Class Predicts Increased Unethical Behavior," *Proceedings of the National Academy of Sciences of the United States of America* 109.11 (2012), 4086.

9. P. Piff, Andres G. Martinez, Daniel M. Stancato, and Michael W. Krau, "Class, Chaos, and the Construction of Community," *Journal of Personality and Social Psychology* 103.6 (2012), 950.

10. *Doomsday preppers* are but one example of this.

11. Piff, Martinez, Stancato, and Krau, "Class, Chaos, and the Construction of Community," 950.

to group resources. In contrast, high ranking non-humans tend to enjoy more grooming partners and increased reproductive opportunities.[12]

Similar to other primates, humans sort themselves into positions of lower and higher ranks that are based on such dimensions as physical attributes, social behaviors, and enduring traits like intelligence and extroversion.[13] As with non-human primates, such class-based patterns affect numerous facets of a human's psychological makeup, including overall psychological health. As humans divide, isolate, and raise their children within the class hierarchies into which they were born, people's perceptions of their own class status in relation to others—both lower and higher—are reinforced along with their psychological development. This leads to profound internalizations and solidifications of class perception. Kraus and Piff write, "Social class is not simply a trait along which individuals vary, but is instead a social context that individuals inhabit in enduring and pervasive ways over time . . . [spending] the majority of their daily lives in contexts that are sorted largely in terms of social class."[14] This blending of class status and a child's psychological development has profound effects on the human psyche. Numerous experiments—as detailed below—have drawn the same general conclusion: those of higher-class status tend to display contempt for those of lower status. Interestingly, as a result of reinforced ideas about their societal potential and roles, people of lower status frequently share that same contempt for themselves.

Relevance of psychological research to biblical studies

The research of these psychological studies is relevant to both exegetical and also hermeneutical readings of biblical texts that address corruption among elites and abuses toward those of low status. Echoing the sentiment of Job's lament in Job 12:5, Piff and his contemporaries have found that the psychological impact of privilege leads those of higher status to frequently exhibit contempt for those beneath them and to display greater tendencies toward such unethical behaviors as cheating and lying for personal gain. The case of Job may appear to juxtapose Piff's work, as Job had once held a higher status than his contemptuous friends. However, it appears that class attitudes toward a neighbor can be developed in an instant. The human propensity for privileged contempt is so powerful that even a temporary simulation of privilege can profoundly affect how one views those who are—in reality—their class peers, as addressed in the following section.

The idea that privilege not only alters a person's perception of those beneath them on the class ladder but also leads to an erosion of one's ethics, offers a new lens through which to interpret the numerous biblical texts that condemn the cruelty

12. Kraus and Piff, "Social Class," 548.
13. Ibid.
14. Ibid., 547.

of rulers, priests, and judges toward their subordinates. This field of study also has the potential to shed new light on biblical stories about people who become corrupt and callous as they climb from lower status to positions of power (e.g., Joseph [Genesis 37, cf. Genesis 47] and David [1 Samuel, cf. 2 Samuel]). Furthermore, the psychology of privilege can open new avenues of biblical interpretation for confronting anti-poor sentiment in Western capitalist states. Considering both the rise of biblical economics as an important sub-field of biblical studies and also increased research on how biblical poverty can connect with modern justice concerns, the discovery of such a tool is timely.[15]

Testing the effects of privilege

The discovery of privilege leading to increased narcissism and an elevated sense of entitlement, on a psychological level, is congruent with the work of sociologist Michèle Lamont. In her research on the moral perspectives of American working-class men, she found that lower-class individuals have a greater propensity to spend time taking care of others and, as such, tend to be more involved in developing and maintaining social networks that facilitate mutual aid.[16] Conversely, those from upper-class backgrounds are more likely to prioritize independence and show less motivation for developing supportive networks.[17]

In relation to community interactions, Lamont references a mechanic, Richard Wrong, who perceived a lack of community interaction between upper- and lower-class people as the result of disparaging attitudes toward the working class, whom he claimed the rich saw as both inferior and also weaker.[18] Another laborer, Tim Williams, saw a disparity between the ethical conduct of higher- and lower-class individuals. Williams attributed this disparity to the nature of competitiveness at the top, observing:

> When you get that almighty dollar, you hate to lose it. So you step on somebody's feet, or somebody's hand, or somebody's head to make sure you stay on top, which is not the greatest thing in the word. [sic] . . . The lower middle class people, they got nothing to lose by being honest.[19]

---

15. A brief list includes of such names as Roland Boer, Marvin Chaney, Norman Gottwald, Crystal Hall, Davis Hankins, Richard Horsley, Monica Melanchthon, Kelly Murphy, Hugh Page, Ron Simkins, Robert Wafawanaka, and Gale Yee.

16. M. Lamont, *The Dignity of Working Men: Morality and Boundaries of Race, Class, and Immigration* (Cambridge, MA: Harvard University Press, 2002), 46–54.

17. M. Kraus and D. Keltner, "Signs of Socio-Economic Status: A Thin-Slicing Approach," *Psychological Science* 20 (2009), 99–100.

18. Lamont, *Dignity of Working Men*, 109.

19. Ibid., 109–10.

Piff has conducted a variety of experiments that have revealed ways in which these attitudes and behaviors manifest themselves.

The hypothetical-situation experiment

In this experiment, subjects were presented with eight scenarios in which a person unjustly takes something or unjustly benefits from a given situation. The subjects were then asked the likelihood that they would engage in such scenarios. The study found that those subjects from privileged backgrounds had a greater tendency to act unethically than their less privileged peers, even when controlling for sex, age, and ethnicity. The results of this experiment suggest that upper-class individuals are more likely to exhibit tendencies toward acting unethically than their lower-class peers.[20]

The driver-pedestrian experiment

Another of Piff's experiments focused on an activity that is part of many Americans' daily routine: driving a car. This study sought to discern the effects of privilege through disparities in the driving habits of upper-class and lower-class individuals. Conducted over three separate weekdays between two and five o'clock in the afternoon, researchers observed the reactions to 152 drivers as they approached an unprotected, but marked, pedestrian crosswalk at a busy intersection in the San Francisco Bay Area.

The observers, blind to the study's purpose, positioned themselves out of drivers' direct lines of sight and recorded the frequency with which vehicles yielded to a pedestrian as they either waited to cross or actively crossed the street; sexes and ethnic backgrounds of the pedestrians were alternated and recorded. Observers also recorded the perceived status of approaching vehicles, based upon make, age, and physical appearance. Other recorded factors included the drivers' perceived sex and age, the time of day, whether or not the driver appeared to have seen the pedestrian, the sex of the pedestrian, and whether or not the driver yielded for the pedestrian or cut the pedestrian off; the latter is a driving offence in the state of California.[21] During the test, several factors were held constant to reduce the risk of confounding the results. As examples, researchers considered whether or not the car was in the lane closest to the pedestrian, they only used examples in which the pedestrian was alone at the crosswalk, they ensured that the pedestrian always entered the crosswalk when the approaching car was fifteen meters away, and they only recorded those cars that didn't have a vehicle in front of them, which may have obstructed the driver's view.

---

20. Piff, Stancatoa, Côtéb, Mendoza-Dentona, and Keltnera, "Higher Social Class Predicts Increased Unethical Behavior," 4087.
21. Ibid., 4089–90.

Regardless of age, gender, time of day, or the amount of traffic present, those in high-end vehicles were nearly four times as likely to cut off pedestrians in the crosswalk than drivers of low-end vehicles. Additionally, researchers found that the drivers of high-end vehicles were about twice as likely to cut off other drivers.[22] The results revealed that privilege does not only affect individuals in situations with clear hierarchical parameters, as found in the floor plan of a business office or in a social function where certain people are assigned to serve others' needs. Rather, the contempt displayed by higher-status drivers, in contrast with the consideration shown by lower-status drivers, was also observable in a scenario in which a system of laws gives clear socioeconomic equity to those using the city streets.

The monopoly experiment

An experiment that Piff described in the TED Talk episode, "Does Money Make You Mean?,"[23] involved pairs of strangers who were made to play the well-known board game, *Monopoly*, for fifteen minutes. Before the game began, a die was cast to determine which player would sit in which chair. What the test subjects had not been told was that one chair had been given a position of greater privilege than the other. The less privileged player was given a single die and received $1,000 when they passed *Go*, while the more privileged subject was given two dice and was awarded $2,000 for passing *Go*. Even though it was obvious that privilege had been given to one of the participants, and that that privilege was neither earned nor real, it took an average of four minutes for the privileged player to exhibit signs of contempt toward the other participant. More obvious signs included trash talking the less privileged player—even though the strangers did not share a rapport that would make such taunting socially acceptable—and avoiding eye contact with them. A more subtle sign was in how the subjects made use of a snack bowl that had been placed on the table; privileged subjects were more likely to indulge in the snacks and with greater frequency.

While these and similar experiments prove neither that an individual with privilege is going to behave contemptuously or unethically toward those of lower-class status nor that an individual of lower status will exhibit ethical conduct, they strongly indicate that privilege shapes our perceptions of *the other* in ways that lead those of higher class-standing toward greater self-interest and a heightened disregard for the well-being of less privileged neighbors.

Piff, Côté, Kraus, and other social behaviorists' findings are not only reflected in Job's lament, "Those at ease have contempt for misfortune," but in the Bible's numerous warnings against the spiritual and societal dangers of social stratification.

---

22. Ibid., 4090.

23. P. Piff, "Does Money Make You Mean?" *TEDxMarin* (2013). Available online at https://www.ted.com/talks/paul_piff_does_money_make_you_mean.

Psychological research into privilege contempt can be of great benefit to readers of the Bible's legal texts that keep privileged abuse in check, prophetic oracles that condemn elites who callously broke such laws, and stories of such abuses in the histories and wisdom literature.

Caveats for reading biblical texts through a psychological lens

The field of biblical studies lacks a particular luxury enjoyed by psychologists and behavioral scientists: live test subjects. Whereas scientists observe people in controlled situations, the primary subjects of biblical scholars have been dead for millennia, and those who would seek to interpret texts on a psychological level have scant hard evidence. While archaeology offers evidence of social stratification through city planning and personal possessions, the ancients' attitudes and thought processes are elusive. Those who wish to discern the psychological underpinnings of biblical texts face numerous challenges.

Multiple authorship

The books of the Bible—and even the passages and verses within—are the products of multiple authors and editors, produced over a great span of time. Texts first composed in a particular setting were later reworked or copied by scribes who lived hundreds of years later. Other texts went through centuries of oral tradition before being written. As a result, it is impossible to examine any biblical text from an individual psychological point of view. Therefore, those applying the heuristic tool proposed here should be mindful that biblical accounts are the product of multiple and divergent psyches and should be read in their collective or generalized contexts.

Biblical characters, laws, and events are not observed candidly

Unlike the observation of an unwitting driver approaching a crosswalk, psychological approaches to biblical texts do not have the benefit of hidden observation. Although some biblical stories take self-demeaning stances toward Israel's history—such as drawing attention to Saul's failures of faith in 1 Samuel or King David's moral failings in 2 Sam. 11–12—biblical texts have been presented in a way that their final redactors intended. In other words, not only are the subjects' works presented largely as they wished to be perceived, but the texts are not even entirely the original subjects' work. This may be comparable to giving someone a Rorschach inkblot test as a take home assignment, and then having a stranger edit the results centuries later. While this issue is not a fatal blow to the use of a psychological approach, as biblical texts reveal very human characteristics and relatable situations, it is important to be aware of this factor as interpreters process their conclusions; results should be considered as general.

Elite authorship of the Bible

A third consideration to be addressed is the fact that the Bible was written by elites, and theirs is the only retrievable perspective. While some biblical authors included non-elite perspectives, (e.g., Naboth's Vineyard [1 Kings 21], the necromancer of Endor [1 Samuel 28], and the Samaritan woman at the well [John 4]), they were written through an elite lens. This problem is not a fatal one, considering that the heuristic tool presented here focuses on elite conduct, but demands consideration.

Limited number of test subjects

Readers of the Bible are faced with a finite number of stories and accounts, that is, test subjects. Any attempt to distill an overarching view of the psychological effects of privilege in biblical authorship—which is not the goal of this chapter but could make for an interesting study—would involve its own host of additional caveats. This chapter, however, is concerned with the value of applying psychological models on privilege to individual texts.

Imposing foreign concepts on ancient texts

It is important to bear in mind that to apply psychological models to the Bible is to introduce foreign concepts that the authors either would not or could not have considered, themselves. Due to differing societal expectations and norms, a twenty-first-century observer cannot expect someone from the Iron Age to exhibit the same psychological reaction to a given stimulus. This caveat does not necessarily represent a problem; applying psychological models is not far afield from applying Marxist, womanist, or queer models to the Bible, which have all been done to great effect. Furthermore, despite the differences between the ancient and modern peoples, in conversations with Piff, he stated that the emerging picture indicates that privileged contempt is a part of a human universal. His assertion is supported by data from the World Values Survey, which reveals that while the cultural norms and structures of some societies may mitigate the severity of privilege's effect on the psyche, privilege seems to translate, psychologically, into a heightened focus on the self and one's independent goals and a lowered sensitivity to others' welfare needs, regardless of culture or society.[24] Evidence of the cross-cultural nature of this pattern—combined with numerous biblical texts that wrestle with the problem—suggests that connections found in the Bible should be explored.

Theological diversity of the biblical anthology

Lastly, those applying the psychology of privilege to biblical texts need to acknowledge the Bible's theological diversity. To assert that the Bible has a

---

24. L. Wang and J. Murnighan, "Money, Emotions, and Ethics Across Individuals and Countries," *Journal of Business Ethics* 125.1 (2014), 163–76.

universal viewpoint on privilege, or any other issue, is to oversimplify both the Bible and the issue itself. Nevertheless, despite the Bible's diversity of theology and its span of composition, biblical texts are permeated with laws, stories, and oracles that advocate the cause of people who were abused by those in positions of higher status.

It is for these reasons, as stated at the beginning of the chapter, that the purposes of this psychological model of interpretation are heuristic, and any exegetical use should be considered speculative in nature.

Relating the psychology of privilege to the Bible

A good place to find evidence of a society's recurring misdeeds is in their laws and legal commentaries. Concerning such texts in the First Testament, the old adage "where there's smoke there's fire" appears applicable to the presence of privileged contempt. The Hebrew authors wrote stories, laws, and oracles addressing powerful people who used their privilege to extract land (Mic. 2:2-4; Isa. 5:8-10), goods (Isa. 10:2; Amos 5.11), and even the lives (Gen. 47:13-26; Prov. 22:7-8) of those vulnerable to their influence. Rather than treated as a trifling or localized matter, the authors continually revisit and comment on this theme, indicating a recognition of connections between systemic poverty's perpetuation and class status.[25] The Second Testament continues the tradition, condemning economic predation among elites. Writings in the Gospels, in the Epistles, and in the book of Revelation denounce contemptuous behaviors displayed against those of lower status, and, like the First Testament, offer systemic solutions to address callousness toward the poor.

The following section examines laws to protect the vulnerable from their higher-class neighbors, subsequent failures to achieve that end, and how current psychological research on privilege may augment our understandings of these texts. The selected passages include the legal texts that address Sabbatical law and the Year of Jubilee, as well as the stories of both Naboth's Vineyard and that of David and Bathsheba.

Biblical measures to protect the vulnerable from the contempt of the elite

The First Testament contains highly developed ways of protecting the less privileged from their elite neighbors. This is mostly achieved by supporting an ethos of community responsibility for the well-being of individuals, which recurs throughout both First and Second Testaments. It is important to note that the

---

25. M. Chaney's collection of essays (*Peasants, Prophets, and Political Economy* [Eugene, OR: Cascade Books, 2017]) offers a number of detailed studies into the systemic nature of poverty in the First Testament.

motivations behind promoting these laws appear to have, at times, been serving the interests of elites. Debt remissions and land protections during the Persian period, for example, were likely used to subvert rival elites in a play for power and influence (Chaney 2017b). Even if this were the case, these laws are rooted in much earlier statutes from Israel's yet further ancient subsistence roots, and they reflect a predominant biblical economic ethic.

Two primary cornerstones of biblical efforts to protect the vulnerable from exploitation by elite neighbors are found in the Sabbatical law of the Deuteronomic Code and the Jubilee laws of the Holiness Code.

Deuteronomic code and the sabbatical year

According to the Deuteronomic Code, YHWH set out a radical expectation for life in the land of Israel: every Israelite was to have all that they needed in the land. Using YHWH's voice, the authors of Deut. 15:4-5 proclaim:

> There will be no poor among you—because YHWH your god will bless you in the land that YHWH your god is giving you as an inheritance to possess—if only you listen to the voice of YHWH your god, to carefully preserve this entire commandment that I charge to you today.

However, only six verses later, the deity predicts that his people will not succeed in their charge, stating, "the poor will never cease to be in your land" (Deut. 15:11). From the outset, the authors acknowledged that any economic system—even one designed by their god—would be abused by those who controlled the reigns. The authors, elites themselves, were well aware of the dangers faced by their lower-class neighbors, when put at the mercy of those in political or economic power. However, rather than a hopeless recognition that the impoverished will always suffer, as 15:11 is frequently interpreted, Norman Gottwald argues that the verse is a call to continual struggle against poverty.[26] His interpretation is supported by YHWH's call to action in v. 11: "I therefore command you: open your hand to the poor and needy in your land." The command is particularly poignant when considering the passage's primary audience: the literate elite who could access it.

The Deuteronomic Code mitigated the bite[27] of debt systems by means of the *sabbatical year*, which canceled debts every seven years. From the perspective of those who had to depend on debts, this dedicated year of remission offered relief

---

26. N. Gottwald, "Early Israel as an Anti-Imperial Community," in *Social Justice and the Hebrew Bible: Volume Two*, eds. Norman Gottwald (The Center and Library for the Bible and Social Justice Series; Eugene, OR: Cascade Books, 2017), 7.

27. The Hebrew word for bite (נשׁך)—as in the bite of a serpent—was the same word used for the taking of interest on debts.

by making debts temporary states of affairs. In addition to demanding observance of the law, Deut. 15:8-9 warns against forgiving debts with a sour disposition:

> You should rather open your hand, willingly lending enough to meet the need, whatever it may be. Be careful that you do not entertain a mean thought, thinking, "The seventh year, the year of remission, is near," and therefore view your needy neighbor with hostility and give nothing; your neighbor might cry to the LORD against you, and you would incur guilt.

Whereas the economic safety net found in Deuteronomy 15 offered assistance to the vulnerable by limiting a debt's lifespan, the year of Jubilee, found in the Holiness Code, offered a safety net that protected a person's access to farmland, upon which most all Israelites depended for their livelihood.

Holiness Code and the year of Jubilee

For members of agrarian societies, financial security is rooted in a person's ability to access arable land, which provides families with food, shelter, and livelihood. The primary answer to ensuring land access—and thereby avoiding social unrest—is found in agrarian societies around the world and across time: making the sale of farmland illegal, religiously taboo, or both.

As found in Deuteronomy 15, the authors of the Holiness Code used YHWH's voice in Lev. 25:23-24. The deity proclaims:

> But the land must not be sold beyond reclaim, for the land is mine; you are but strangers resident with me. Throughout the land that you hold, you must provide for the redemption of the land.

While the command appears clear, it would be dangerous for families during crises in which portions of land must be exchanged for desperately needed foodstuffs (e.g., during successive crop failures). To protect families who found themselves in such straits, and thereby vulnerable to those with the means to acquire their land, permanently, vv. 25-28 offered a series of protections to ensure that the family plot would be returned to the original holder.

The first safety net opens with YHWH proclaiming, "If your kinsman is in crisis and has to sell part of his holding, his nearest redeemer shall come and redeem what his kinsman has sold" (Lev. 25:25). In other words, if a struggling farmer had to sell a portion of his land to a wealthier farmer for goods, it was the sacred duty of the struggling farmer's closest kin to buy the land back and restore usufruct. Notice the absence of stipulations to be met for such a remission to be enacted; whether the land was lost due to bad luck or poor decisions, the struggling farmer's nearest relative is responsible for restoring the family's usufruct, if able.

The second safety net commands that if the nearest kin is not able to reclaim the land, but the struggling farmer falls upon good fortune, he is to repurchase the land's usufruct, himself (Lev. 25:26-27). However, the purchase price will reflect the remaining value of the contract. If the struggling farmer sold the plot for ten years of use in exchange for ten units of grain but is able to buy it back after five years, he only owed the creditor five units of grain, since the creditor enjoyed five years of the land's productive capabilities. Unlike capitalist economics, this lending system's objective is equity and mutual benefit, not the production of capital.[28]

Should the first two safety nets fail to protect the struggling farmer's usufruct, Lev. 25:28 offered a final line of defense: the Year of Jubilee. Since YHWH was deemed to be the land's owner, no Israelite had the right to make a permanent sale. Consequently, only the land's productive value was to be exchanged, and for a maximum forty-nine years. After this time, the land's usufruct was to revert to the original holder. Farmers who needed to sell their family's usufruct might not live to see the Jubilee, but their families would not be left in perpetual poverty.

Jubilee's treatment of real estate within city walls, and therefore non-productive, was handled quite differently from farmland. Leviticus 25:29-30 states that city dwellings either needed to be reclaimed within a year, or the house would "belong to the purchaser in perpetuity" (25:30). Such a distinction between city and rural real estate highlights Jubilee's primary intent: preventing those with greater means from exploiting their less-affluent neighbors. Just as much of Jubilee had been designed to support access to land, it was also designed to keep those in power from usurping the land and livelihood of disempowered families.

Laws prohibiting the removal of boundary markers

Further protections for land usufruct are found in prohibitions on the removal of boundary markers. Deuteronomy 19:14 proclaims, "You will not move your neighbor's boundary marker, which was set up by previous generations, in the property that YHWH, your God, is giving you to possess." This prohibition is intensified in 27:17, which offers the threat, "Cursed be he who moves his neighbor's boundary marker." Outside of Torah, Prov. 22:28 and 23:10 also forbid tampering with ancestral markers; the latter adds emphasis to the dire consequences of such actions for the vulnerable: "Do not encroach on the field of orphans." In Job 24:2, Job refers to those who shift boundary markers as the first benchmark for "the wicked."

While in a theological context such usufruct protections were to protect God's promise of land to Abraham's descendants (Gen. 15:18-21), such stipulations were not unique to Israel; they are also found in Babylonian and Assyrian legal texts. Whereas the leasing of fields in ancient Babylon was common, the Babylonian

---

28. For a treatment on the differences between credit and debt systems, see R. Boer's *The Sacred Economy of Ancient Israel* (Library of Ancient Israel; Louisville, KY: Westminster John Knox, 2015), 157-63.

record offers no evidence of sales, claims of land as assets, and even the use of landholdings as collateral. This suggests that land was not used in legal exchanges.[29] Land records from Mari and Nuzi reveal that the land rights were protected by keeping the right to access arable land within the family;[30] this is a common practice in agrarian societies around the world.[31]

The legal protections of Deuteronomy 15 and Leviticus 25 had the potential to subvert social stratification—and perhaps the psychosocial effects of privilege—thoroughly preventing people from either climbing too high or falling too low, economically. Whether or not rulers upheld these laws, their ethos is reflected throughout both the Bible and also throughout numerous other societies. But even if the rulers of Israel made concerted efforts to enact Sabbatical and Jubilee—a topic of debate—the question remains: Could such protections have worked? The Bible offers scant evidence of their successes, but it does accounts for numerous failures.

To emphasize, despite the presence of a biblical ethos of care for those who are less fortunate—supported by texts found throughout the Bible—there are numerous examples of people breaching these laws in the Bible; sometimes the perpetrators are known to be good people, on the whole. In addition to attesting to the presence of privileged contempt in the biblical world—which comes as no surprise—the psychology of privilege offers new insights into why these laws were required and needed to be emphasized throughout the First Testament.

Stories of privileged disdain for those of lower status

The usefulness of the psychology of privilege to biblical studies is well highlighted by two stories that share some similarities yet are quite different: Naboth's Vineyard and David and Bathsheba. Naboth's story involves the misdeeds of an inherently

---

29. J. Ranger, "Institutional, Communal, and Individual Ownership or Possession of Arable Land in Ancient Mesopotamia from the End of the Fourth to the End of the First Millennium B.C.," in *Symposium on Ancient Law, Economics, and Society, Part II*, eds. J. Lindgren, Geoffrey P. Miller, Martha Roth, James Whitman, James Lindgren, and Laurent Mayali (Chicago, IL: Chicago-Kent College of Law and Illinois Institute of Technology, 1995), 296–97.

30. A. Malamat, "Mari and the Bible: Some Patterns of Tribal Organizations and Institutions," *Journal for the American Oriental Society* 82 (1962), 143–50; P. Purves, "Commentary on Nuzi Real Property in the Light of Recent Studies," *Journal of Near Eastern Studies* 4.2 (1945), 69.

31. A. Johnson and T. Earle, *The Evolution of Human Societies: From Foraging Group to Agrarian State* (2nd ed.; Stanford, CA: Stanford University Press, 2001); M. Coomber, *Re-Reading the Prophets Through Corporate Globalization* (Piscataway, NJ: Gorgias, 2010), 179–84.

wicked king who grew up in privilege. The second, by contrast, is about a relatively good king who grew up without privilege yet engaged in foul activities just the same.

The example of Naboth's vineyard in 1 Kings 21

The psychology-of-privilege illuminates the story of Naboth's vineyard in 1 Kings 21, which can be used to consider the effects of status on a person's psychological development from childhood. What makes this particular narrative so striking is that it pits a stark power play of deeply ingrained privilege against the Hebrew ethos of the community's responsibility for the well-being of the individual, which is reflected in the First Testament. Unfortunately for Naboth, privileged contempt wins the day.

The story opens with the wicked King Ahab seeking to plant a vegetable garden next to his palace in Jezreel. Since Naboth's family holds a vineyard adjacent to the palace, the king asks to buy it. On the surface, the transaction appears fair; the king offers Naboth either fair payment or a better vineyard in exchange. However, Naboth—a pious man—refuses his king's offer by referencing ancestral inheritance laws similar to those in the Holiness Code: "YHWH forbids me to give you my ancestral inheritance" (1 Kgs 21:3). Rather than dealing harshly with Naboth's rejection, as one may expect from a tyrannical king, Ahab returns to his palace, despondent, to sulk on his bed. While this portrayal of a farmer reprimanding his king may emphasize the socio-religious power that the ethos of community responsibility held, the story reveals that any such authority was no match for entitled privileged.

King Ahab's wife, Jezebel, a Phoenician princess who had not been raised with this Hebrew ethos, unleashes violence upon Naboth. Proclaiming such legal restrictions to be beneath a king, she sets out to resolve the problem. The rhetorical question that Queen Jezebel puts to Ahab, "Do you now govern Israel?" (21:7), highlights her belief that neither laws nor ethics apply to rulers. Drawing upon her influence and wealth, she employs "scoundrels" to falsely accuse Naboth of blasphemy (21:8-14). As a result of the charge and Naboth's subsequent execution, King Ahab seizes his land and plants his garden. The authors make it clear, however, that both Ahab and his queen would pay dearly for their transgression (1 Kgs 21:17-29)

This story's power, and where privileged contempt comes to the fore, is found in what was not at stake. Naboth's death was neither some matter of national security nor to protect the king from some scandal. Ahab simply wanted a garden and, disappointed he could not attain this mundane luxury, sat by as his wife murdered a man who, according to the ethos found in Leviticus, had obeyed the laws that the king was to uphold. Understanding human predisposition to callousness toward those of lower class gives greater nuance to the story by shedding light on Ahab's callousness. While Ahab's socio-religious sensibilities left him impotent in the face of Naboth's rejection, he did not mind Jezebel's murderous intervention, until faced with dire consequences (21:27). A psychological-interpretative lens gives another angle through which to read such callousness and greater depth in drawing upon this story, hermeneutically, to relate it to callous leaders, today.

Comparable to Naboth's fate, inflicting grievous harm on others to reap minor luxuries can be seen throughout Western economies and markets: for example, the blood diamonds that fill jewelry stores and the sweatshop clothes that are sold at stores ranging from Walmart to Prada. A reading of 1 Kings 21 through this lens can also serve as a warning to the privileged in society to be mindful of how status predisposes them to contemptuous and unethical activity. As a story originally written by elites for an elite audience, the conclusion's image of dogs consuming King Ahab and Queen Jezebel serves as a powerful warning against abusing subjects to the point of revolt. The same can hold true for today. An exceedingly powerful individual, like movie mogul Harvey Weinstein, whose alleged sexual crimes were brought to light after decades of abuse, may believe that his or her privilege shields him or her from the consequences of wrongdoing, but this can be true only to a degree. The story of Naboth's vineyard, after all, asserts that anyone who breaches another's right to livelihood could expect divine punishment: even the kings among us.

Exegetically, a consideration of the psychology of privilege opens new doors through which to understand 1 Kings 21. Shining light on Jezebel's response to her despondent husband, readers may be able to develop a more nuanced understanding of her disregard for the ethos that had stopped Ahab in his tracks. Raised in great privilege as the daughter of the King of Tyre, it can be speculated that she would neither have been dependent upon nor valued the sorts of social networks upon which many people depend.

The potential value of psychological studies on the effects of privilege does not end with how we read either the stories or the lessons from the Bible itself; it can also shed light upon numerous interpretations of these stories.

The example of David and Bathsheba in 2 Sam. 11–12:25

Like 1 Kings 21, David and Bathsheba's story offers a powerful example of the dangers of privileged contempt. However, whereas 1 Kings 21 examines a wicked king, born into privilege, who abused his power, 2 Sam. 11–12:25 considers the murderous contempt of a king who had been born of humble means and set up to be pious and selfless (1 Samuel) prior to his rise to power. Research on the effects of privilege gives greater nuance to King David's moral fall, and also highlights the story's value for addressing privileged contempt today.

The sins of David, as they are manifest in the contemptuous ways in which he deals with those beneath him in 2 Samuel 11, are numerous. First, whereas ancient Near Eastern kings were expected to fight in battle with their soldiers, 2 Samuel 11 sets the stage by placing David at home, while Israel warred with the Ammonites. Rather than fulfilling his duty at the siege of Rabbah, David remained engaged in lechery on his palace rooftop (vv. 1-2); not only does David fail to fight, he uses his time to spy on his soldiers' bathing wives. Second, King David's disregard goes to the extreme when he sees Bathsheba—identified as the wife of Uriah the Hittite (11:3)—summons her to his palace, has sex with her, and impregnates her.

By modern American standards, not only did David leave Bathsheba vulnerable to divorce or death on a charge of adultery, he raped her. Considering the power disparity between a king and a (possibly foreign) soldier's wife, David's advance on Bathsheba was comparable to making advances on a passed-out individual. There are numerous reasons as to why Bathsheba was in no position to refuse; the king lived with near impunity and had power over her and her husband's lives.

David attempts to cover up Bathsheba's pregnancy by bringing Uriah home from battle and ordering him to "go down to your house and wash your feet,"[32] adds another serious crime in the story's historical cultural context; usurping another's family line. When David asks why his soldier refused to go home to his wife, Uriah responds,

> The ark and Israel and Judah remain in booths; and my lord Joab and the servants of my lord are camping in the open field; shall I then go to my house, to eat and to drink, and to lie with my wife? As you live, and as your soul lives, I will not do such a thing. (2 Sam. 11:11)

Uriah's words create a powerful contrast between the privileged king and his subordinate. Whereas Uriah's reasoning highlights David's depravity, it also reminds the reader of the younger and more innocent David, before he rose to power. Rather than being awakened by this confrontation, David's contempt for his subjects sinks to a yet deeper level.

With complete disregard for the married couple and for Uriah's life, David attempted to hide his crimes through having Uriah killed in a battlefield conspiracy. However, this act victimizes even more of his subjects as soldiers die in the execution of the plot, presumably leaving widows and orphans behind.

After the bereaved Bathsheba finishes her mourning, David marries the war widow, whom he victimized both sexually and also martially. In contrast to the sins of King Ahab, from whom treachery is expected, this story reveals the menacing transformation of a once-pious David. The story culminates in 2 Samuel 12 with yet another victim: David and Bathsheba's infant son dies as a direct result of David's treachery.

The work of Piff and his colleagues, which reveals that privilege renders people more prone to unethical activity and decreased empathy toward those beneath them, offers new insights into David and Bathsheba's story. It gives an explanation of how a character like the humble and unassuming shepherd boy of 1 Samuel—who had so strongly believed in and adhered to a moral matrix—transformed into the king of 2 Samuel 11. It gives an explanation of how status could have so deeply blinded David to the extent of his fall that when the prophet Nathan confronted

---

32. The Hebrew word for "feet" (רגל) served as a euphemism for genitalia.

him, David seemed surprised, responding rather stupidly, "I have sinned against the Lord" (2 Sam. 12:13). In addition to adding layers of understanding to the story, the psychology of privilege can emphasize the story's warning: the power of privilege can not only corrupt; it will corrupt even the best of us. The psychology of privilege helps to further open passages like 2 Samuel 12 and 1 Kings 21 by both giving readers a better understanding of where such contempt is rooted and creating paths through which we can connect such cautionary tales to the contempt of the privileged today. The following section considers how privileged contempt and systemic poverty connect in the twenty-first-century United States, and how the biblical ethos of collective responsibility for the well-being of the individual—combined with Piff's research—can create effective interpretive tools for confronting this issue.

Connecting contempt for misfortune in the Bible to the twenty-first century

One reason that the Bible is such an incredibly useful collection of texts is that regardless of a reader's faith or non-faith perspective, the problems and challenges that it addresses are relevant to almost any time or location. While the societal and economic circumstances of the twenty-first-century United States are vastly different from the cultures in which the Bible is rooted, its stories of exploitation and extraction are not foreign. Elites feeding their insatiable hunger for even greater wealth—at the cost of those who can barely survive—is a predominant characteristic of ancient and modern cultures alike. Whether in the cities and villages of the Bible or on the internet, today, one does not need to look far to find the privileged displaying contempt and callousness toward the poor. This section considers the prevalence of privilege contempt and anti-poor sentiment in US society as a guide to how a psychology-of-privilege-hermeneutic may be useful for addressing systemic poverty today.

The American Dream and anti-poor sentiment

Comparable to the way in which Eliphaz, Bildad, and Zophar's disdain toward Job was rooted in a predominate worldview of their time, US anti-poor sentiment appears to be connected to an American Dream worldview. In some cases, this modern paradigm is even superimposed upon the Bible.[33] While there is great power in the American Dream's idea of a person being able to achieve financial stability if they are willing to work hard enough, a closer look at the societal trajectory of the United States tells another story. Nevertheless, ongoing adherence

---

33. In the United States, it is not unusual to hear the Algernon Sidney quote, "God helps those who help themselves," incorrectly attributed to the Bible.

to this dream facilitates anti-poor sentiment among both the nation's wealthy elite and the poor.

When compared to France, impoverished white American workers show greater disdain toward their poor contemporaries. Lamont writes that only 7 percent of white collar and 37 percent of blue-collar French workers hold negative views of the poor. By contrast, 67 percent of white collar and 50 percent of blue-collar Americans display anti-poor disdain.[34] The French were also more likely to identify societal mechanisms as partially to blame for poverty, leading to a sense of solidarity with the poor.[35] But if the American Dream is seen as the hallmark of the American success story, how does one know if they have achieved it?

When I ask my students what comes to mind when they hear "The American Dream," the whiteboard quickly fills with a wide range of items. But the three things that appear in every class, without fail, are

1. Homeownership
2. Car ownership
3. Having a satisfying career.

For many US citizens, attaining a satisfying career involves a college education, which has been shown to be a key factor in helping people to avoid poverty, especially during sudden economic downturns.[36] I then ask my students how many Americans can achieve even one of these benchmarks without becoming heavily indebted. Of course, the answer is "hardly any." Few US citizens can buy new cars—or reliable used cars—without the aid of loans. Only the wealthiest Americans can purchase a home without a mortgage. And a college education can frequently cost even more than a house, demanding the use of student loans. Therefore, unless a US citizen is among the highest echelons of the economic elite, achieving the American Dream demands a crippling amount of debt. And for those who control the systems of lending, this is a highly profitable position. Unfortunately, as was the case in the biblical world, our lenders' approach is rarely rooted in the interests of community well-being or mutual benefit. Instead, the path to the American Dream winds through systems of debt and extraction that reinforce our economic hierarchies at the expense of those who are in the greatest of need. The example of student loans, in particular, highlights anti-poor sentiment in the United States.

Since those who attend college choose to do so, and thereby incur debt voluntarily, it could be argued that the massive debts that students accrue are just. The benefits of their education, however, are not theirs alone; they benefit all

---

34. Lamont, *Dignity of Working Men*, 234.
35. Ibid.
36. R. Fry, "The Growing Economic Clout of the College Educated," *Pew Research Center* (2013). Available online at http://www.pewresearch.org/fact-tank/2013/09/24/the-growing-economic-clout-of-the-college-educated.

Americans. College graduates go on to become medical practitioners, engineers, journalists, artists, and educators, who will help to carry the nation forward. Yet with the average debt for an undergraduate degree at $30,100—the national student debt level is currently at $1.5 trillion—American students' financial burdens will delay major life choices, including such intimate ones as at what time to begin having a family. In addition to the rising costs of higher education, however, an injustice of student debt is found in how it is managed and exchanged. While most college graduates will pay for their debts in full, their student loans are commonly traded behind closed doors for pennies on the dollar.[37]

Although debt has become a central component of American capitalism and a natural part of American life, it carries a heavy sigma for those who struggle under its weight: often labeled as *financially reckless* by both their wealthy and impoverished neighbors.[38] The myth that most people in debt ended up in their situation due to recklessness is not merited. Bad choices can certainly lead to debts. However, in a society where homeownership, car ownership, and student loans are often promoted as essential, most of our nation's personal debt results from playing by the rules. Although many who struggle with debt are looked down upon with moral indignation, the system that put them there, and those who profit from the interest to be earned, often escape either scrutiny or disparagement.

The dysfunction inherent in the handling of debt and resources in the United States is found in the numbers. A 2016 Federal Reserve study found that 71 percent of US citizens did not expect to see wage increases in 2017, 49 percent of part-time workers were in need of more work, and 47 percent of Americans—almost half the citizens of the world's wealthiest nation—were unable cope with a four-hundred-dollar emergency.[39] Perhaps most startling of all was that in 2015, one in five US citizens under the age of eighteen lived in poverty.[40] This indicates that the system helps those at the top while many who seek to achieve the societal standards of success must both take on debt while also suffering under its stigma. Despite these ominous economic signs, the idea that sheer grit can get you anywhere is still very much alive.

---

37. J. Kasperkevic, "Occupy Activists Abolish $3.85m in Corinthian Colleges Students' Loan Debt," *The Guardian*, September 17, 2014. Available online at https://www.theguardian.com/money/2014/sep/17/occupy-activists-student-debt-corinthiancolleges.

38. This problem is explored in-depth by Neal Gabler's article ("The Secret Shame of Middle-Class Americans," *Atlantic*, May 2016) in which he uses his own experiences with debt to address the economic fragility of even those who are not considered impoverished by US standards.

39. Federal Reserve, Board of Governors, "Report on the Economic Wellbeing of U.S. Households in 2015," (2016). Available online at https://www.federalreserve.gov/2015-reporteconomic-wellbeing-us-households-201605.pdf.

40. S. J. Schwarzenberg, A. Kuo, J. Linton, and P. Flanagan, "Promoting Food Security for Children," *Pediatrics* 136 (2015), 1432.

At the height of the Great Recession, 50 percent of Americans between the ages of eighteen and twenty-nine believed that someday they would join the upper class.[41] In reality, however, the largest forecaster of a US citizen's future earning potential is not grit, but their parents' income. Forty percent of Americans are not only in the same class bracket as their parents but also their grandparents, and income disparity is growing. The poverty rate is at its highest level in decades and income inequality is greater than at any time since 1929. This is not likely to improve, considering that the wealthiest four hundred Americans control one half the nation's wealth, and in the past three decades, income among the wealthiest 20 percent has risen by 45 percent. Conversely, the income of those among the nation's bottom 20 percent has dropped by 11 percent.[42] Nevertheless, the natural conclusion for many in the United States is that the poor are impoverished due to laziness, irresponsibility, or both.

A predominate interpretation of the American Dream suggests that the impoverished can become financially stable, if they only work harder. Ironically, blind adherence to this ideology impedes a realization of the American Dream by limiting our ability to challenge those factors that trap people in poverty, despite their best efforts to escape. While I have served those who were impoverished due to apathy toward work and saving, they are the exceptions. For most of the impoverished people with whom I have worked, their hardships are not rooted in a lack of grit, but in larger systems that lie outside of their control. In addition to being an academic, I am a priest who has served churches with families who cannot make ends meet, despite being intelligent, hardworking—often at multiple jobs—and frugal. Their poverty is often the result of having a child with special needs, a layoff, or an unexpected medical emergency. But similar to the cognitive dissonance faced by Job's friends, these families endure poor-shaming—both from others and also self-inflicted—despite clear evidence of increasing income disparity and shady lending practices of the financial sector that serves the needs of the wealthiest citizens.

American Dream and the Bible

The question that naturally arises is, how can ancient Near Eastern texts on debt exploitation and attitudes toward the poor find relevance in the economic realities of the twenty-first century? The paradigm-shaking dissonance sitting between the poverty statistics of the United States and the idea that hard work reaps all rewards is not dissimilar to that experienced by Job's friends, as their righteous friend's suffering forced them to choose between holding onto a faulty paradigm or reevaluating its merit. Like Job's friends, many choose to attack the victim in order to protect the paradigm, and perhaps psychological connections between privilege and callousness make that an easier choice to make. The anti-poor sentiment that assumes poverty is the result of personal failure and a lack of drive manifests itself both through what is here termed *systemic* and *direct contempt*. As in the First Testament, contempt for

---

41. L. Miller, "The Money Empathy Gap," *New York* 45, July 1, 2012, 20.
42. Ibid.

the impoverished is best highlighted in contrast to the efforts made to assist those of lower economic status.

Assistance for underprivileged US citizens

The most obvious contrast between biblical poverty and poverty in the United States rests in the divergent economic environments of the ancient and modern worlds. In the post-industrial landscape of the United States, farm and ranch families account for less than 2 percent of the population, and only 15 percent of the US workforce is involved in agricultural production, at any level.[43] Since access to land and a person's livelihood are no longer synonymous in the United States, the lens through which systems of poverty alleviation are viewed requires adjustment. In the US context, speaking in terms of access to shelter, food, and employment—those things that the ancients gained from arable land—is more suitable. Since the laws of Deuteronomy 15 and Leviticus 25 were compulsory, comparisons can be found in tax-funded services, which oblige US citizens to be their brothers' and sisters' keepers. Below are a few examples of such obligatory care in the American economic landscape.

In terms of access to shelter, US taxpayers fund the Department of Housing and Urban Development (HUD), which provides poor, disabled, and elderly people access to affordable and transitional housing. HUD also assists US citizens in fighting foreclosure due to financial hardship.

As to ensuring access to food, one of the ways in which citizens collectively ensure their impoverished neighbors' access to food is through the Supplemental Nutrition Assistance Program, or SNAP. The SNAP program helps scores of millions of Americans to buy groceries.[44] The Federal Breakfast Program is another tax-funded service that offers daily morning meals to nearly fifteen million children.[45]

There are also programs to help the next generation of US citizens access a livelihood. Tax dollars fund our public education system, which is to ensure that all Americans can access an education that will prepare them for their future in the workforce and with such skills as literacy, which make it easier to attain and retain employment. In addition to a guaranteed kindergarten through twelfth-grade education, Head Start assists young children in gaining skills and knowledge that will help them to get the most out of their education.

---

43. Bureau of Labor Statistics, "Employment by Major Industry Sector," (2015). Available online at https://www.bls.gov/emp/ep_table_201.htm.

44. USDA, "Supplemental Nutrition Assistance Program Participation and Costs," (2016). Available online at https://www.fns.usda.gov/pd/supplemental-nutrition-assistance-program-snap.

45. USDA, "School Breakfast Program Fact Sheet," (2017). Available online at https://www.fns.usda.gov/sbp/fact-sheet.

While the ways in which livelihood in the ancient world and in the United States differ greatly for most, the United States has created laws and programs—to varying degrees of success—that align with an ethos of collective responsibility for the individual's well-being.[46] However, even with such mandates to be one's brothers' and sisters' keepers, like Jezebel, many Americans fight their responsibility. In recent years, efforts to ensure the well-being of America's most vulnerable citizens have been attacked through an unlikely marriage of financial elites and populist movements.

Privileged attacks on collective responsibility in the United States

Privileged contempt among the US elite toward the impoverished can be found in political decisions that either diminish or eliminate protections for the country's most vulnerable citizens. Connected with the idea that anyone can get ahead if they are willing to work hard enough, these cuts either ignore or outright deny the presence of systems that create poverty.

While the SNAP program serves as the sole food source for 8.5 million American families (roughly 41 million individuals), and costs less than 2 percent of the federal annual budget at $70.9 billion,[47] Speaker of the House Paul Ryan proposed more than $23 billion in cuts to the program during the 2016 election campaign. President Trump's budget proposal for 2018 called for $192 billion in cuts over a ten-year period. Going even further, Iowa Senator Joni Ernst called for an end to food stamps altogether. During her 2014 campaign, Ernst told audiences that her parents "taught her to live within her means," even though her family collected $463,000 in federal farm subsidies between 1995 and 2009.[48]

In a move toward ending the SNAP program, Ernst and Florida senator, Marco Rubio, introduced the Economic Mobility, Prosperity, and Opportunities with Waivers that Enable Reforms for States (EMPOWERS) Act to the Senate floor in 2017. This bill would allow states to transfer monies budgeted for funding both SNAP and also its sub-programs, Women, Infants, and Children (WIC), the Emergency Food Assistance Program (TEFAP), the Temporary Assistance for Needy Families program (TANF)—as well as other child welfare, job training, and housing programs—toward other spending priorities. The bill would effectively eliminate the 1996 safeguards that were put on the waiver authority that states

---

46. For a more detailed study on this, see M. Coomber, "Seeking Community in a Capitalist Age: A Collective Response to Poverty and Debt, from the Bible to Today," *Journal of Religion and Society* 16 (2018), 92–108.

47. N. Goodkind, "Trump's Food Stamp Cuts Will Leave More Americans Hungry," *Newsweek*, February 22, 2018. Available online at http://www.newsweek.com/trump-food-stampssnap-hunger-815327.

48. M. Hiltzik, "Sen. Joni Ernst Learned to 'Live within Her Means'—on the Taxpayer's Dime," *Los Angeles Times*, January 23, 2015. Available online at http://www.latimes.com/business/hiltzik/la-fi-mh-sen-joni-ernst-learned-20150123-column.html.

already enjoyed, allowing them to both impose unlimited benefit cuts and remove large numbers of current recipients from eligibility.[49]

Ernst's views toward welfare, indicated by her assertion that learning to live within one's means would cure the nation's poverty problem, align with her campaign benefactors, financial elites David and Charles Koch. During David Koch's 1980 vice-presidential run on the Libertarian ticket, he promoted an end to welfare, Social Security, and to public education altogether. Today, the two brothers fund political ads and races that are in line with the goals of the Libertarian Party, who have declared a "War on the War on Poverty." In early 2017 the Libertarian Party's website proclaimed,

> We should eliminate the entire social welfare system. This includes food stamps, subsidized housing, and all the rest. Individuals who are unable to fully support themselves and their families through the job market must, once again, learn to rely on . . . family, church, community, or private charity to bridge the gap.

Those words, *once again*, reflect a myth that—perhaps a golden age in which— US citizens were ever entirely self-sufficient. This is simply not true. The federal government has funded unemployed citizens as far back as the late eighteenth century. The 1862 Civil War Pension Program provided benefits for disabled Union veterans and their families. Many European Americans' ancestors received government aid via land grants, made possible through stealing land from Native Americans. European settlers also enjoyed tax-funded infrastructure projects that enabled them to get their goods to market. While US citizens have always relied on community responsibility for the well-being of the nation's individuals, a false narrative of an entirely individualistic American history remains powerful.

Another prime example of indirect anti-poor sentiment is found in the handling of the 2008 financial crisis. While the reckless lending and investment practices of financial giants were at the heart of the crisis, our economic system allowed borrowers to bear the greatest weight of the collapse. As millions of households endured the trauma of losing their jobs and their homes to foreclosure—many of those foreclosures committed illegally in the *robo-signing* scandal—the CEO of J.P. Morgan, Jamie Dimon, who was a major architect of the bailout, negotiated a taxpayer-funded sale of Bear Sterns that put him in a position to reap a handsome stock profit of $90 million.[50]

---

49. L. Schott and D. Rosenbaum, "'Superwaiver' Bill Threatens Key Low-Income Programs," *Center on Budget and Policy Priorities*, September 28, 2017. Available online at https://www.cbpp.org/research/poverty-and-inequality/superwaiver-bill-threatens-key-lowincome-programs.

50. T. Meyers, "Open Letter from Thomas A. Myers to Occupy Wall Street," *Journal of International Business Ethics* 5.1 (2012), 63.

Examples of direct contempt for the underprivileged in the United States are found in the nation's political discourse, from talk of *anchor babies*[51] to Mitt Romney's false and disparaging comments about the poor to a room of wealthy campaign donors, alluding to the allegedly 47 percent of Americans "who are dependent on the government, who believe that they are victims, who believe the government has a responsibility to care for them, who believe they are entitled to health care, to food, to housing, to you-name-it . . . [yet] pay no income taxes."[52] While the leaking of this video shook the Romney campaign, its contents are not surprising; Romney's words reflect an anti-poor sentiment that is acceptable in much US political and social discourse.

Direct contempt—which can become systemic—is found in legislation to give welfare recipients drug tests. According to Jim DeMint's Heritage Foundation, these laws are made in the spirit of "reciprocal obligation" proclaiming, "in return [for receiving support, recipients] should engage in responsible and constructive behavior as a condition of receiving aid. Requiring welfare recipients to stop using illegal drugs is a core element of reciprocal obligation."[53] The foundation's rationale is contemptuous on many levels. First, it assumes the underprivileged require social engineering so as to develop *responsible and constructive behavior*, vilifying the character of the poor on no other basis than class status. Second, the statement ignores systemic causes of poverty, deflecting any responsibility from abusive systems onto their victims: consider the bank bailouts and illegal foreclosures of the Great Recession. Third, supporting an absolutist view of the American Dream, DeMint's statement fails to consider that people can be simultaneously responsible and live in poverty. Finally, DeMint's statement assumes drug offences among the impoverished, as a whole. Before passing such a drug-test law in North Carolina, an amendment was proposed to require testing for state senators, who receive tax dollars for their salaries; the amendment never made it onto the bill.

These examples of how anti-poor sentiment eclipses compassion and leaves "those at ease with contempt for misfortune," are reminiscent of Job's friends' decision to attack the victim rather than reassess their own worldview. As legal scholar Lawrence Mitchell laments, the individualism tied to the American Dream has created an image of individual strength that "drowns out our ethic of care."[54]

---

51. A derogatory term for the children of non-citizens who, being born in the United States, are granted automatic citizenship, and thereby are feared to give their alien parents a path to residency or citizenship.

52. J. Rutenberg and A. Parker, "Romney Says Remarks on Voters Help Clarify Position," *New York Times*, September 8, 2012. Speech available online at https://www.youtube.com/watch?v=M2gvY2wqI7M.

53. K. Bradley and R. Rector, "Hunger and Food Programs: Reforming the Food Stamp Program," *Heritage Foundation* (2012). Available online at http://www.heritage.org/node/12241/print-display.

54. L. Mitchell, *Stacked Deck: A Story of Selfishness in America* (Philadelphia, PA: Temple University Press, 1998).

The value of biblical warnings against abuses of privilege is underscored when considering that privilege can predispose our minds to hold contemptuous attitudes toward those of lower-class status, leading to unethical behavior.

The examples of anti-poor sentiment in this section offer a glimpse into the ways in which a psychology-of-privilege hermeneutic can shed light on the circumstances that surround privileged contempt in the ancient texts of the Bible, while also offering new insights into how these texts may connect to modern anti-poor sentiment. Efforts to diminish or eradicate impoverished citizens' access to food assistance and end public education—often under a rationale that condescends the character of the poor while ignoring systems that keep them impoverished—can be understood in new ways through the psychology of privilege. When brought into the field of biblical studies, a psychology-of-privilege hermeneutic can shed light on the profound relevance that such stories as Naboth's vineyard, David and Bathsheba, and Nehemiah's Nobles, prophetic oracles like Mic. 2:1-2 and Isa. 5:8-10, and the laws of sabbatical and jubilee can find in confronting anti-poor sentiment—and its dire consequences—in the modern world.

Conclusion

The words of Job 12:5 ring as true today as they did in the ancient world. Millennia before psychologists would explore the effects of privilege on the human mind, ancient Near Eastern societies perceived the dangers of privileged contempt, and biblical authors—for various reasons—adopted earlier subsistence-based traditions into their legal codes to protect against such callousness. Additionally, numerous biblical tragedies and prophecies cautioned against the abuse of those of lower status, which often resulted in God's divine anger and punishment.

The work conducted by psychologists like Paul Piff provides an opportunity to reread biblical texts with a greater understanding of their psychological underpinnings, while also inviting biblical interpreters to consider new ways in which the Bible's ancient texts might confront poverty in the modern world. As Eliphaz, Bildad, and Zophar's worldview was challenged by Job's suffering, perhaps this heuristic tool can help to challenge paradigms that shame the victims of systemic poverty in the United States and beyond.

Chapter 7

A TASTE FOR WISDOM: AESTHETICS, MORAL DISCERNMENT, AND SOCIAL CLASS IN PROVERBS

Mark Sneed

Over the last three decades, literary and philosophical approaches to the wisdom literature have become popular. Of the former, one can point to Robert Alter as the father of literary approaches to poetry in the Hebrew Bible, including the wisdom corpus. My favorite chapter in his book, *The Art of Biblical Poetry*, is the one on Proverbs he titles "The Poetry of Wit."[1] There, he delineates intricacies of the parallelism within sentences (the short bicolon genre found in two collections [Prov. 10–22:16; 25–29]) demonstrating that their meanings are made emphatic by their terseness.[2] But recently, Knut Heim published a large tome on the sophistication of the sentences exploring the phenomenon known as "twice-told proverbs," or proverbs that involve the repetition of proverbs found elsewhere in the book of Proverbs.[3] He argues that this strategy creates a dialectic in which parts of one proverb resonate with the other proverbs that share similar or identical parts. This goes beyond the contextual analysis of proverbs in clusters and extends the context to the book as a whole.[4] Both these and other studies have contributed much to scholarly understanding not only of the proverbial material but also how biblical poetry works distinctly within the wisdom literature.

As for the philosophical, I am referring to the trend in the last two decades to draw on virtue ethics and the notion of character to interpret the wisdom literature. Instead of the form of this literature, they focus on its content, particularly the ethical principles that are inculcated in it. Most recognized is Bill Brown, whose book *Character in Crisis* (1996) has spawned interest in how Israelite wisdom literature can be illuminated by comparing it to Greek philosophical treatments

---

1. R. Alter, *The Art of Biblical Poetry* (New York: Basic Books, 1985), 163–84.
2. Ibid., 165–68.
3. K. Heim, *Poetic Imagination in Proverbs: Variant Repetitions and the Nature of Poetry* (BBRSup 4; Winona Lake, IN: Eisenbrauns, 2013).
4. See, especially, ibid., 30–35.

of ethics.⁵ Brown argues that the wisdom literature should be viewed as aiding in the character formation of its readers. So, it is not about content so much as helping the original reader mature in character formation. Brown uses the analytical tools and definitions developed concerning virtues of ancient philosophers like Plato and Aristotle and the medieval philosopher, Aquinas, to help better understand the goals of wisdom literature.⁶ Again, this is an important contribution for better discerning the intent of the wisdom writers, and it helps hermeneutically to connect the ancient Near Eastern sapiential tradition with our modern, Western culture, which has been heavily influenced by Greek philosophy. However, rarely do the representatives of literary or philosophical ethics approaches treat the question of how the two phenomena they focus on connect to particular societies and cultures, that is, their social context, which is the source for both literary and ethical phenomena. Understanding those phenomena for studies beyond those limited to literary and philosophical concerns are critical, as Benedict Anderson exposes, for understanding how language and meaning are co-opted within cultural articulations of identity.⁷

In her book *Poetic Ethics in Proverbs*, Anne Stewart combined literary and philosophical strategies by arguing that the aesthetic sophistication of the sayings and longer poems in Proverbs was intentional to facilitate moral formation. She maintains that poetry, pedagogy, and ethos are all intertwined in Proverbs.⁸ She points out that poetry in Proverbs would be more difficult for students to read than narrative but that its difficulty is intentional in order to hone skills in moral discernment.⁹ With that, she critiques other scholars who use virtue ethics to interpret Proverbs while emphasizing the importance of narrative, not poetry, in the formation of moral character. Proverbs, she argues, does not simply etch out the correct moral path for the student to take; it helps develop general moral discernment so that when the student matures socially and morally, he will be prepared to make the best moral decision required by the situation.¹⁰ Stewart has also published a recent article using the theorization of Mark Johnson to argue that Proverbs employs various metaphors involving prototypes. According to that theory, those prototypes are deliberately flexible and generic so to aid the reader in imagining moral possibilities that will serve her in ethical decision-making in

---

5. See, for example, C. Ansberry, "What Does Jerusalem Have To Do with Athens?: The Moral Vision of the Book of Proverbs and Aristotle's Nicomachean Ethics," *HS* 51 (2010), 157–73, and M. Fox, "Ethics and Wisdom in the Book of Proverbs," *HS* 48 (2007), 75–88.

6. See W. Brown, *Character in Crisis: A Fresh Approach to the Wisdom Literature of the Old Testament* (Grand Rapids, MI: Eerdmans, 1996), 9–12.

7. Cf. Anderson, *Imagined Communities*, Kindle ed., locations 1429–80.

8. A. Stewart, *Poetic Ethics in Proverbs: Wisdom Literature and the Shaping of the Moral Self* (Cambridge: Cambridge University Press, 2016), 1–8.

9. Ibid., 41–43.

10. Ibid., see 50, 55, 59, 66–69.

the future.[11] All of this is illuminating and Stewart's work certainly pushes the state of research in the area forward, but she too falls short of the greater need that I've identified: she never clearly connects the sapiential aesthetics and ethics of Proverbs with its original audience in its social context. To be fair, in her article, she does indicate how the prototype of moral authority legitimizes the contemporary power structures but, unfortunately, she never explores this further.

Bridging literary and philosophical approaches

In the following discussion I want to explore two questions tangentially related to Stewart's work that she never explores. First, how would the wisdom treated in Proverbs differ from the wisdom used outside the book within Israelite society? That question will connect with Stewart's focus on aesthetics. Second, why does Proverbs seem to fixate on morality and piety, or why is this the focus in the wisdom literature in general? It is one thing to argue that Proverbs is primarily about character formation, but it is an entirely different matter to ask why it focuses so much on that issue. Along those lines, another needed question is whether or not a fixation on piety, as the composers of Proverbs seem to have, was something shared more commonly.

The theorist best to answer those questions, in my opinion, is not a biblical scholar but a French sociologist: Pierre Bourdieu.[12] Bourdieu is often designated as the successor of Max Weber, especially in that Bourdieu embraces Weber's important notion of *Stand* or status over against social class, which is a purely economic category.[13] This particular nuance distinguishes both Weber and Bourdieu from Marx. Status is especially significant for an ancient society like that of the Israelites where one's honor and reputation were of the utmost significance. I am not the first to use Bourdieu to illuminate Proverbs. At least other two scholars, of which I am aware, have also seen the relevancy of his theories for clarifying something about

---

11. A. Stewart, "Wisdom's Imagination: Moral Reasoning and the Book of Proverbs," *JSOT* 40.3 (2016), 351–72.

12. For introductions to Bourdieu's thinking, see D. Swartz (*Culture & Power: The Sociology of Pierre Bourdieu* [Chicago, IL: University of Chicago Press, 1997]; P. Bourdieu, *Outline of a Theory of Practice*, trans. R. Nice [Cambridge Studies in Social and Cultural Anthropology 16; Cambridge: Cambridge University Press, 1977]; *Sociology in Question*, trans. R. Nice [Theory, Culture & Society 18; London: Sage, 1993]; *Practical Reason: On the Theory of Action* [Stanford: Stanford University Press, 1998]).

13. See M. Weber, *Economy and Society: An Outline of Interpretive Sociology*, eds. G. Roth and C. Wittich, trans. E. Fischoff, H. Gerth, A. M. Henderson, F. Kolegar, C. W. Mills, T. Parsons, M. Rheinstein, G. Roth, E. Shils, and C. Wittich (2 vols; New York: Bedminster, 1968; repr. Berkeley, CA: University of California Press, 1978), 302–07, 927–40; R. Swedberg, *The Max Weber Dictionary: Key Words and Central Concepts* (Stanford, CA: Stanford University Press, 2005), 38.

the book. Joseph Scrivner, for example, completed a Princeton 2007 dissertation under C. L. Seow entitled "Wisdom as Cultural Capital: Textuality and Moral-Social Reproduction in Proverbs 1-9." Drawing on Bourdieu's work, Scrivner argues that wisdom is a type of cultural capital and with which young Israelite scribes were inculcated through study. In addition, he argues that the book of Proverbs served to form scribes morally and bodily simultaneously and also was a significant means of reproducing the scribal guild professionally. His analysis is helpful, but it never really situates the scribal elite within the larger Israelite social stratification, which would make the study truly Bourdieusian in that Bourdieu always connects his particular analysis with the larger social stratification, that is, the complete pecking order.

Another example is Greg Goering, who uses the metaphor of taste to illuminate wisdom in Proverbs.[14] Goering emphasizes the sensorial embodiment of wisdom by its original readers. He[15] utilizes Bourdieu's theory of practice (citing Bourdieu's *Outline of a Theory of Practice*[16]) that explores how "Israelite pedagogy inscribes its values on the body"[17] which entails disciplining the senses, particularly hearing and seeing. In another study,[18] Goering focuses on the sense of taste and argues that in Proverbs taste is metaphorical for moral tastes. Here Goering draws on Bourdieu's important work *Distinctions*,[19] which argues that social classes reproduce themselves and maintain their place within the social pecking order by creating a sense of taste that correlates with and supports class delineation.[20] Bourdieu's analysis is based on surveys he did in the 1960s France. Goering[21] indicates that taste becomes concretized in the distinction between wise and fool in Proverbs. For example, in Prov. 26:11, an incorrigible fool is compared to a dog eating its own vomit.

Goering's distinction of the wise man and the fool provides a nice segue into my own argument. For Bourdieu, morality and aesthetics are two ways that the lower echelons within the upper class could compensate for inferior social positions over against the highest echelons of the same class. Both class ethos and aesthetics form two sides of the same coin of what Bourdieu calls "cultural capital," as opposed to economic capital. In that, Bourdieu distinguishes himself from Marx and clearly reveals his Weberian leanings. Economic capital is equivalent to Marx's notion of capital, where all social facets can be reduced to economics. But Bourdieu, following Weber, believes that there is such a thing as cultural capital that can

---

14. G. Goering, "Attentive Ears and Forward-Looking Eyes: Disciplining the Senses and Forming the Self in the Book of Proverbs," *JJS* 66.2 (2015), 242–64.

15. Ibid., 248, 257–61.

16. Bourdieu, *Outline of a Theory*.

17. Goering, "Attentive Ears," 257.

18. G. Goering, "Honey and Wormwood: Taste and the Embodiment of Wisdom in the Book of Proverbs." *HBAI* 5 (2016), 23–41.

19. P. Bourdieu, *Distinction: A Social Critique of the Judgment of Taste*, trans. R. Nice (Routledge Classics; London: Routledge, 2010).

20. Goering, "Honey and Wormwood," 36.

21. Ibid.

actually be identified as in some ways the opposite of economic capital, though even with Bourdieu, as with Marx, economic capital is always primary. Cultural capital represents capacities that compensate for the lack of economic capital among members of the upper classes. For example, intellectuals and other petite bourgeoisie can compensate for their dominated position under the bourgeoisie by focusing on their educational skills and knowledge, which provides them leverage over against the truly rich and powerful, who do not need such qualities to retain their superiority.[22] That leverage can result in a sense of superiority over the truly wealthy and powerful. Bourdieu shows that the petite bourgeoisie often compensate by fixating on piety or morality, a type of "aristocratic asceticism"[23] which is reflected in the surveys he conducted. They can then pride themselves in taking the high road morally in contradistinction to the Machiavellian actions taken by the truly aristocratic, who are quite comfortable in their lifestyle and have few scruples about their (mis)use of power.

This suggests another more basic tension: that between the working class and poor and the upper classes, including intellectuals and the petite bourgeoisie, Bourdieu argues that a sense of taste is directly connected with the social class into which one is born. All social classes, according to Bourdieu, have their own tastes and preferences in style and manner, and, it is these more than anything else that define particular classes over against others. The main difference between the higher and lower classes is that the lower classes are constrained by necessity, whereas the higher classes are so unconstrained[24] that they can actually waste resources, what American sociologists call "disposable income" or "conspicuous consumption." They can also waste time and deliberately, whereas the lower classes cannot afford such luxuries. They also focus more on form than substance. For example, the wealthy focus more on the aesthetics or form of the food and its quality. But the working class usually favors heavy, hearty, cheap food—the focus is on quantity. So, the typical taste of a manual laborer is not really by choice, as he or she might think, but has been determined by the class within which he/she was born into and enculturated.

The same goes for art, in which the wealthy tend to relish form over substance.[25] These dynamics play out within the upper-class factions. For example, modern artists push this to its limit with emphasis on the symbolism of their art rather than any dominant realism. One often hears the working class complaining that modern art is chaotic and simply splattering paint on canvas, but to the artistic world these comments are simply the words of a philistine who does not

---

22. See P. Bourdieu, *The Field of Cultural Production. European Perspectives* (New York: Columbia University Press, 1993). On the role of intellectuals in Bourdieu's sociology, see D. Swartz, *Symbolic Power, Politics and Intellectuals: The Political Sociology of Pierre Bourdieu* (Chicago, IL: University of Chicago Press, 2013).

23. Bourdieu, *Distinction*, 217.

24. See ibid., 46–50.

25. See ibid., 195.

appreciate great art. The working class generally prefers portraits of still life to abstract expressionism. What is intriguing about Bourdieu's theorization here is that taste, of all the varying types, serves not only to distinguish and identify differences between the various classes and subclasses. It also serves to reproduce the class divisions and reinforce the social pressures to remain in one's class, to know where one's place is and not venture beyond the proper boundaries. In other words, taste can be one of the major ideological vehicles for oppression, entailing what Bourdieu calls symbolic power or capital, but real and effective, nonetheless. Now it is time to apply some of Bourdieu's theory for illuminating the book of Proverbs.

The aesthetics of the sentences in proverbs

In her book, Stewart provides some examples of the aesthetic sophistication of Proverbs 1–9 and how statements within those passages are connected with moral formation.[26] Of course, Alter has almost comprehensively demonstrated the literary finesse of the sentences (mainly in the collections, e.g., 10:1–22:16) and how this reinforces the principles taught in them.[27] We will focus on the contrast between the sentences in Proverbs and a related genre, folk proverbs found within biblical narratives, and how the difference between the two points to the broader social context within Israelite society. A clear contrast exists between the sentences in Proverbs and examples of folk proverbs in the Hebrew Bible, in terms of form. Of course, several scholars view the sentences in Proverbs as being actual folk proverbs. Friedemann Golka[28] has argued that the sentences in Proverbs are in fact actually oral proverbs from the common people that have been collected and recorded, or at the least, the sentences preserve vestiges of folk proverbs in their current literary form. Similarly, R. N. Whybray also sees some of the collections originating among "petit peuple" or even farmers.[29] And Tremper Longman comes to a similar conclusion, maintaining that, based on the topics discussed in Proverbs, the social contexts of the sentences vary from courtier to farmer.[30]

But there is no evidence that the Israelites collected and recorded oral proverbs like paremiologists today. To assert otherwise is quite anachronistic. In fact, the superscriptions of the collections in Proverbs clearly indicate that their collectors viewed these "proverbs" as epigrams and not folk proverbs that might have been

---

26. Stewart, *Poetic Ethics in Proverbs*, 43–69.

27. Alter, *Art*, 163–84.

28. F. Golka, *The Leopard's Spots: Biblical and African Wisdom in Proverbs* (Edinburgh: T&T Clark, 1993).

29. R. Whybray, *Wealth and Poverty in the Book of Proverbs* (Sheffield: JSOT Press, 1990), 60–61, 68, 92–93, 100, 103, 114–17.

30. T. Longman, Jr., *The Fear of the Lord Is Wisdom: A Theological Introduction to Wisdom in Israel* (Grand Rapids, MI: Baker Academic, 2017), 197–98.

current among the masses. The superscriptions to the collections ("the epigrams of Solomon" [10:1]; "the wise men" [22:17]) point to this material as not being current among the people, as in a folk proverb. If they were current, why would Israelite scribes waste their time copying them, except perhaps for posterity's sake? But this is an anachronistic notion. Israelite scribes were not paremiologists who recorded and collected proverbs to be published. But a perhaps more serious problem with this kind of speculation about social matrices is that it is impossible to identify the composers of epigrams (or proverbs) from the topics treated in them. As Richard Clifford states, "One can speak 'of cabbages and kings' without being a cook or a courtier."[31] It is doubtful that an Israelite scribe would have had much difficulty coining an epigram that alluded to farming techniques. That is because he lived in an agrarian economy, with animals and fields only a few yards away from the table he copied scrolls on. And if there are folk proverbs embedded in these sentences, they have certainly been refined in the process of their integration within the framework of the dominant cultural identity.[32]

The difference in form, at least, between the folk proverb and epigram is clear in the few instances where we find folk proverbs. We will first compare 1 Sam. 24:13, a proverb cited by David, with Prov. 10:1, the very first epigram of the Solomonic collection of sentences (chs. 10–22:16). But before we look at these, I want to briefly discuss "proverb performance" or how folk proverbs function in social contexts. In Africa, for comparison, proverbs have been used rhetorically in forensic settings to persuade a jurist to take the side of the plaintive or defendant,[33] or to teach young people morality.[34] Elías Barajas, for further example, has investigated the usages of proverbs among Mexican migrant workers in order to determine their function in discourse.[35] He identifies four ways proverbs are typically used in particular social situations:[36]

1. "to support an argumentative claim concerning behavior"
2. "to teach or promote reflection by way of advice"
3. "to establish interpersonal rapport"
4. "to entertain via verbal creativity, which is viewed as a supplement to the above functions."[37]

31. R. Clifford, *The Wisdom Literature* (IBT; Nashville, TN: Abingdon, 1998), 49.

32. Compare Anderson, *Imagined Communities*, locations 1498–519.

33. J. Messenger, "The Role of the Proverb in a Nigerian Judicial System," *Southwestern Journal of Anthropology* 15 (1959), 64–73.

34. E. Arera and A. Dundes, "Proverbs and the Ethnography of Speaking Folklore," *American Anthropologist* 66.6 (1954), 70–85.

35. E. Barajas, *The Function of Proverbs in Discourse: The Case of a Mexican Transnational Social Network*, ed. J. Fishman (Contributions to the Sociology of Language 98; Berlin: De Gruyter Mouton, 2010).

36. This is what C. Fontaine ("Proverb Performance in the Hebrew Bible," *JSOT* 32 [1985], 87–103) describes as "proverb performance," how proverbs are actually used in mundane circumstances among persons.

37. Barajas, *Function of Proverbs*, 70.

For our purposes, an example of each of the first three functions of proverbs provided by Barajas will prove helpful in analyzing the biblical examples. The first involves the use of a proverb in an argument regarding behavior. A mother-in-law rebukes her son-in-law when he accuses her daughter of infidelity, when in fact he was the actual culprit.[38] She exposes him publicly before other members of the family. The woman's husband admits that she was in the right to rebuke the son-in-law but not publicly. She responds to her husband with this proverb: "When the saint needs the candle, one must light it." The proverb justifies her behavior and simultaneously challenges the traditional role of women as passive before male authority. That challenge fits what Anderson would describe as a "revolutionary" activity within the vernacular to affect a "national" consciousness.[39] In this case, the woman clearly wins the argument.

An example of using a proverb for advice involves Barajas himself and the parents of a son.[40] They speak of their son who is boastful about his control over everyone, though they point out that this does not apply to his wife. The father recites this proverb: "Don't spit at the sky that which to your face will fall." The father disapproves of his son's boastfulness, but this is not the function of the citation since the son was not present. The proverb was actually intended as advice for Barajas because he was the younger of the trio and less experienced.

The third example of using a proverb to establish rapport involves a young man who defends an older man for leaving his common law wife, who constantly disrespects him.[41] After squandering all his savings, the older man decides to leave and take what few possessions he has left. The woman then accuses him of theft. The young man defends the older man to his aunts with this recitation: "Better to be alone than in bad company." This usage is not didactic because the young man was less experienced than his aunts. It also involved no critique of the woman's behavior because she was not present. Rather, the proverb is used as an identity marker for the interlocutors present. It is the young man's way of expressing to his aunts that they share the same values.

1 Sam. 24:13 versus Prov. 10:1

מרשעים יצא רשע

"Out of the wicked comes forth wickedness." (1 Sam. 24:13)

בן חכם ישמח־אב ובן כסיל תוגת אמו

"A wise son brings joy to his father, but a foolish son is the grief of *his* mother." (Prov. 10:1)

---

38. Ibid., 75–77.
39. Anderson, *Imagined Communities*, location 1549.
40. Barajas, *Function of Proverbs*, 85–86.
41. Ibid., 93–94.

Our first biblical example is 1 Samuel 14, and the context is David's flight from Saul's pursuit of him. Saul goes into a cave of En-Gedi and relieves himself as David's men suggest that he slay Saul. Instead, David cut's the corner off of Saul's tunic. After Saul leaves the cave, David confronts him with the evidence that he had a chance to slay the Lord's Anointed but didn't. David then cites a proverb that is actually identified as a folk saying: "ancient proverb." It is only three words in length: "Out of the wicked comes forth wickedness." The proverb makes the point that people act according to their heart's character, similar to Jesus's citation of the proverb about a good or bad tree that produces according to its nature (Lk. 6:43-49). David's citation, thus, functions according to Barajas's number one: "To support an argumentative claim concerning behavior." David, thereby, justifies his behavior as demonstrated by his actions over against Saul's criminal behavior in trying to kill David. The proverb serves to cinch David's argument or point because a proverb already has built-in agreed upon truth that it expresses.[42] Its truth represents the cumulative wisdom of the past generations to which the current generation adheres.

As far as aesthetics, this proverb doesn't have much. There is a repetition of the stem for "wicked," which makes the proverb easier to remember, but other than that, there is clearly no sophistication to the proverb orally. It is simply a one-colon popular saying.

Now to Prov. 10:1. While this is not the most sophisticated example of a sentence in the collection, it certainly reveals its distinction from the folk proverb. It is longer due to its bicolon form, a clear marker of distinction. As Alter has pointed out, the bicolon form of the sentence is what provides it its pizazz and punch.[43] The cola echo each other and interact to produce a meaning that goes beyond the two cola. And their terseness serves to create other interesting effects. No such interaction or supplementation is possible with a single colon folk proverb. Here this is achieved in two ways. First, the type of parallelism this sentence reflects is known as antithetical, where opposite concepts are used to convey the same principle. Here "wise" opposes "foolish," "father" opposes "mother," and "joy" opposes "grief." And then in the second colon there is what Alter calls "specification."[44] We progress from the broader term "father" to the more particular "his mother." Also, the shift from the verb in the first colon to its ellipsis in the second also reveals the subtle sophistication of this epigram. Here form takes dominance over content.

The message is banal: grow up to be a wise child and bring honor to your family. In other words, honor your parents by being wise. The original audience, say a scribe, who read or heard this wouldn't have been receiving anything new in

---

42. See R. Abrahams, "Proverbs and Proverbial Expressions," in *Folklore and Folklife: An Introduction*, ed. R. Porson (Chicago, IL: University of Chicago Press, 1972), 119, 122; cf. R. Abrahams, "A Rhetoric of Everyday Life: Traditional Conversational Genres," *Southern Folklore Quarterly* 32 (1968), 48.

43. Alter, *Art*, 173.

44. Ibid., 19.

terms of information or profundity of insight. Surely his childhood socialization engrained this principle into him because this is one of the core tenets of an honor/shame society. Rather, the aesthetics of the epigram would have caught his attention and simultaneously served to reinforce this principle that he already knew well.

So, the function that comes closest to Barajas's typology would be both numbers two and four: "To teach or promote reflection by way of advice" and "to entertain via verbal creativity." It would be more the latter than the former because, as just said, the principle is rather banal and already inculcated. Thus, the principle is to be wise but it's wrapped in a beautiful package that might help keep the student's interest as he either heard someone else read, perhaps the scribal teacher and/or he read this epigram himself within the collection. The principle of living wisely is a type of wisdom that anyone could seek to embody and live by, not just elite scribes. However, the ability to appreciate the aesthetic beauty of Prov. 10:1 would not be a skill that an Israelite peasant could value. Their world was the world of David where folk proverbs were used in daily interaction and argumentation. Short and sweet suited their tastes. Not so the Israelite scribe, who through his study of wisdom literature and other modes of literature learned to appreciate the nuances of literary sophistication, such techniques as parallelism, intensification, specification, assonance, and alliteration, among many other joys of poetry. This is the kind of wisdom identified in the prologue to the book of Proverbs that one could describe as scribal wisdom, certainly an elite form of wisdom in which only they could engage: "To understand a *mashal* (epigram) and a figure, the words of the wise and their riddles" (1:6).

Judg. 8:21 versus Prov. 9:17

כאיש גבורתו
"As the man, so is his strength." (Judg. 8:21)

מים־גנובים ימתקו ולחם סתרים ינעם
"Stolen water is sweet, and secret bread tastes good." (Prov. 9:17)

Judges 8:21 provides another example of a folk proverb used orally in a social context. Gideon tried to convince his son to kill the captured Midianite kings, Zebah and Zalmunna. But the boy was afraid and couldn't do it. So the two kings exclaim to Gideon, "As the man, so is his strength," indicating that this is a man's job, not a boy's. Ultimately, they wanted to avoid dying at the hands of a youth, a very shameful way to die in the context of the Israelite honor/shame culture. The proverb is only two words in Hebrew. There is no focus here on form for form's sake, except in the terseness of the proverb, which is one of the defining characteristics of a proverb. The function of this proverb would be the same as David's: "To support an argumentative claim concerning behavior," Barajas' number one. The Midianite kings are essentially challenging Gideon's tactic in order to persuade him into allowing them at least to die honorably as valiant men.

We will now look at an epigram (Prov. 9:17) that in itself is more sophisticated than the above proverb, but its chief sophistication is in the way it is used in its literary context. This context is Woman Folly attempting to seduce young men to come follow her. While Woman Wisdom invites the same young men to a grand banquet, Woman Folly only invites to a metaphorical meal that involves illicit sexual gratification.[45] The proverb is more sophisticated than the one cited by Zeba and Zalmunnah, chiefly because of its bicolon form. It has six words divided into two cola. The second colon parallels the first synonymously. This allows the paralleling of "water" and "bread." Water and bread were staples of the Israelite meal. Thus, this allows a clearer allusion to the consumption of food/drink as metaphorical for sexual gratification, here illicit because it is "stolen" and "secret," which makes it that more appealing since it is taboo. Compare 5:15-17, "Drink water from your own cistern, flowing water from your own well. Should your springs be scattered abroad, streams of water in the streets? Let them be for yourself alone, and not for sharing with strangers." Here it is licit. The epigram in Folly's mouth describes the enticement of forbidden things. In other words, there is pleasure in folly or sin, else it would not be a temptation. Here in its literary context, this epigram is being used to seduce the young men, pointing to its reward, while obscuring its dangers. However, the epigram alone, without a literary context, would imply the very opposite: though the forbidden is alluring, avoid it! This creates a tension in its current context, because Woman Folly is using the epigram against its normative intent, to allure instead of to detract! Such interesting possibilities are not possible with the folk proverb on the lips of the Midianite kings.

It is doubtful anyone would ever quote the epigram of Prov. 9:17 in a particular social context, as one finds with Woman Folly, part of fictive context. Rather, the epigram sans context serves only to teach Barajas's second function. Its message would have been significant for a young scribe because sexual peccadillos could ruin the career of a governmental official, which many scribes aspired to be. The concern to avoid illicit sexual affairs is a topos found frequently in the wisdom literature of the ancient Near East. But the epigram alone does not necessitate a particular social situation beyond that between teacher and student, or the student himself, who could read it from a scroll and be instructed. Either way, without its literary context in Proverbs 9, it would have been used to teach young scribes the dangers of forbidden pleasures, especially that of the adulterer. Here, without its literary context, this epigram's power is its message and less its form, yet its form is more sophisticated than the proverb cited by the Midianite kings. Within

---

45. For a deconstructive analysis of the two figures that delineates a darker side to Woman Wisdom, see M. Sneed, "'White Trash' Wisdom: Proverbs 9 Deconstructed," *JHebS* 7 (2007), article 5. http://www.arts.ualberta.ca/JHS/Articles/articl_66.pdf. Accessed April 24, 2011.

its literary context, of course, the literary sophistication is on the extreme, as indicated above.

1 Kgs 20:11 versus Prov. 11:22

אל־יתהלל חגר כמפתח
"One who puts on armor should not brag like one who takes it off." (1 Kgs 20:11)

נזם זהב באף חזיר אשה יפה וסרת טעם
"A gold ring in the nose of a pig, a beautiful woman who departs from discretion." (Prov. 11:22)

In our last example of a folk proverb, 1 Kgs 20:11 is directed at Benhadad, who has besieged Samaria where Ahab reigned. Benhadad had offered him vassalage in order to lift the siege. Ahab agreed but then Benhadad demanded to inspect his residence. Ahab refused this demand and then sent back Benhadad's messengers with this proverb. The point of the proverb is similar to our own proverb: "Don't count your chickens before they're hatched." It, of course, was insulting to Benhadad, but Ahab scored points in the use of a fitting proverb in his riposte. This proverb fits Barajas's category of using a proverb to support an argument regarding behavior. Again, it is short: only four words and there is no focus on form, except for its brevity. Its sophistication is rather in pairing the opposites of putting on and removing armor, which is clever. One can even detect a sense of humor here, as the braggart will have to eat his own words.

Yet its form cannot compare with our new example, Prov. 11:22, a riddle according to Alter, one of the most sophisticated kinds of epigrams.[46] One imagines that the first colon was read out loud or cited by a scribal teacher, who then hesitated, creating dissonance in the novice scribes' minds. The first colon has a built in tension that only becomes released with the revelation of the second colon. Thus, the cognitive movement is tension and then relief. The tension in the first colon here is not formal but semantic. What could be more incongruent than a pig with a gold ring in its nose? Who would waste their wealth doing such a thing? But when the second colon is revealed, it all makes sense. The riddle involves a comparison between two incongruities, the punch line constituting the second colon. Its message is profound and would serve to teach its original scribal audience or cause it to reflect Barajas's number two. Beauty is fleeting and wisdom is more valuable. This epigram might have served as advice to young scribes as they contemplated a future wife, whether selected by his parents or himself. A wise woman is to be preferred over one who is beautiful, a quality which is ephemeral. But, again, the social situation implied by this riddle (epigram) here is either between a teacher and student as the teacher recites the

---

46. Alter, *Art*, 169, 176.

first colon and asks the student(s) to solve it or it is the student alone who ponders the epigram as recorded on a scroll. It does not involve the type of dialog or give and take associated with the use of a folk proverb in a complex social situation. Thus, while the social situation of the riddle is simpler than the proverb cited by Ahab, the aesthetics and the topic of the riddle is more complex than those of the folk proverb.

While the message is profound in the riddle, the creativity, and, thus, the focus on form over content is clear here. Here we have an epigram with a double the punch! One can easily imagine the scribes enjoying the recitation and pondering of riddles in their training and subsequent lives as intellectuals.

Piety trumps power

In the prolog to Proverbs it emphasizes "gaining discipline in comprehending righteousness, justice, and fairness" (1:3). This correlates with the moral principle found in 10:1 of living wisely so as to honor parents. Almost all the sentences in Proverbs are about morality or mores. The significant question then is: Why did the scribal apprentices need to read all of these sentences whose moral messages were often banal and no doubt had been ingrained in them since they were little? Bourdieu's sociological theory may provide us an answer. Morality is a way for a social class that is inferior to compensate for this liability through noneconomic means—which it lacks—again, what he called "cultural capital," a form of symbolic capital. The social location of scribes reveals such a lack. The scribes who composed and studied the Israelite wisdom literature—and this is true also for the Mesopotamian and Egyptian scribal guilds—would have been part of the retainer class, the class that served the interests of the governing class: the king, his family, the nobility, the military leaders, among others. The one realm in which they could have exceled, in addition to aesthetics, was piety. They could live wise and pious lives, and since they had relatively comfortable lives with ample leisure time, they could excel at this better than any of their superiors or inferiors.

Brian Kovacs, in his 1978 dissertation at Vanderbilt University, deftly perceives the sages' sensitivity to how they differed from the other classes.[47] By closely analyzing Prov. 15:28–22:16, Kovacs uses phenomenological sociology to detect the ways the wise define formal structures for their worlds, find them meaningful, and how this strategy fits with their social locations.[48] Kovacs especially analyzes the way the wise in Proverbs conceive of space and how this elicits the notion

---

47. For an analysis of the class culture of Proverbs, see M. Sneed, "The Class Culture of Proverbs: Eliminating Stereotypes," *SJOT* 10.2 (1996), 296–308.

48. The following is a summary of chap. 5 of his dissertation (B. Kovacs, "Sociological-Structural Constraints Upon Wisdom: The Spatial and Temporal Matrix of Proverbs 15:28–22:16," [PhD diss.; Vanderbilt University, 1978], 317–515).

of demesne or social domain. Particular groups have their areas of control and boundaries in which they operate and often define themselves in terms of these areas of control.[49]

He first discusses the wise men's ethic of restraint and self-discipline (e.g., Prov. 17:27-28). The wise use this to neutralize the powers of the un-wise and those more powerful than themselves, for example, the king (16:14). The wise sense the power of knowledge.

Kovacs points out that the bribe sayings (e.g., 19:6; 18:16) indicate that the wise of necessity have to use less-than-savory means to influence the rich and powerful. The sayings that extol the king (e.g., 20:26) show that the wise generally support the royal establishment in spite of its liabilities. But while the wise respect power, they value wisdom more highly (e.g., 21:22). Wealth and power are valued chiefly as means of security from the manipulations of others. Wealth is to be shared with the poor (e.g., 22:9), so the wise see themselves as distanced from both the rich and poor. This, Kovacs describes as noblesse oblige, but the wise go beyond this responsibility. One's disposition is more important than one's economic status (e.g., 19:1). They are not "mere custodians of the status quo" (e.g., 22:2). The proverbs against being surety for others and borrowing (e.g., 17:18; 20:16) show that the sages avoided being dependent on others. In other words, they protect their social space and avoid attempts by others to violate it or by their own to stray from it. Kovacs maintains that the wise define themselves by what they are, not by what they do, as do the powerful.

He then examines various social institutions the wise make reference to. He shows how numerous proverbs (e.g., 17:17; 19:7) demonstrate that family (parents, siblings, and their own children) and friends were important to the wise, and they formed a relatively closed group. The law court was also apparently a place where they served (e.g., 18:17). They refer also to the cult (e.g., 21:27), the market (e.g., 20:10), the countryside (e.g., 22:8), the battlefield (e.g., 18:11), and school (e.g., 17:16). Kovacs then concludes about the wise:

> When they look outside their realm, their language and imagery become stereotypical, symbolic, and sometimes banal. Their attention seems to be focused on a fairly restricted sphere... much of the social life is missing, because it did not occupy the attention of the wise... The life of the lower classes and the world outside the city... scarcely appears.[50]

Kovacs points out there is a significant aesthetic dimension to wisdom that makes it an elite demesne—many are excluded, such as the ignorant and the poor.[51] This elitism is built not on power but character and insight.

---

49. Ibid., 393; see also, again, Anderson, *Imagined Communities*, locations 1429–80.
50. Kovacs, "Sociological-Structural Constraints," 392.
51. Ibid., 436.

In another work, Kovacs delineates a sense of class ethic in Proverbs as a whole that could be described in sociological terms as an in-group morality.[52] In the context of pointing out that the wise did not slavishly support the status quo, Kovacs concludes,

> Thus, even if the wise man is oriented toward the acknowledged Hebrew goods of life (long life, success, progeny, and recognition), he may not seek them directly, nor by the path of his own planting. Only by pursuing wisdom for its own sake, so that it is good and valuable in its own right, rather than instrumentally, by means of the discipline of restraint, can he succeed. It is only a slight exaggeration to say that the wise could seek success only by giving it up.[53]

Kovacs's incisive perception that the sages saw themselves as choosing wisdom for its own sake is exactly what Bourdieu means by symbolic capital compensating for a lack of economic capital. Though the sages delude themselves into thinking they are taking the moral high road, in fact, they are simply unconsciously compensating for their own lack of the very thing they seek to distance themselves from (power and wealth). Thus, the sages do not really value wisdom for its own sake but employ it as a form of cultural capital they excel at over against the capital employed by the other social factions and classes within ancient Israel. A taste for wisdom, then, is essentially a jockeying for superior positioning in disguise, providing the sages with a sense of moral superiority over everyone else in Israelite society.

Conclusion

The new literary and philosophical (virtue ethics) approaches have brought much illumination to the study of the book of Proverbs. However, neither approach has seriously engaged the social context of this literature and what this signifies about its producers in terms of social stratification in ancient Israel. A social theoretical approach does not just take at face value the reality of a focus on formal aesthetics and morality (piety) but asks the more fundamental question, why? This means it searches for a broader, more comprehensive, perspective for understanding the book of Proverbs. I have compared three maxims, in each case, one of folkish origin, the other elitist. While the Israelite folk proverb and epigram share certain social functions, they do so in different ways and involving different social strata. By this comparison, I have attempted to expose the social significance of the focus on form over substance in the sentences in Proverbs and simultaneously have suggested why Proverbs as a whole also focuses almost exclusively on morality and

---

52. B. Kovacs, "Is There a Class-Ethic in Proverbs?" in *Essays in Old Testament Ethics*, eds. J. Crenshaw and J. Willis (New York: Ktav, 1974), 173–89.

53. Ibid., 183.

ethics. Through these two means, the sages have constructed their identity over against the other factions of ancient Israel, the truly wealthy and powerful above them and the poor and oppressed beneath them. Developing a taste for wisdom, whether in terms of sophisticated poetry or in the form of aristocratic asceticism, then, was not some innocuous, disinterested activity detached from the rest of Israelite society. It was much, much more.

Chapter 8

BIBLICAL STRATEGIES FOR REINTERPRETING CRISES WITH "OUTSIDERS"

Jeremiah W. Cataldo

The nation is imagined as *limited* because even the largest of them, encompassing perhaps a billion living human beings, has finite, if elastic, boundaries, beyond which lie other nations.[1]

Let me acknowledge here my starting premise: "the biblical texts" are historical artifacts; "Bible" is the symbol against which a, and quite often *the*, horizon of meaning is based for modern Judeo-Christian communities. Ethics, values, moral, contours of identity and ideology are measured against it. In its combined form both as artifact and symbol, it considers the outsider to be a threat. How then might the Bible be read in light of conflicts with outsiders? Is the history of its interpretation too much to overcome for the disenfranchised minority?

Without doubt, the question is multifaceted and complex. And in many ways, my project here is an attempt to come to terms with the complexity of this question, which exposes the frayed margins of biblical studies. To approach the beginning of an answer, I focus here on how identity is "imagined," along the lines of insider-outsider distinctions, against the Bible as both artifact and symbol. This pursuit is not new in itself. In their own ways, liberation and postcolonial theories[2] have pursued similar questions, and because of that both will be helpful here.

Together with those questions, Benedict Anderson's study of how communities imagine themselves as unified bodies offers a helpful framework, though limited perhaps in obvious ways, for reading the biblical texts and the relics of group identities they preserve. In its identification of a dominant sociopolitical narrative as the basis for imagined identity, it also exposes the ways prejudices fill in gaps between the (social) center and the margins. It pursues how they do so with restrictive vocabulary and concomitant categorical limitations upon the "other," who may

---

1. Anderson, *Imagined Communities*, Kindle ed., location 227.
2. My emphasis here is on theologies of liberation and postcolonialism. I would also include other theories such as queer theory, feminist theory, and similar.

take the form of a resident, foreigner, or immigrant. On a functional level for the majority, prejudices reinforce community boundaries. They emphasize differences in ways that a minority subject is seen as the antithesis to the majority and its sense of a stabilized community. Consequently, the emergence of critical methods that resist the dominant interpretive tradition, among which one would include facets of postcolonialism and black liberation thought, demand that we acknowledge that the interpretive world of the Bible has been a tool for prejudice and oppression.

So what does that mean for biblical interpretation? My question in this study is a big one. It seeks avenues for a "relational discourse" that openly acknowledge differences among interpreting communities without seeking to undermine those differences in favor of a singular interpretive strategy and concomitant identity. Such a discourse must also be open to perspectives that may seem reductive, exclusionary, or otherwise myopic. At some points, it must be willing to weave perspectives and stories of the past with those of the present, which creates greater space for marginalized and colonized communities. It must forego the pursuit of a singular "truth" or meaning in favor of listening to what a conversation conveys about the experiences of others. It must set the popular and profane in conversation with the sacred, the colonized with the colonizer, and so on, without assuming priority of position. It must be comfortable with accepting that different communities may reappropriate the biblical texts in unique and sometimes startling ways. To illustrate that, it is my attempt in this contribution to demonstrate what a relational discourse might look like while also acknowledging my own perspective as an academic. I have resisted cleaning the frayed edges of argumentation and highlighting a single moral, interpretation, or truth. I have included popular narratives with academic ones, current voices with historical ones, and discourses shaped by a majority with responses from minority perspectives. I have included tangentially related issues or stories to serve as reminders that meaning is generated through dialogue and engagement with others, *and that sometimes the most profound meanings are found when our expectations are slightly subverted.* My attempt here is not simply to describe relational dialogue but to do it.

To be effective, one must also develop interpretive strategies that accept that prejudices are found in both text and interpreter, artifact and symbol, and that prejudices express boundaries, perceived and real, in social identity. In knowing that prejudices are preserved along the margins of constructed identities, interpreters might converse with those margins in a type of "relational discourse," which assumes that differences cannot be homogenized but are instead productive of a more comprehensive strategy of relationship. It resists the dominance of *identity* and emphasizes *identities*. Or, as Roland Boer argues in this volume, though without the terminology of "relational discourse," productive conversation begins by recognizing not *nationality* but *nationalities* as a reflection of diversity within an otherwise singular sociopolitical body. What often gets overlooked by biblical interpreters, however, is that there are many (sub-)groups within a sociopolitical body, each with its own perspective, or narrative, on identity and what a supporting social world would look like. Was there a singular "Israel" or multiple communities *imagining* the identity from their own perspectives, as Boer also asks?

That said, there are several seemingly conflicting obstacles: (1) the biblical texts were largely written from the perspective of minority communities looking to establish themselves in a position of power, namely through the restoration of an *Israelite* kingdom, which entailed a specific *imagined* collective identity; (2) central orthodoxies and values of Judeo-Christianity, those that later shaped the contours of "legitimate" biblical interpretation, have become the products of a dominant interpretation from a Western majority;[3] and (3) the biblical texts *also* reflect the position of a majority—expressed as the patriarchal Israelite male over the subordinate "other," which theoretically includes everyone else.

Toward an explanation of the first point, the biblical texts reflect a sentiment common to communities under the yoke of an imperial or otherwise restrictive power—"restrictive" in the sense of a limit upon sociopolitical autonomy, the existence of which might confirm prejudice on the part of the group defining community boundaries. Responses on the part of minority communities have produced what the majority tradition has neatly categorized, for but a few examples, as postcolonial and black liberation interpretive strategies (one should also include feminist theory, queer theory, womanist theory, and others that emphasize social-justice ideological frameworks).

For biblical, and artifactual, example of that main point, Neh. 9:36 expressed the sentiment of restriction, "Lo! We are slaves today! And the land that you gave to our fathers to eat of its fruit and its goodness, lo, we are slaves in it!"[4] It is generally true that chafing under oppressive yokes, communities typically, and understandably, imagine liberation and a renewed, independent community, often in a reversal of the position and relationship between majority and minority. That was true for the psalmist who wrote, "And Yahweh said to my lord, 'Remain at my right hand until I make your enemies a footstool for your feet'" (Ps. 110:1).[5] When "imaginings" that make space for divisions and prejudices are not divested from religious practice, and when biblical interpretation, as a practice, fails to recognize that it may tend toward preserving systematic prejudices, imagined communities tend to preclude any possible dismantling of a majority-minority dichotomized structure. When that happens, a sociopolitical body may also fracture further along internal lines legitimated by religious and political ideologies, as Brad Crowell's contribution to this volume strategically exposes.

---

3. As M. Westphal describes, we perpetuate this through prejudices shaped by the traditions to which we belong (*Whose Community? Which Interpretation? Philosophical Hermeneutics for the Church*, The Church and Postmodern Culture [Grand Rapids, MI: Baker Academic, 2009], 71). Note also his summary of Gadamer, "The prejudices we inherit from tradition are at once the conditions of possible experience and its limit" (75).

4. Translation mine.

5. Ibid.

Since the following section deals extensively with the issues of the second "obstacle," I'll offer now a quick explanation of the third: the biblical texts reflect the perspective of a majority as heterosexual, patriarchal male—*after all, how often do women or gay men, for but two minority groups, get to speak for themselves?* Why is this important? Because it speaks to some of the ways in which uncritical interpretation has preserved the prejudices of the author and his community, preserved within their shared, imagined identity. In turn, the uncritical conflation of both artifact and symbol permits modern prejudices to fill in the spaces once occupied by historical prejudices instead of closing them.

To expose problematic intersections between artifact and symbol along more familiar lines, note the following example: why is it that even God and the angels have an ignorant understanding of conception? Is barrenness *always* the fault of the woman (cf. Gen. 11:30; 25:21; Judg. 13:3; Ps. 113:9), while the patriarchal male remains ever potent? Even God's understanding of it seems to be shaped by an agrarian metaphor: the man plants the seed and the woman as a field receives it. What that perspective also betrays is a patriarchal perception *and* a cultural strategy for casting blame: when something goes wrong, blaming the minority, which reinforces lines of legitimated prejudices,[6] tends to offer the majority the strongest alleviation of the disruption or dissonance. And it wasn't just the failure of women to fulfill their divinely imposed obligation of childbearing (cf. Gen. 3:16) that was reason for concern. Women who sought knowledge or experiences outside their imposed stations were considered threatening. As Carolyn Alsen argued in this volume, for example, Tamar's playing with the symbolic meaning of the veil took on a more dynamic impact *because* of her self-initiative despite deeply rooted prejudices against women as minorities. That is also, for further instance, one of the underlying assumptions in 1 Kgs 11:1-8. Not only had Solomon married *foreign* women, but he *listened* to them when what they had to say led the king away from Yahweh, the god of an Israelite, patriarchal community. Prejudices against foreigners *and* women were adopted as preventative measures against disobedience to the national deity in that narrative.

To bring the main points of this section together, this chapter focuses on introducing a type of discourse strategy that avoids the colonialist tendencies in traditional biblical interpretation and scholarship. As such, it highlights important issues and questions that should be given focused attention as more individuals take part in a pervasive strategy of "relational discourse." The following discussion will pursue that idea(l) in more detail.

---

6. Cf. the study of Christian S. Crandall and Amy Eshleman, "A Justification-Suppression Model of the Expression and Experience of Prejudice," *Psychological Bulletin* 129.3 (2003): 414–46.

The Bible as an imperial tool and as a tool against empire: Early Christianity as a brief case study

In considering the direction indicated in the section heading, it is important to recognize that dominant interpretations of the Bible have frequently been employed, as seen from a minority perspective, as "a tool" of empire in the more modern world.[7] Take, for example, the eventual rejection of the Bible and an imperial culture by indigenous peoples of the Andes and America in a letter to Pope John Paul II:

> We, the Indians of the Andes and America, decided to take advantage of John Paul II's visit to return to him his Bible because in five centuries it has given us neither love, nor peace, nor justice. Please, take your Bible and give it back to our oppressors, because they need its moral precepts more than we. Since the arrival of Christopher Columbus the Bible was imposed upon America with force: European culture, language, religion, and values. The Bible came to us as part of imposed colonial change. It was the ideological arm of the colonial assault. The Spanish sword, which by day attacked and assassinated the body of the Indians, by night changed itself into the cross which attacked the Indian soul.[8]

Describing biblical interpretation as a tool of empire is not meant to become mired in the emotionalism of sweeping, cutting accusations.[9] Although, as Sugirtharajah points out, within the framework of postcolonialism, such accusations are sometimes necessary from the perspective of the "colonized other," who is oftentimes forced to speak for herself *through* the dominant vocabulary of the colonizer (albeit with the purpose of eventually subverting it).[10]

Some of the monotheistic tendencies expressed in Christianity, and its interpretation of the Bible (as a symbol), can be explained partly by its early

---

7. Sugirtharajah, *Exploring Postcolonial Biblical Criticism*, 7–27.

8. Cited in Elsa Tamez, "The Bible and Five Hundred Years of Conquest," in *Voices from the Margin: Interpreting the Bible in the Third World*, ed. R.S. Sugirtharajah, 25th Anniversary (New York: Orbis Books, 2016), 3–18, 10, who gets the letter from Pablo Richard, "Hermenéutica Bíblica India: Revelación de Dios En Las Religiones Indígenas Y En La Biblia (Después de 500 años de Dominación)," in *Sentido Histórico Del V Centenario (1492-1992)*, ed. Guillermo Meléndez (San José, CA: CEHILADEI, 1992), 45–62.

9. But note for further reference what E. Tamez says about the above letter: "The above letter, according to [P. Richards], expresses the traumatic experience of the Indigenous peoples because, in the conquest and colonization, the Bible was an instrument of domination. Today 'this trauma becomes deeper' with the fundamentalist use of the Bible and its manipulation against Indigenous tradition" ("Bible and Conquest," 10). Her observation seems to include the assumption that missionary activities tend to be conducted by conservative and fundamentalist believers.

10. Sugirtharajah, *Exploring Postcolonial Biblical Criticism*, 48–54.

development and the solidification of fundamental doctrines as the basis of a more "universal" identity under imperial rule and culture. This reflects the problem of divestment that I described earlier. During its historical development, early Christianity historically modeled aspects of itself after empire (or imperial culture), adopting and translating them to meet the needs of its early communities.[11] That much is apparent through careful analysis of the development of Christianity—in terms of the development of communities and a shared collective identity, and the centralization of orthodox doctrines and theologies—under the Roman Empire.[12] One can see examples in conflicts over orthodoxy, whether in the form of *homoousia*, other aspects of the Trinity, about the nature of God, justifications for land acquisition through conquest of the "barbarian," and more. In each of those conflicts were rooted concerns to articulate a dominant, shared identity, and to transform the peoples of the "uncivilized" world into either contributing members or those dependent upon the community of members for their own sense of well-being.[13]

How does this affect the "other"? Conscious of it or not, early Christian communities established the basis for collective identity on the model of the imperial citizen as a method for drawing out unity amid conflict.[14] Out of that emerged a dominant interpretive tradition, handled by the materializing majority in the Church. Today its descendants unconsciously preserve that legacy of dominance in various ways including by re-appropriating the concerns of the minority as the majority's own, filtering, sterilizing, and reinterpreting them in ways to make sense of them within its own value and meaning systems. Doing that destroys the more "natural" boundaries of communities; it privatizes concerns of minority voices and issues them within the "absolute" nature of revelation as defined by a dominant interpretive tradition. Or, as Ukachukwu Chris Manus put it: "This cultural invasion through colonial rule and missionary indoctrination has wrecked havoc on African culture to such an extent that the *homo Africanus* is now groping in a state of flux and utter confusion in quest for cultural identity."[15]

Before Manus's accusation, can we afford to ignore the colonialism moving behind Western Christianity? Such that in the United States, nationalism and Christian identity are often equated? Take, for example, the motto, *In God we trust!* As an assumed national motto, it takes for granted that heterosexual, ableist, wealthy, Christian white men are imagined to be the ideal citizens. That identity was culturally assumed and used to discriminate against African American identity during the civil rights movement, to the point that Malcolm X declared, "The entire civil-rights struggle needs a new interpretation, a broader

---

11. See also the sustained discussion in Jeremiah W. Cataldo, *A Social-Political History of Monotheism: From Judah to the Byzantines* (London: Routledge Press, 2018).

12. See again, ibid.

13. This argument is made at length in ibid.

14. Ibid., passim.

15. Ukachukwu Chris Manus, *Intercultural Hermeneutics in Africa: Methods and Approaches*, Biblical Studies in African Scholarship (Nairobi: Acton Publishers, 2003), 9.

interpretation.... The only way you can get involved in the civil-rights struggle is give it a new interpretation. That old interpretation excluded us. It kept us out."[16]

Then, is there salvation in the Bible?

Maybe. The Bible is, as Mark Sneed's focus on the book of Proverbs shows, a dominant symbol at a complex intersection of cultural, religious, political, social, and even ethnic identities. A product of divine truth or of human experience, its value and meaning have been reinterpreted beyond its original communities. Yet what the history of monotheism has shown us is that orthodoxy, including the prejudices that inform and restrict it, tends to control interpretation for the benefit of a majority.[17] With the help of Anderson's theory one can develop a helpful tool for developing strategies of relational discourse within biblical interpretation. Toward that end, I believe, the Bible *can* become a religious-cultural strategy—better, religious-cultural *strategies*—for renegotiating the current dominant Western Judeo-Christian discourse about minorities and outsiders.[18] But it can only become that when access to ontological and other fundamental truths are no longer restricted to a singular dominant script, language, or interpretive tradition.[19] Such restrictions depend upon an overly dichotomized world of member and nonmember that will always see things in terms of a majority-minority binary at the heart of access to the truths a particular community guards.

I accept that it is an ambitious methodological strategy. Even with Anderson's theory as the guiding framework it must incorporate strategies from multiple areas, such as postcolonial biblical criticism, African American biblical criticism, hermeneutics of liberation, and other social-scientific theories on cultural identity and behavior. The purpose must be to synthesize different perspectives along the majority-minority dichotomy as equal voices in the process of imagining community and thereby disrupt the dichotomy. It is to attempt to avoid what Hjamil A. Martínez-Vázquez describes as the "standard normative" in religious history: "It is important to dis-cover the silences that have been perpetuated by the standard narrative, but in order to give these silence voices the opportunity to

---

16. Malcolm X, "The Ballot or the Bullet" (Cleveland, OH, 1964).

17. This historical tendency has been explored in Cataldo, *Social-Political History*; Jeremiah W. Cataldo, *Biblical Terror: Why Law and Restoration in the Bible Depend upon Fear* (New York: Bloomsbury T&T Clark, 2016).

18. Manus demands a similar approach is his call for recognition of different christologies in different cultures in the African continent (cf. *Intercultural Hermeneutics*, 210–11). G. Okihiro argues for a sharable national identity constructed in acknowledgment of difference to replace the margin-mainstream binary (*Common Ground: Reimagining American History* [Princeton, NJ: Princeton University Press, 2001], xii, xiv).

19. Anderson describes this in more general terms not linked directly to the Bible or biblical interpretation (see *Imagined Communities*, location 660).

speak about their own situation [sic] and in their own terms, we need new theories and methodologies that do not serve the colonial agenda."[20] To avoid that while also acknowledging the importance of voices such as young Andrés Jiménez, whose practice of and perspective on religion will change in light of his father's deportation.[21] After all,

> studies have shown that the threat of deportation causes severe stress and anxiety among children with undocumented parents or siblings. A 2013 report by Human Impact Partners found that nearly 75% of undocumented parents reported that their children had experienced symptoms of PTSD.[22]

Such a strategy must be aimed at constructing subversive discourses that confront the dominant canon or normative and elevate subaltern voices.[23] It would mean, for example, looking—regardless of whether something is found, the act alone is enough to open our own perspectives in productive ways—for the voice of the Canaanites slaughtered in the conquest of the land under Joshua, of the Native Americans under the justification of Manifest Destiny, of the frustration of unwelcomed refugees, of children of undocumented immigrants threatened with deportations, and of Palestinians under Israeli expansionist policies. How often, for instance, have the words of Palestinian rapper Ibrahim Ghunaim (MC Gaza) been *really* heard:

> Everybody's standing in silence / And I'm still gazing / A human inside me is calling / Who sympathizes with me? / [In Gaza and Aleppo] Stay in your place, resistant but patient / Together we'll watch our fucked up Arab reality.[24]

Such a strategy would also mean giving Sarah a chance to comment on Abraham's character, and Rebekah a chance to describe her feelings about Isaac's inability to satisfy her. It would mean elevating "relational discourse" over uniform interpretation and leaving the symbolisms and values in the Bible open to

---

20. Hjamil A. Mártinez-Vázquez, *Made in the Margins: Latina/O Constructions of Us Religious History* (Waco, TX: Baylor University Press, 2013), 4.

21. Lauren Gambino, "Orphaned by Deportation: The Crisis of American Children Left Behind," *The Guardian*, US News, October 2014.

22. Ibid.

23. A need also identified in Mártinez-Vázquez, *Made in the Margins*, 4–5. Martinez-Vazquez claims that postcolonialism is capable of shouldering that burden. I would argue that postcolonialism alone cannot but that it must be joined by representatives from other minority interpretive traditions as well as self-aware representatives from a majority tradition.

24. MC Gaza, "From Gaza to Aleppo," video posted on YouTube, 2016. https://youtu.be/ah1nzHJjKzc. Accessed October 19, 2017.

translation in different ways by different communities.²⁵ It would react, as Matthew Coomber argues in this volume, to privileged rejection of collective responsibility for the (economic, gendered, etc.) "other." Only with flexibility in the symbolic meanings of "Bible" and only by accepting that different interpretations and theologies are equally valid, equally truthful, might a truly inclusive community be imagined. One in which differences are not reasons for exclusion and prejudice but the strength of an identity that emphasizes that the best of humanity is its ability to engage in relational discourse, to listen, to speak, to appreciate, and to be appreciated. To be free, to be obligated, to love, to hate, but above all to understand and to respect that my freedoms are also yours. And maybe then will the enterprise of biblical interpretation see and cherish its own internal changes that have resulted from minority perspectives changing "the time, the space and the subject of . . . enquiries within biblical scholarship."²⁶ But that it does so in a way that (re)writes the categorical distinction of "minority" out of needed use.

Put bluntly, relational discourse rejects the privatization of morality, truth, and God by any singular religious tradition. It encourages vocabulary based on shared ownership. It encourages crossing boundaries from a position of dichotomy into a more "public square," in which the operating vocabulary and framework of meaning is shared, democratized into a discourse strategy giving equal voice to majority and minority. It seeks to avoid the trap of a methodological mirrored image of the "other," which manifests, as Irvin Schick writes, within "the tendency to analyze patriarchal oppression through the paradigm of colonization."²⁷ It is fueled by mutual respect. Most importantly, it emphasizes a return to reason and consensus through validating the position and opinion of others. It accepts protest

25. Such a strategy would be supportive of Manus's call, "It is no longer sensible for Africans to continue reading the Bible from alien perspectives. Though many an African biblical scholar has brought home Western methodologies and taught them in African Seminaries and Universities, the time has come to re-focus the curriculum on the African cultural and religious heritage. For much too long, African theological education has been integrated into the mainstream European and North American academic tradition, neglecting the norms, values, principles and insights inherent in African culture" (*Intercultural Hermeneutics*, 1). Compare that with G. West's observation that what has happened in South Africa is that minority communities develop their own interpretive strategies as a type of "hidden transcript," in which the Bible is made relevant for the community rather than the community changing to fit the interpretive demands of a dominant, colonizing community (*Biblical Hermeneutics of Liberation: Modes of Reading the Bible in the South African Context*, The Bible & Liberation [2nd ed. New York: Orbis Books, 1995], 52–58).

26. Tat-Siong Benny Liew, "When Margins Become Common Ground: Questions of and for Biblical Studies," in *Still at the Margins: Biblical Scholarship Fifteen Years after the Voices from the Margin*, ed. R. S. Sugirtharajah (New York: Continuum / T&T Clark, 2008), 41.

27. Irvin Cemil Schick, *The Erotic Margin: Sexuality and Spatiality in Alteritist Discourse* (London: Verso Books, 1999), 2.

as an awakening, after all, revelation is itself a genre of protest.[28] It accepts protest but expects protest to transition into participation in a shared discourse.

The *first* step for biblical scholars, who preserve the colonial apparatus through the dominant culture and expectations in the institution of scholarship and academia, is to look at their own bibliographies.

But that strategy also acknowledges the sordid past of biblical interpretation and the dominance held by specific groups over definitions of community and identity. It must. And, it must renegotiate such definitions by acknowledging the social and political ideologies that shaped them in both the past and the present. Colonizer and oppressor must hold up their own signs acknowledging the legitimacy of a new discourse, a new *imagining*. This process is necessary; after all, the historical roots of the Judeo-Christian concept of community, the identity of which crossed existing cultural boundaries and replaced an active culture with one of its own, are found in the sociopolitical realities of empire. Christianity owes much to Roman imperial culture for its own self-perception and its perception of "others."[29] With its expansion, it simultaneously expected behavior among its sociopolitical agents to be a singular, "civilized" identity. Those that did not, or could not, invest themselves in that identity were considered a "barbarian other." In doing that, it preserved the distinction between insider and outsider by forcing the outsider to take on an identity expressed in terms of the values and ideals of the majority. Yet it also preserved the imperial pattern for imagining identity.

We must also renegotiate the influence of the quintessential (Christian) monotheistic strategy: "Go therefore and make disciples of all nations, baptizing them in the name of the Father and of the Son and of the Holy Spirit, and teaching them to obey everything that *I have commanded you*" (Mat. 28:19).[30] One can see a similar ideology of sociopolitical citizenship in the form and intent of the early Christian councils that emerged, as well as the orthodoxies emerging during the second, third, and fourth centuries CE. Both council and orthodoxy reflect the early emphasis upon articulating a singular, dominant identity defined by a superior power—in this case, God—and that the superior power will eventually rule the entire world, bringing the community's enemies to their knees. Yet what that must also accept is that while in modern Judeo-Christian communities such forces are generally forgotten, their centripetal force and the centrality and dominance of the

---

28. Divine revelation and presence as a form of protest is an idea echoed in Cone's work, "To know God is to know God's work of liberation on behalf of the oppressed. God's revelation means liberation, an emancipation from death-dealing political, economic, and social structures of society. This is the essence of biblical revelation" (*A Black Theology of Liberation*, 40th anniversary [New York: Orbis Books, 1970], 48).

29. Incidentally, an emphasis upon a common creed over a shared blood line as the basis for collective identity and unity was also one of the reasons why Muhammad was successful in the seventh century CE.

30. NRSV, emphasis mine.

Bible are presupposed.[31] Put more simply, the past may be forgotten, but it haunts us yet today through the institution of Judeo-Christianity and the symbolic force of the Bible.

Early Christian identity was once the identity of a minority community, or communities, on the margins of sociopolitical power, it is no longer. And that is true despite the best efforts of individuals from the conservative, Evangelical Christian Right to convince their audience that Jim Crow laws are back and that conservative Christians are now the ones being oppressed.[32] Such claims are absurd while also intentional. They are examples of an avoidance strategy that co-opts and mutes the voice of the real victimized "other" and legitimates avoidance of any possible relational discourse.[33] Consequently, for minoritized "others" to adopt Christian identity means to be measured against the dominant interpretive tradition of Western, and white, Christianity and community. Control over a dominant tradition of interpretation is exercised through acknowledgment of who can participate fully in debate or conversation, such as a member or "citizen," and a concomitant silencing of the profane "other." Moreover, in Western cultures, one cannot avoid being influenced by the weight that Christianity, and its dominant biblical interpretive tradition, imposes upon definitions of citizen, rights, ethics, and freedoms, even the value of the individual life.[34] Or put differently, one cannot engage in public debate without also engaging vocabulary and discourses that have

---

31. M. Westphal refers to this tendency as "naïve realism," which rejects the possibility of different interpretations. But, "the multiplicity of interpretations stems not from the indeterminacy of the object but from the way it exceeds the ability of any limited perspective to grasp it in its totality. . . . It is precisely the inability of human understanding to grasp reality in its totality that led Kant to downgrade human understanding in comparison with divine" (*Whose Community*, 26).

32. Cf. Bryan Fischer, *Focal Point*, January 10, 2013.

33. I am drawing from D. Smith-Christopher's comment on white, liberal strategies of biblical interpretation: "A white liberal may desperately search for a place that claims a share of victimization so that listening to others is implied to be unnecessary. . . . I treat attempts to borrow victimization with the same suspicion that I treat attempts to identify with, or seek ex-officio membership of, minority groups (to be 'accepted by the tribe'). Expropriating minority perspectives without maintaining a clear sense of respecting and honouring difference amounts to what one might call 'exegetical minstrelry'" ("Abolitionist Exegesis: A Quaker Proposal for White Liberals," in *Still at the Margins: Biblical Scholarship Fifteen Years after the Voices from the Margin*, ed. R. S. Sugirtharajah [New York: Continuum / T&T Clark, 2008], 128–38, 136).

34. W. Webb, for example, seeks to navigate the resulting dichotomy between member and nonmember by separating "kingdom values" from "cultural values." The problem, as postcolonial criticism has already observed, is that "value" itself is a culturally defined term and that definitions of "kingdom values" have tended to be those proffered by the dominant majority (cf. *Slaves, Women & Homosexuals* [Downers Grove, IL: InterVarsity Press, 2001], 22–24).

been shaped and influenced by Christianity, the Bible, and the dominant tradition of biblical interpretation. And that is the beast that hermeneutics of liberation struggle against continually.[35] On the part of the dominant, it is a defensive strategy. Preserving the "myth of objectivity," and so the "true interpretation" over which the dominant majority lays claim, allows one to retreat to already determined issues and values outside those exposed through postcolonial and postmodern discourses that challenge the dominant normative.[36]

Even in the seemingly innocent act of reading, one is guilty of this, for example, when reading passages such as Ezra 6:19-22 as reference to Israel as a religiously faithful community and the ancestor to Jewish and Christian identities reflecting the dominant traditions in each respective community. Yet Ezra uses the term "Israel" with exlusionary intent. In vv. 19-22, to provide a specific example, Ezra describes Israel as observing the Passover, which commemorated the radical event in which Yahweh selected his people from the surrounding peoples and killed the firstborn of the outsiders. The firstborn of the chosen people, however, was saved as long as families smeared the blood of a sacrificial lamb on the door frame of the familial house. That act constituted a public declaration of commitment to the community. It was a family's proclamation of allegiance to the community and to its emerging dominant normative, the behavioral norms that constituted the identity of "Israel." The book was written in a particular historical context, but as a part of the Bible, it has taken on a more diachronic meaning. In the modern context, the Bible as a "unified whole,"[37] in its function as a symbol, is being interpreted by the majority community in each epoch as being written for it, that the actions of God are meant to preserve that community, such as through the acquisition of land or political ascendency, and that the "other" must accept her rejection as seen against the contours of the dominant majority. And this makes the Bible susceptible to group prejudices along the

---

35. As Renita Weems puts it, "Re-reading for liberation is the work of people reaching out to one another across the gulf of their real flesh-and-blood painful gender, racial, national, religious, and geo-political differences.... It means hearing people out, respecting the way they read and interpret stories, making room for them at the table, and sharing power with them. For what is liberation without power? And what is power? Power is the ability to take one's place in whatever discourse is essential to change and having the right to have one's story matter regardless of how it is told, not matter how rambling the story, no matter how unconventional the telling, no matter how irritating the inflections, and sometimes no matter how unthinkable the tale" ("Re-Reading for Liberation: African American Women and the Bible," in *Voices from the Margin: Interpreting the Bible in the Third World*, ed. R. S. Sugirtharajah, 25th Anniversary [New York: Orbis Books, 2016], 19–32, 31).

36. Smith-Christopher, "Abolitionist Exegesis," 137.

37. For but a couple of examples arguing the unity of the Bible, see Daniel P. Fuller, *The Unity of the Bible: Unfolding God's Plan for Humanity* (Grand Rapids, MI: Zondervan Publishing House, 1992); Nancy Pearcey, *Total Truth* (Wheaton, IL: Crossway Books, 2004).

lines of insider-outsider dichotomies. In response, the minority must often present herself and her differences as being within the tolerable limits of what the majority views as not too disruptive of its internal stability. The relational fluidity of that dichotomy is at the heart of Kyong-Jin Lee's contribution in this volume: Nehemiah 5 reflects an attempt, through socioeconomic reform, to legitimate the "remnant" community as a majority in its context, while also acknowledging the established imperial dichotomy between ruler and ruled.

The Passover ritual in Ezra reaffirmed the *imagined* identity of the community, which included the dominant expectation that members of the community expressed, within the dominant meaning framework, loyalty to the community and its god. Such loyalty could be seen in preserving the distinction between member and nonmember, as with the policy against intermarriage in Ezra-Nehemiah. Intermarriage was considered so great a threat that violent actions were taken to prevent it or break apart existing mixed marriages.[38] The intensity of that position on intermarriage may have been the consequence of strong xenophobic attitudes in the community represented by the author.[39] It was reinforced by drawing a line between those who could "join Israel" and those who could not. These activities, as well as the rejection of Ammonites and Ashdodites in Nehemiah, reflect a collective reaction to what Anderson describes as a fundamental shift in (re-)imagining community.[40] Ezra-Nehemiah depicts some attempts to *resist* the changes fundamental to sociopolitical identity while also embracing the change in the center of power, from kingdom-specific to imperial. In that sense, Ezra-Nehemiah is a schizophrenic text; it tries to syncretize competing strategies of resistance and acceptance while also preserving the distinction between its community and others.

According to Ezra, the Passover lamb was eaten by the people of Israel, who had returned from exile, *and* by those who had joined them, separating themselves from the pollutions of the nations of the land to worship Yahweh, the god of Israel. If as dominant shared symbols deities represent the most cherished values and ideals of their respective communities,[41] what takes place is that others committed themselves to becoming "Israelite." Yahweh, as the god of Israel, was still a *political* symbol, as much as or perhaps even more than he was in the past. In Ezra, as also

---

38. One should also note that Ezra-Nehemiah's concern over intermarriage was also driven by an attempt to control access to private property as well as the collective identity of the people of Yahweh. See, for instance, Lisbeth S. Fried, *The Priest and the Great King: Temple-Palace Relations in the Persian Empire*, 10 (Winona Lake, MI: Eisenbrauns, 2004), 211; Jacob Myers, *Ezra Nehemiah*, ed. William Foxwell Albright and David Noel Freedman (*AB*, vol. 14; Garden City, NY: Doubleday & Co., 1965), 77.

39. Cf. Mary Douglas, "Responding to Ezra: The Priests and the Foreign Wives," *BI* 10 (2002): 1–23, 1; Peter R. Bedford, "Diaspora: Homeland Relations in Ezra-Nehemiah," *VT* 52 (2001): 147–65, 156.

40. Cf. Anderson, *Imagined Communities*, location 467.

41. See also the discussion in Cataldo, *Breaking Monotheism*, 213.

occurred in other books such as Isaiah, Yahweh took on a new power, becoming a god capable of manipulating empires. As such, he extended the boundaries that once constrained him to the traditional kingdom of Judah. With the yoke of a foreign imperial rule, and a belief that an imperial power was necessary to counteract an empire, Yahweh took on qualities of an imperial ruler and god. The changing perceptions of Yahweh were due to the increasing emphasis upon imperial-political ideologies to navigate the international contours of the ancient Near East. Yet as is the risk that threatens modern interpreting communities, when the marginal community becomes the mainstream, such strategies of alleviating the dissonance of oppression are frequently transformed into tools of oppression when they are not revised to fit changed power relationships in new situations.

Imagining a new identity must challenge traditional models of identity

A number of postcolonial studies have moved toward this goal in different ways, which is one of the primary reasons I am incorporating them alongside Anderson. I'm also reminded of Theophus Smith's work, *Conjuring Culture*, in which he described the Bible as "a conjuring tool."[42] Through it, minority communities and oppressed communities could liberate the Bible from the dominance of a ruling or controlling majority and give relevance to the different needs of ruled or oppressed communities. The Gikuyu of Kenya did this, for example, when they centralized polygamous patriarchs from the Old Testament as examples that validated polygamy in their own community. And they did this in direct contrast to the "white man's" authority and the imposed interpretive strategy, one consistent with Ezra-Nehemiah, of missionaries that sought, from the Gikuyan perspective, to break up their families and so also their community.[43] For Smith, who follows a similar strategy of making the Bible relevant to the community, but unlike the Gikuyu who maintain a certain sense of objectivity, there is no objective, symbolic truth in the Bible. Neither does there exist objective meaning or value. It is not confined by the myth of objectivity, which for Smith submits that the Bible might be "privatized" by a dominant community. Objectivity is not the real reason behind the Bible's status and role as a sacred object. Instead, its ascended role as a sacred object—an *imagined* position—which could be described as something more akin to a totem, was due to its function and role as an object that different communities could approach and *create* meaning relevant to their

---

42. Cf. Theophus H. Smith, *Conjuring Culture: Biblical Formations of Black America*, (Religion in America) (Oxford: Oxford University Press, 1995), 3–16.

43. As recounted in R. S. Sugirtharajah, *The Bible and Empire* (Cambridge: Cambridge University Press, 2005), 156–57. Sugirtharajah states that the missionaries unsurprisingly thought this interpretive strategy to be pertinent and a rejection of the morality that the missionaries advocated (see ibid., 157).

own perspectives and needs. And in his emphasis upon postcolonial readings of the Bible, R. S. Sugirtharajah offers a similar strategy for biblical interpretation:

> Postcolonialism is used here as an interventionist instrument which refuses to take the dominant reading as an uncomplicated representation of the past and introduces an alternative reading. Postcolonialism allows silenced and often marginalized people to find their own voices when they are at loggerheads with the dominant readings.[44]

Interpretive strategies must translate the Bible as a shared symbol into the meaning and value framework of the community, not the community into the framework of the Bible. *That* is an anti-imperial or postcolonial reading. To be sure, Benedict Anderson doesn't go as far as Martinez-Vázquez, Smith, or Sugirtharajah; to be clear, Anderson doesn't address the Bible, though I am putting his theory to work on biblical interpretation in my own analysis. What Smith and Sugirtharajah touch upon is the process of identity realization and expression with the Bible at the center. They, as Anderson does, talk about *imagining community* in fundamental ways around a shared, cultural object or idea; ways that might include the creation of "national" rituals, such as in Ezra: "The Sons of the Exile kept the Passover on the fourteenth [day] of the first month" (6:19).[45] As Smith and Sugirtharajah point out, objects, ideas, even rituals function as central magnets drawing together and legitimating expressions of collective identity. As, for instance, in Ezra, two verses later, "the sons of the exile" become the Sons of Israel, "The Sons of Israel, who had returned from Exile and all who separated themselves from the impurities of the people of the land, ate" (v. 21).[46] Because the Bible is a central object to many communities, discourse about it must be discourse that knows how to engage others in discourse as equal partners. It must acknowledge that insider and outsider, and mainstream and marginal are relative terms that are dynamic and not static.[47]

Relational discourse is an open expression of imagined identity

According to Anderson, identity-confirming discourses are from the position of a speaker, or subject, based on frames of reference characterized by categories, hierarchies, and meanings from the subject's cultural origin.[48] And this reflects the interpretive problem mentioned earlier, and it is one that Ehud Ben Zvi touches upon in his contribution in this volume: the biblical texts were written from the

---

44. Ibid., 3.
45. Translation mine.
46. Ibid.
47. Liew, "When Margins," 47.
48. Cf. the basis for his argument in Anderson, *Imagined Communities*, locations 300–424.

vantage point of a minority's utopian *imaginings* but the dominant form of biblical interpretation, despite the best efforts of postcolonial criticism and its offshoots, continues to reflect in Western societies the interpretive tradition and position of the majority. Moreover, as Anderson points out, nationality, or communal identity, is unavoidably a cultural artifact.[49] That means for him that there is nothing that is essentially a nationality, or a communal identity. What constitutes such identities is specific to each culture and the demands that each culture has. Those demands, and the specifics of what it means to be an obedient and committed citizen of the community, are oftentimes the very things that help flush out the fullness of what deities represent as shared collective symbols.

It is also important to note that the term "imagine," in reference to imagined communities, according to Anderson, reflects that the resulting members of a community will likely never know everyone else in the community but will still view themselves as sharing a bond in contrast to outsiders.[50] The ideas and forces that define the similarities are also those that define the differences. And it is those differences, by which we know ourselves (such that *you are not me*) that provide the basis for shared prejudices. In Ezra, the others who joined in the Passover were more likely Judeans who had been left behind and who could be members of the community. But Ezra-Nehemiah as a whole makes it clear that people who came from outside of the traditional boundaries of the Judean community, the foreigners, such as Assyrians, Egyptians, Moabites, Ammonites, Ashdodites, etc., could not be members of the community. The boundaries needed to be closed in order to preserve the identity as it was imagined. However, it is in the act of closing those boundaries, in creating an ideology of closure, that prejudices are also given legitimation.[51]

But that need not be the end of it, because it is in acknowledging differences, in holding up our signs, in a productive and respectful manner that we can learn from each other and allow the true identity of the "other" to emerge.[52] Failure to do so will result in exclusion. Excluding the "other" as speaker, and so also possible alternative interpretations, means that the dominant culture takes for itself the position or identity of empire. And marginalizing the voices of minority communities, who develop response strategies to the pressures and impressions imposed by a dominant interpretive tradition, rather than listening is itself an act of oppression. The same is true both in religion and in politics.

---

49. Ibid., location 191.

50. Ibid., location 215.

51. As C. Crandall and A. Eshleman note, legitimated prejudices are not genuine prejudices, which are raw and unfiltered but are those, in contrast to collectively suppressed prejudices, that have been deemed necessary or allowable by the community (cf. "A Justification-Suppression Model," 414–46).

52. Smith-Christopher refers to this type of strategy as "abolitionist exegesis" (see "Abolitionist Exegesis," 136).

A strategy of relational discourse embraces an evolving nature of meaning behind primary symbols, characters, and ideas within the Bible. It releases, for example, "Jesus," "Israel," "body," "blood," and so on, from any singular dominating meaning or interpretation. Let Jesus be a Syrian woman. Let the body of Christ be fried chicken. Let Israel be the remnants of Palestine. Let human communities intersect at their engagement of a shared object or symbol whose meanings and values are open. It permits individuals from different positions, from margin to mainstream, from grass roots to ivory tower, to have equal voice, to be heard but also to listen. It means contributing to a conversation about oppression by engaging the voices of "others" while also contributing one's own. It means accepting, as even Stalin once acknowledged, that unity produces unexpected diversity.[53] It means recognizing one's sociopolitical position and consciously acknowledging how the differences shape one's perspective, even if reductively. It means recognizing how differences strengthen the conversation that should consume us all: in all our love, our hate, our differences, our passions, our prejudices, our greed, we are human. Maybe then we can more effectively reach out to people like Nazand Begikhani, who wrote:

> I am not you, you are not I
> God you are, but not yourself
> I am not you, you are not I
> We are two beings
> Together forming the God you created against me
> Together we are humanity.[54]

---

53. Joseph Stalin, "The Political Tasks of the University of the Peoples of the East: Speech Delivered at a Meeting of Students of the Communist University of the Toilers of the East, May 18, 1925," in *Works*, vol. 7 (Moscow: Foreign Languages Publishing House, 1925 [1954]), 140–42.

54. From the poem "Man, the Sinful God," cited in Jennifer Langer, ed. *Crossing the Border* (Nottingham: Five Leaves, 2002), 205–07.

Chapter 9

MULTINATIONALITY AND THE UTOPIAN PROJECT: THE CASE OF ACTUALLY EXISTING ISRAEL

Roland Boer

How might the relation between utopianism and "nationalism" be understood? A more usual approach would be to suggest that utopia indicates an ideal or perfected form of collective existence, while a nation is an "imagined community"[1] that may become the object of such a utopian ideal. A budding utopian nation in such a situation careens toward a trap with two outcomes: either it is unrealizable, since the step toward its material realization is too great, or it becomes dystopian, since the required effort to realize it betrays it by failing to live up to the initial ideal that inspired it. The seeming inevitability of this trap has produced a range of responses: impatient dismissals of any form of utopian project; the distinction between undesirable utopian projects and desirable scientific projects;[2] the refusal to acknowledge any actual effort at constructing an alternative society in the name of a "genuine" and ideal utopian break that really changes the foundations of social existence.[3]

Given the seeming conflation of both utopianism and nationalism in the Bible, which makes the "trap" a significant risk for modern interpreters, I undertake a different approach to these terms, with specific reference to ancient Israel. To wit, while utopia is predicated on incompletion or imperfection, dystopia is predicated on completion and perfection. This approach challenges common assumptions concerning utopia: it is supposed to be a situation in which change is no longer

---

1. As defined by Anderson, *Imagined Communities*.
2. F. Engels, "Socialism: Utopian and Scientific," in *Marx and Engels Collected Works* (vol. 24; Moscow: Progress Publishers, 1880 [1989]), 281–325.
3. S. Žižek, *Revolution at the Gates: Žižek on Lenin: The 1917 Writings* (London: Verso, 2002); S. Žižek, "A Leninist Gesture Today: Against the Populist Temptation," in *Lenin Reloaded: Towards a Politics of Truth*, eds. S. Budgen, S. Kouvelakis, and S. Žižek (Durham, NC: Duke University Press, 2007), 74–98. Žižek's effort in particular is lifelong, being part of the curious myopia of "Western" Marxism (see D. Losurdo, *Il marxismo occidentale: Come nacque, come morì, come può rinascere* [Rome: Editori Laterza, 2017]).

needed, which entails closure to any further change in the material and ideological systems that define the identity of the social-political body. Such closure assumes that contradictions and tensions, if not forces of interruption and challenges to the newly stabilized status quo, as well as multiplicity, by which difference is unavoidably introduced into the system, and uncertainty in any social-political stability have all been "shut out." The catch is that any attempt to realize a utopian situation that is predicated upon such assumptions breaks down into dystopia. By contrast, I argue that utopia is actually determined by a *lack* of closure, an irresolvable *in*completion. It is an ongoing and uncertain process, radically incomplete and multifarious. It should be added that the utopian desire is predicated on two key features: sustained criticism of the bitter realities of contemporary societies and the construction of an imagined alternative, usually in another location from the present one.[4]

As for the idea of a nation, I argue that it is a distinct group within a state—which should really be called a nationality—rather than a state or country (or as it is often called, a "nation state"). Or, as Anderson writes, "It is an imagined political community . . . imagined because the members of even the smallest nation will never know most of their fellow-members."[5] But members are bound by their shared commitment to a greater ideal. This means that any state is, on the level of identity, a multinational state. Consequently, a national utopian project depends upon an incomplete national identity, so much so that it produces a multiplication of nationalities and diversity.

Obviously, my effort to reshape the key terms requires more explanation, which I undertake in the first two parts of this study. How it relates to Israel is the concern of the third part. In a nutshell, my argument is that the narrative effort (my focus is on the texts of the Hebrew Bible) to produce a distinct and unified nationality known as "Israel" opens the possibility of a multiplicity of nationalities. In other words, the utopian project of Israel turns out to be multiple, incomplete, and open.

Imperfect utopias

I draw the idea of an imperfect utopia from the work of Ernst Bloch and Fredric Jameson but I add a distinctive "Chinese twist." Jameson has argued consistently that the danger of utopias running aground means that we must look elsewhere for a viable theory of utopia.[6] So he begins with a more dialectical approach, locating the possibility of utopia within dystopias of even the worst kind. His interest lies not so much in the *content* of dystopias as in the formal and collective effort to

---

4. Anderson, *Imagined Communities*, 69; F. Jameson, *The Ideologies of Theory* (London: Verso 2008), 386–414.

5. Anderson, *Imagined Communities*, 6.

6. Jameson, *Ideologies*, 386–414; F. Jameson, *Archaeologies of the Future: The Desire Called Utopia and Other Science Fictions* (London: Verso, 2005).

imagine (and we might recall Anderson here) an alternative world. And the role of collective imagination leads him to propose a multiplicity of potential utopias, each of them incomplete and open. It follows that the longevity or otherwise of a utopia is not a sign of "failure," but that the possibility they may last for shorter or longer periods is a feature of such utopias. Jameson adds that, with a nod to some form of democratic expression, one may opt out of one in favor of another. Clearly, Jameson is less interested in subjective dimensions, concerning the ideological content of such utopias or indeed the nature of their construction by human intention, and more in the objective, formal features. However, for my purpose in this chapter, I am less interested in the anarcho-syndicalist dimension of Jameson's proposal, with its multiple voluntary utopias, and more in his insistence on the incompletion of such utopias.

As for Bloch, his simultaneous hermeneutics and philosophy of utopia draw upon the wealth of biblical, literary, and cultural references to capture glimpses of utopian desires and wishes.[7] These remain irrepressible but unfulfilled, which the forces of reaction are unable to suppress no matter what they try.[8] (It is worth noting that Bloch seeks to develop a notion of agency that goes well beyond human agency. It includes non-human and material agency.) Most importantly for my purposes, Bloch proposes what he calls the "non-contemporaneity" (*Ungleichzeitigkeit*) of the present, or the "contemporaneity of non-contemporaneity."[9] This means that any mode of production (socioeconomic system) always contains traces of earlier modes of production, traces that exist at different levels and modalities simultaneously in the present. They function as types of economic, political, and cultural "groundwater," which lies closer to or farther from the surface, depending on the time and place. But they also challenge and resist the present, contradicting "the Now; very strangely, crookedly, from behind."[10] Bloch's immediate interest is to account for the rise of fascism in Europe, which he analyzes in terms of its ability to construct reactionary resistance through false myths and hopes drawn from the past. But the most significant implication of his analysis concerns socialism: this non-contemporaneity also creates the possibility for socialist revolution in

---

7. E. Bloch, *The Principle of Hope*, trans. N. Plaice, S. Plaice, and P. Knight (Cambridge, MA: MIT Press, 1995); E. Bloch, *The Spirit of Utopia*, trans. A. Nassar (Stanford, CA: Stanford University Press, 2000); E. Bloch, *Traces*, trans. A. Nassar (Stanford, CA: Stanford University Press, 2006 [1930]).

8. Anticipating Negri's constitutive resistance: "Even though common use of the term might suggest the opposite—that resistance is a response or reaction—*resistance is primary with respect to power*" (M. Hardt and A. Negri, *Multitude: War and Democracy in the Age of Empire* [New York: Penguin, 2004], 64; see also Y. Moulier, "Introduction," to A. Negri, *The Politics of Subversion: A Manifesto for the Twenty-First Century* [Cambridge: Polity, 2005]), 1–44.

9. E. Bloch, *Heritage of Our Times*, trans. N. Plaice and S. Plaice (London: Polity, 1991 [1935]), 97–116.

10. Ibid., 97.

which the unattained hopes of earlier forms link with present anticipations. More dialectically, the revolutionary impulse of the present, which emerges from class struggle and generates expectations of a "prevented future" and the unleashing of the forces of production, gains "*additional revolutionary force* precisely from the *incomplete* wealth of the past."[11] Bloch calls for a multi-temporal and multi-spatial dialectic in order to make philosophical sense of this potential, but it also indicates the distinct possibility, if not necessity, that the contradictions and tensions in question would be exacerbated in any utopian project in process. In other words, in any utopian construction, the process would become even more complicated and incomplete.

Mao Zedong's "On Contradiction" offers this discussion a unique "Chinese twist."[12] Mao draws heavily on Lenin's "Philosophical Notebooks"[13] to develop his arguments concerning the universality but also the particularity of contradiction, as well as the primary and secondary contradictions in any given situation. Further, the primary contradiction has a more important and less important pole, with the relationship changing in light of circumstances. From the wealth of his argument, what I want to stress for my purpose here is the unity of contradictions. That unity, including the assumption of a possible unity itself, reveals a distinctly Chinese transformation of dialectics—as his quotation of a popular Chinese saying indicates: "*xiangfan xiangcheng*" (Things that oppose each other also complement each other).[14] This reality of mutual cooperation within contradictions runs deep in Chinese philosophical thought and cultural assumptions: from the mundane everyday matters of food and drink, through Lao Zi's point that what is in opposition is transformed into its opposite, to the universal principle of the interpermeation of *yin* and *yang* (from the *Yi Jing* and *Dao De Jing*). Indeed, the fabled Confucian category of *datong*, thoroughly reinterpreted by Kang Yuwei, assumes not an overcoming of contradictions but a situation in which they are able to exist side by side, in mutual cooperation, without being disruptive.[15] While Mao transforms these traditional elements in light of the dominant framework of dialectical materialism,[16] I am particularly interested in the point that utopia

11. Ibid., 115–16. Italics in original.

12. Mao Z. "On Contradiction," in *Selected Works of Mao Tse-Tung* (vol. 1; Beijing: Foreign Languages Press, 1937 [1965]), 311–47.

13. V. Lenin, "Philosophical Notebooks," in *Collected Works* (vol. 38; Moscow: Progress Publishers, 1914–1916 [1968]).

14. Mao, "On Contradiction," 343. By the time Mao quotes this saying, which appears only in the revised version of the essay, it was already 1900 years old. It was first coined by Ban Gu's *Hanshu* (*Book of Han*), from the first century CE.

15. Y. Kang, *Ta T'ung Shu: The One-World Philosophy of K'ang Yu-wei*, trans. L. Thompson (London: Routledge, 1958).

16. N. Knight, *Mao Zedong on Dialectical Materialism: Writings on Philosophy, 1937* (Armonk: M.E. Sharpe, 1990), 50–51; N. Knight, *Marxist Philosophy in China: From Qu Qiubai to Mao Zedong, 1923-1945* (Dordrecht: Springer, 2005), 167–69.

(by which Mao, and indeed the others, mean communism) does not entail some impossible perfection, but the continuation of contradictions, or what some would call "imperfections." Indeed, what counts as utopia is precisely these contradictions, tensions, even imperfections, rather than a completed and perfected project.

Redefining nation and nationality

Thus far I have sought to reshape the understanding of utopia, so now I seek to revise the way nation and nationality may be approached. Indeed, I prefer the terminology of "nationality," since the term "nation" is now so closely bound up with the idea of a state that it is difficult to imagine another usage. When one thinks of the "nations" of, say, Japan, Indonesia, and the Philippines, one usually calls to mind the political entities known as states or "countries." Indeed, "nation state" has become the assumed way of speaking about them, especially as an "imagined community."[17] This approach may be acceptable in the geopolitical situation of the twentieth century and later, but the terminology has its own distinct and relatively brief history. This means that it is problematic to apply this terminology to the ancient world. Any close examination of that world would show that collective political bodies were far from "nations," in the modern sense, let alone "nation states." In order to develop an alternative terminology that may be used for such a situation, I turn to debates about the particularities of such terminology that happened among socialists at the turn of the twentieth century. These debates were known as "the national question" and drew the attention of socialists in states with multiple groups—which are now erroneously called "ethnic groups"—such as Austria and Russia.[18]

In the early twentieth century, the burgeoning European socialist movement was vexed by the issue of nationalities. Opinions tended to fall into two groups. One side was represented by Karl Kautsky, who argued in favor of class solidarity at the expense of cultural and national difference. Nations, argued Kautsky, were produced historically by economic forces, especially under capitalism and the bourgeoisie: the breaking down of territorial, cultural, and linguistic barriers led to modern nations as economic, political, and military entities with official languages.[19] Thus far, the participants in the debate agreed, but Kautsky went

---

17. Anderson, *Imagined Communities*.

18. This crucial debate is missing from M. Brett's ("Interpreting Ethnicity: Method, Hermeneutics, Ethics," in *Ethnicity and the Bible*, ed. M. Brett [Leiden: Brill, 2002], 3–22) North Atlantic focus when attempting to set the context for debates over ethnicity and biblical interpretation.

19. The historical production of nations and nationalism is common to all these positions, foreshadowing the later proposals (K. Deutsch, *Nationalism and Social Communication* [2nd ed.; Cambridge: MIT, 1966]; E. Gellner, *Nations and Nationalism* [Ithaca, NY: Cornell University Press, 1983]; Anderson, *Imagined Communities*; R. Suny, *The Revenge of the*

a step further, suggesting that socialism would continue the process, breaking down national barriers to the point where global socialism would eventually require a common language, albeit one that was already known rather than a new one.[20] On the other side were those who urged that national and cultural issues were central. This side included the Austro-Marxists, Otto Bauer and Karl Renner (Rudolf Springer), the Bund (General Jewish Workers' Union of Lithuania, Poland, and Russia), and branches of the Caucasian Social-Democrats (especially the dispersed Armenians). Building on Renner's practical political proposals, Bauer argued for a historicist culturism, in which an intangible "national culture" was contingent upon historical and economic forces.[21] Practically, this meant a need for "cultural-national autonomy," in which cultural communities lived in a multinational state, safe-guarded by autonomous self-administration and democratization, but without territorial sovereignty. Crucially, ethnicity was not regarded as a major feature of such groups—an agreement among all involved in the debate. The Bund and some of the Caucasian Social-Democrats followed Bauer's lead, deploying the terminology of both "national cultures" and "cultural-national autonomy." The Bund did so with much struggle, for it was riven with debate between the internationally minded members, who felt that any deference to national issues was an incipient form of nationalism, and the nationally minded, who argued that the Bund should represent Jewish workers within a federated social democratic organization and then—after a socialist revolution—that nationalities should have jurisdiction over cultural matters, but not political, economic, or territorial autonomy within a federated state. The latter were instrumental in formulating the Bund's position that the Jews form a "nation" (fourth congress of 1901), which is entitled to "free cultural development" with self-government (sixth congress of 1905).[22]

A major contributor to these debates was none other than Stalin. His early position would become over time the basis for policies in the Soviet Union and

---

Past: Nationalism, Revolution, and the Collapse of the Soviet Union [Stanford, CA: Stanford University Press, 1993], 1–19; Y. Brudny, *Reinventing Russia: Russian Nationalism and the Soviet State, 1953-1991* [Cambridge, MA: Harvard University Press, 1998], 5).

20. K. Kautsky, "Die moderne Nationalität," in *Die Neue Zeit: Revue des gcistigen und öffentlichen Lebens*, 5 (1887), 392–405, 442–51. http://library.fes.de/cgi-bin/neuzeit.pl?id=07.00427&dok=1887&f=1887_0392&l=1887_0405; K. Kautsky, "Nationality and Internationalism, Part 1," *Critique: Journal of Socialist Theory* 3.37 (1907 [2009]), 371–89; K. Kautsky, "Nationality and Internationalism, Part 2," *Critique: Journal of Socialist Theory* 1.38 (1907 [2010]), 143–63.

21. O. Bauer, *The Question of Nationalities and Social Democracy*, trans. J. O'Donnell (Minneapolis: University of Minnesota Press, 2000 [1907]); see also G. Egry, "Social Democracy and the Nationalities Question," in *Regimes and Transformations: Hungary in the Twentieth Century*, eds. I. Feitl and B. Sipos (Budapest: Napvilág Kiadó, 2005), 95–118.

22. J. Frankel, *Prophecy and Politics: Socialism, Nationalism, and the Russian Jews, 1862–1917* (Cambridge: Cambridge University Press, 1981), 195, 220, 247.

indeed other socialist states throughout the world. Stalin responded to these culturist positions in two ways that are important here.[23] First, he proposed a definition in which he relegated the cultural factor to the unimportant final place: "A nation is a historically constituted, stable community of people, formed on the basis of a common language, territory, economic life, and psychological storehouse [sklada] manifested in a common culture."[24] It is also worth noting that Stalin agreed with all the other participants in the debate that ethnicity is not a determining factor of a nationality. Second, his overriding emphasis was on unity, whether of the social democratic movement or the state after a socialist revolution. But how was such unity to be achieved? Not through the federalism suggested by those advocating "national-cultural autonomy."[25] Instead, Stalin argued for class as the primary category, compared to which a "national-cultural" approach "substitutes for the socialist principle of the *class struggle* the bourgeois '*principle of nationality*.'"[26] The point is not that an external category—class—determines the nature of national identification, but that one must move dialectically: only through a focus on class as an international category can national aspirations be reconfigured, leading to the production of regional autonomy and recognition of dispersed minorities.

Let me take this further, focusing less on the content than the dynamic of his argument. Unity is not to be imposed on diversity, whether through policies of assimilation or a grudging awareness of national diversity, as some have suggested.[27] Instead, Stalin argues dialectically that unity produces hitherto

---

23. Culturism identifies an intangible "culture" (often laced with religious factors) as the basis for collective identity.

24. I. V. Stalin, "Marxism and the National Question," in *Works* (vol. 2, Moscow: Foreign Languages Publishing House, 1913 [1953]), 307; I. V. Stalin, "Marksizm i natsional'nyĭ vopros," in *Sochineniia* (vol. 2, Moscow: Gosudarstvennoe izdatel'stvo politicheskoi literatury, 1913 [1946]), 296 (translation modified).

25. Like the anatomist, who must know the whole to understand its parts (I. V. Stalin, "The Social-Democratic View on the National Question," in *Works* [vol. 1, Moscow: Foreign Languages Publishing House, 1904 (1954)], 46-47; I. V. Stalin, "Kak ponimaet sotsial-demokratiia natsional'nyĭ vopros?" in *Sochineniia* [vol. 1, Moscow: Gosudarstvennoe izdatel'stvo politicheskoi literatury, 1904 (1946)], 47-48).

26. Stalin, "Marxism and the National Question," 342; Stalin, "Marksizm i natsional'nyĭ vopros," 330-31.

27. G. Guins, *Soviet Law and Soviet Society* (The Hague: Martinus Nijhoff, 1954), 213-25; R. Pipes, *The Formation of the Soviet Union: Communism and Nationalism, 1917-1923* (Cambridge, MA: Harvard University Press, 1964 [1954]); B. Pinkus, *The Jews of the Soviet Union: A History of a National Minority* (Cambridge: Cambridge University Press, 1988), 50-51; T. Martin, "Modernization or Neo-Traditionalism? Ascribed Nationality and Soviet Primordialism," in *Stalinism: New Directions*, ed. S. Fitzpatrick (London: Routledge, 2000), 348-67; T. Martin, "An Affirmative Action Empire: The Soviet Union as the Highest Form of Imperialism," in *A State of Nations: Empire and Nation-Making in the Age of Lenin and Stalin*,

unexpected diversity.[28] This argument would appear in many situations, but perhaps the best example—pertinent to my analysis of Israel in the biblical texts—relates to nationalities and languages:

> Until now what has happened has been that the socialist revolution has not diminished but rather increased the number of languages; for, by stirring up the lowest sections of humanity and pushing them on to the political arena, it awakens to new life a number of hitherto unknown or little-known nationalities. Who could have imagined that the old, tsarist Russia consisted of not less than fifty nations and national groups? The October Revolution, however, by breaking the old chains and bringing a number of forgotten peoples and nationalities on to the scene, gave them new life and a new development.[29]

In summing up this debate, let me draw out the key features for the present argument. To begin with, ethnicity was not a factor regarded as central to identifying a nationality because it potentially confused matters. Instead, the main factors were history, economics, community, territory, language, and culture, with participants differing in their emphases. More significantly, the question of unity and diversity loomed large, in which diversity was produced out of a primary drive to unity. I will interpret this point as the question of utopia. One may suggest that diversity within unity is utopian, with the former valorized in light of the dystopian—"totalitarian"—threats of the latter. This would be a liberal utopia, which manifests itself in the debate as "cultural-national" diversity and which would come to form the basis of later Western European programs of multiculturalism. Or should one suggest that the unity of nationalities is the

---

eds. R. Suny and T. Martin (Oxford: Oxford University Press, 2001), 67–90; E. Van Ree, *The Political Thought of Joseph Stalin: A Study in Twentieth-Century Revolutionary Patriotism* (London: Routledge Curzon, 2002), 64, 77–78; T. Weeks, "Stalinism and Nationality," *Kritika: Explorations in Russian and Eurasian History* 3.6 (2005), 567–68. Notable exceptions include T. Rakowska-Harmstone, "The Dialectics of Nationalism in the USSR," *Problems of Communism* 3.23 (1974), 1–22; and, R. Suny, "Nationalism and Class in the Russian Revolution: A Comparative Discussion," in *Revolution in Russia: Reassessments of 1917*, eds. E. R. Frankel, J. Frankel, and B. Knei-Paz (Cambridge: Cambridge University Press, 1992), 219–46; Suny, *Revenge of the Past*.

28. I. V. Stalin, "The Political Tasks of the University of the Peoples of the East: Speech Delivered at a Meeting of Students of the Communist University of the Toilers of the East, May 18, 1925," in *Works* (vol. 7, Moscow: Foreign Languages Publishing House, 1925 [1954]), 140–42; I. V. Stalin, "O politicheskikh zadachakh universiteta narodov Vostoka: Rech' na sobranii studentov KUTV, 18 maia 1925 g," in *Sochineniia* (vol. 7, Moscow: Gosudarstvennoe izdatel'stvo politicheskoi literatury, 1925 [1952]), 137–40; S. Yekelchyk, "Stalinist Patriotism as Imperial Discourse: Reconciling the Ukrainian and Russian 'Heroic Pasts', 1939–45," *Kritika: Explorations in Russian and Eurasian History* 3.1 (2002), 55.

29. Stalin, "Political Tasks," 141.

utopian dimension, entailing all manner of assimilation programs in different parts of the world? Either option is problematic, with the constant threat of dystopian elements. Since neither option is satisfactory, I propose that the more dialectical argument offers the best approach: the way to foster diversity is precisely through an alternative and indeed totalizing unity. Or in the terminology used in my analysis of utopia: this emphasis on unity produces not a closed dystopia (in the name of utopia) but a utopian project that is ever more open, diverse, and incomplete.

It is perhaps less well known than it should be that this approach to nationalities became—through much trial and error—the basis for the Soviet Union's affirmative action program concerning nationalities,[30] as well as the anti-colonial drive that enabled what is now called postcolonialism.[31] It also became the basis for similar programs in other socialist countries. Indeed, as a transition to my analysis of ancient Israel, I would like to provide a specific example from China, which—after a thorough revision in the 1990s—has taken the approach to its fifty-five minority nationalities to a level beyond that achieved in the Soviet Union, emphasizing the increased autonomy of these nationalities and the inviolability of China's borders.[32] The example concerns the Hui people, who were initially invited by the Tang emperors some thirteen centuries ago to come to the ancient capital of Xi'an, since they had a reputation for hard work and the fostering of exchange. But were they an identifiable ethnic group at the time? Not at all. As with all such groups, their history is mixed.[33] The Tang, Song, and Yuan dynasties encouraged immigration to China of Muslim peoples from more western parts of the world, as far as Persia. A long history of intermarriage with Han people led to the development of what is now known as the Hui. But the Hui include converts to Islam among the Han, as well as other Muslim groups on Hainan island, among the Bai people and Tibetan Muslims. The key to their identification is religion, even if such identification is restricted to certain customs, dietary patterns, and dress, rather than religious practice per se. The vast majority of the Hui speak Mandarin and most of their customs are common to the Han. However, I cannot emphasize enough that the identification of the Hui as a nationality was a state

---

30. T. Martin, *The Affirmative Action Empire: Nations and Nationalism in the Soviet Union, 1923-1939* (Ithaca, NY: Cornell University Press, 2001).

31. C. Petterson, "The Second World: Cold War Ideology and the Development of Postcolonial Criticism," Unpublished manuscript.

32. C. Mackerras, *China's Ethnic Minorities and Globalisation* (London: RoutledgeCurzon, 2003); R. Boer, "The State and Minority Nationalities (Ethnic Groups) in China," in *The Palgrave Handbook of Ethnicity*, ed. S. Ratuva (Singapore: Springer, 2019), 1–17.

33. The best historical study of the Hui remains that of M. Dillon (*China's Muslim Hui Community: Migration, Settlement and Sects* [London: Routledge, 1999]). With some caveats, see also D. Gladney (*Muslim Chinese: Ethnic Nationalism in the People's Republic* [Cambridge, MA: Council on East Asian Studies, Harvard University, 1991]).

decision, made after the liberation of China and the establishment of the People's Republic. Earlier uses of Hui (dating back to the Song Dynasty a millennium ago) referred to Chinese speaking people with foreign and Muslim ancestry. But the designation, in the 1950s, as a distinct nationality has produced a strong national consciousness among the Hui. This means that the complex and overlaid history of the Hui, with migration, intermarriage, state decisions, and policies, has led to, if not produced, a strong sense of national identity *within* a larger state.[34] The point is that such a process is dialectical: it is not so much a distinction between "from above" and "from below," but rather a situation in which both are entwined with one another, defining each in turn. The official identification of the Hui as a nationality would not have happened without their gradual arrival in China from different parts further west. But their self-identification as a nationality, of which they are enthusiastic, would not have happened without a distinct decision by the state, based on extensive research. I would like to emphasize this point in two respects, for the Hui are not unique. First, as with any such group, its identity is the result of a long history of movement, intermingling, and development, so much so that no such group is "pure," for what counts as such a group is really a history of intermingling with many other groups, which are themselves the result of further mingling. Second, the unified identity of the group as a distinct nationality is the result of a distinct program, whether the decision of a state and its ensuing policies, or indeed—as we will see—of a literary narrative that seeks to produce such an identity. In this light, we may redefine Anderson's notion of an imagined community as one that involves a dual process, one that moves at the intersections of above and below.

Israel: A dialectic of unity and multiplication

Now I can turn to the question of Israel, as both a nationality and as a utopian project. The utopian dimension would seem to be easy to identify via the texts: an ideal that is developed in the wilderness, following faithfully the divine laws and the form of the state delineated. The problem, of course, is that the utopian community is never realized, for the people are represented as constantly falling short of the ideal, worshipping "foreign" gods and inter-breeding with "foreigners." In light of my earlier observations, this biblical image of an ideal Israel—developed particularly in the Torah—is problematic, for it leads to dystopia. In order to find an alternative approach, I will work through the question of nationality. Not only does it turn out that the nationality in question is actually quite diverse and the intersection of multiple nationalities, but the very effort to identify a distinct nationality also produces even more diversity, both within and without.

The archaeological and sociological arguments for the multifarious origins of Israel are by now reasonably well known. Let me begin with Gottwald some forty

---

34. Gladney, "Muslim Chinese," 323.

years ago,³⁵ with the proposal that early Israel may well have been composed of amorphous groups such as a Levitical Moses group from Egypt, bands of *'apiru*, Shosu, Rechabites/Kenites, disaffected Canaanite peasants, debtors, and outlaws, who gathered in the Judean highlands and made use of new technology, invented during the long economic "crisis" of the turn of the first millennium BCE. Since then, archaeological field surveys have confirmed that new settlements in the highlands did indeed take place during this time.³⁶ But who were they? Foreigners, settled pastoral nomads, an ethnically distinct group, Canaanites, Israelites, economic refugees making the most of the absence of imperial overlords and their extractive palatine regime, people of mixed backgrounds?³⁷

The initial impression is that such a historical reconstruction is analogous with the example of the Hui (see above), at least in historical terms focused on the question of origins. But the catch with this approach is that it entails a narrative that moves from multiplicity to unity, in which the former is the initial problem and the latter is an attempt at unity. I would like to examine a different approach, which I attempted earlier in relation to the Hui: Can we identify a dialectic of unity and diversity in the way "Israel" developed? In order to answer this question, I focus on the texts. At first sight, they seem to be stitched together with an overarching narrative of uniqueness, which can be traced back to the legendary ancestors: Abraham, Isaac, and Jacob. A more careful consideration of the text reveals a somewhat different picture, in which various nationalities turn up in the midst of what the text claims as ancient Israel. Already early in the convoluted and constructed narrative we find that Abram's father, Terah, comes from Ur of the Chaldeans,³⁸ which he then leaves for Canaan with his family in tow (Gen. 11:31; Neh. 9:7), although he does not arrive, having settled and then died in Haran. When it comes time for Isaac to find an appropriate partner, it is back to "my country and my kindred" (Gen. 24:4), to which Abraham's slave is sent. Is this country Chaldean or something else? Rebekah, it will turn out, is the "daughter of Bethuel the Aramean of Paddan-aram" (Gen. 25:19). And to keep it all in the family, Jacob-Israel himself returns to "Paddan-aram to the house

---

35. N. Gottwald, *The Tribes of Yahweh: A Sociology of Liberated Israel 1250-1050 BC* (Reprint with new Preface ed.; Sheffield: Sheffield Academic Press, 1999 [1979]).

36. I. Finkelstein and N. Silberman, *The Bible Unearthed: Archaeology's New Vision of Ancient Israel and the Origin of Its Sacred Texts* (New York: Free Press, 2001), 106–07.

37. Ibid., 111–13; I. Finkelstein and A. Mazar, *The Quest for the Historical Israel: Debating Archaeology and the History of Early Israel* (Leiden: Brill, 2007); R. Coote and K. Whitelam, *The Emergence of Early Israel in Historical Perspective* (Sheffield: Almond, 1987); P. Davies, *In Search of "Ancient Israel"* (Sheffield: Sheffield Academic, 1995); K. Whitelam, *The Invention of Ancient Israel: The Silencing of Palestinian History* (London: Routledge, 1997); A. Faust, *Israel's Ethnogenesis: Settlement, Interaction, Expansion and Resistance* (London: Equinox, 2006).

38. Daniel-Belteshazzar's identity is also unclear, suggesting that he is both Hebrew and Chaldean (Dan. 1:6-7).

of Bethuel, your mother's father" (Gen. 28:2), to seize a woman or two from the daughters of his maternal uncle, Laban (Genesis 29). Although this mythical narrative repeatedly emphasizes that the women in question were not to be seized from the "Canaanites," Esau (brother of Israel) and his descendants become the embodiment of the Edomites (Gen. 25:30; 36; Num. 20:24; see also Deut. 23:7). He also marries women from among the "people of the land," the Hittites (Gen. 26:34) or indeed Canaanites (Gen. 36:1), the same land in which Sarah and then Abraham, Isaac, Leah, Rachel, and Jacob are buried (Gen. 23; 25:9-10; 49:29–50:14). Even more, the offspring of Lot (grandson of Terah and nephew of Abraham) and his daughters become the Moabites and Ammonites (Gen. 19:30-38; see also Deut. 2:19),[39] and Judah marries an unnamed Canaanite woman (Gen. 38:2) and then has two sons, Perez and Zerah, by Tamar, his widowed daughter-in-law who also seems to be a Canaanite. Simeon too has a son by a "Canaanite woman" (Exod. 6:15), while Manasseh's unnamed Aramean concubine bears Machir the father of Gilead (1 Chron. 7:14). To add to mix, Joseph marries an Egyptian woman given to him by Pharaoh, Asenath daughter of Potiphera, priest of On, who bears two sons, Manasseh and Ephraim (Gen. 41:45; 50-52). Thus, the ancestors are already—as far as the text is concerned—a distinct mix of Chaldean, Aramean, Edomite, Egyptian, Moabite, Ammonite, Hittite, and Canaanite.[40] The complexity of what counts as "Israel" only increases, but it does so precisely when a distinct identity begins to be asserted. In other words, diversity intensified the more unity is asserted. Already in the first chapter of Exodus, this identity appears, in both the narrator's voice (Exod. 1:7) and in the mouth of the new king of Egypt (Exod. 1:8). Yet, as this distinctness becomes a narrative feature, the diversity of its leader becomes intriguingly complicated. Is Moses an Egyptian, as Exod. 2:9 suggests,[41] with a distinctly Egyptian name (Exod. 2:1-9, 19) and marrying a Midianite, Zipporah (Exod. 2:21-22)?[42] And who is Moses's father-in-law? Is it Reuel, the priest of Midian (Exod. 2:17) and son of Hobab (Num. 10:29), or Jethro, also a priest of Midian (Exod. 3:1; 4:18-20; 18), or Hobab the Kenite (Judg. 1:16; 4:11)? Multiple names, multiple wives, shifting identities, textual disruptions—I suggest

---

39. J. Skinner quaintly observes of the incident: "The habit is said to have persisted till modern times in that region" (*A Critical and Exegetical Commentary on Genesis* [The International Critical Commentary; Edinburgh: T&T Clark, 1910], 313). He seems to be referring to living in caves.

40. In this light, it is somewhat misleading to refer to Abraham and Isaac "among the nations" (T. Brodie, *Genesis as Dialogue: A Literary, Historical, and Theological Commentary* [Oxford: Oxford University Press, 2001], 254–64).

41. J. Assmann, *Moses the Egyptian: The Memory of Egypt in Western Monotheism* (Cambridge, MA: Harvard University Press, 1997).

42. "When Moses claims the mantle of being 'an alien in a foreign land,' we as readers may wonder which foreign land does Moses have in mind when he makes that statement" (D. Olson, "Literary and Rhetorical Criticism," in *Methods for Exodus*, ed. T. Dozeman [Cambridge: Cambridge University Press, 2010], 39).

9. Multinationality and the Utopian Project 157

that these shifts act as symptom of the deeper issue of the diversity of national identity, for even the pivotal figure of Moses is decidedly mixed: precisely the one who brings about the narrative unity of the people as Israel.

The point should by now be clear: time and again, the textual strands indicate that what counts as "Israel," as a textual item, an imagined community and as a social-political identity, is actually an intersection of many nationalities. Let me add a few more examples: Ruth is a Moabite and also the great-grandmother of David (Ruth 4:17), a relationship David exploits later (1 Sam. 22:3-4), while the Canaanite sex worker, Rahab, becomes part of the people (Josh 6:25; see also Mat. 1:5). Repeatedly, we find Ammonites (Zelek and Zabad), Hittites (Uriah and Ahimelech), Moabites (Ithmah and Jehozabad), Gittites (Obed-edom), and Edomites (Doeg) among Israelite army, temple staff, and court (1 Sam. 21:7; 22:9; 26:6; 2 Sam. 6:10-11; 11; 23:37, 39; 1 Chron. 11:39, 41, 46; 16:5, 38; 26:8, 15; 2 Chron. 24:26). Further, the account of the conquest of Palestine reveals the continuance of a significant number of groups, especially Canaanites and Hittites (Josh 13:1-6; 15:63; Judg. 1:19-36; see also 1 Kgs 9:20-21). And Solomon has a distinct fondness for Egyptian, Moabite, Ammonite, Edomite, Sidonian, and Hittite women (1 Kgs 3:1; 11:1), while the people are constantly marrying Edomites, Midianites, Canaanites, Hittites, Perizzites, Jebusites, Ammonites, Moabites, Egyptians, Amorites, and Ashdodites (2 Sam. 11:3; Numbers 25; Ezra 9–10; Neh. 13:23-27).

Let me sum up the point I have been making this far with three texts that capture well the sheer diversity of Israel. The first observes: "So the Israelites lived among the Canaanites, the Hittites, the Amorites, the Perizzites, the Hivites, and the Jebusites; and they took their daughters as wives for themselves, and their own daughters they gave to their sons; and they worshiped their gods" (Judg. 3:5). If this text still harbors the desire for a clear identity for the nationality of Israel, then the next is even more direct: "Your origin and your birth were in the land of the Canaanites; your father was an Amorite, and your mother a Hittite" (Ezek. 16:3), or as Deut. 26:5 puts it, more simply, "a wandering Aramean was my ancestor." In this light, the observation of Exod. 23:9 expresses the textual situation well indeed: "You know the heart of an alien [*nepeš haggēr*]." The text in this case postulates that one should treat foreigners well, since the people themselves were once foreigners in Egypt. But the text also betrays another sense, in which the heart itself knows what it is like to be foreign, to be an alien.

Although the contexts are quite different, Israel seems to be very much like the Hui I discussed earlier. But this is only the first step, leading to the relatively mundane point concerning unity out of diversity—at least as far as the narrative structure is concerned. The tendency toward diversity increases when unity begins to be asserted. The patriarchal and matriarchal accounts in Genesis may seek to distill a form of unity out of diversity, but when the narrative begins to assert the distinctness of the people, or indeed the nationality of Israel in Exodus onwards, diversity increases. I have noted Moses's multiple identity, the man born in Egypt with an Egyptian name, raised by the Pharaoh's daughter, and then disappearing in the land of Moab (Deut. 34:1-8), let alone the multiplicity of his father(s)-in-law.

This intensified diversity follows two paths after Moses. The first is internal, with all manner of "foreigners" in the midst of Israel: Ammonites, Edomites, Moabites, Hittites, and Gittites. The second is external, with the very same nationalities—from Joshua through to Kings/Chronicles—attacking Israel, with varying levels of success or failure, and with some being wiped out again and again only to return in ever greater numbers (especially the Amalekites, descendants of Eliphaz, son of Esau, and Timna—Gen. 36:23). The prophets too call down curse and destruction against all manner of nationalities, if not the occasional empire.

Thus far, the nationalities in question are somewhat known entities. At the fringes are Gittites (reputedly from the Philistine town of Gath), Jebusites (from Jerusalem), Perizzites (apparently part of the Canaanites), Hivites (descendants of Canaan), but they already indicate an intriguing multiplication of nationalities. More and more appear, such as the Geshurites and Maacathites of the Transjordan (Deut. 3:14; Josh 12:1-6; 13:11-13), or the Girzites (1 Sam. 27:8).[43] By the time we get to the list of warriors in 2 Sam. 23:24-39 and 1 Chron. 11:26-47, we find even more: Paltites, Hushathites, Ahohites, Arbathites, Hararites, Gilonites, Arbites, Ithrites, Pelonites, Gizonites, Mithnites, Ashterathite, Aroerites, Tizites, Mahavites, and Mezobaites.[44] One may make valiant efforts to identify and categorize such groups, whether in terms of town names or tribes and clans within a people, or indeed as "petty communities."[45] But I would like to emphasize a somewhat different point: they increasingly designate the diversity of nationalities, with ever more found within what appears to be a nationality. Even Israel is subject to this process, in which the "tribes" are given names reserved for nationalities—from Reubenites to Benjaminites. It would seem that this multiplication is the dialectical result of the increasing emphasis on the unity of Israel. As I indicated earlier, this insight appeared theoretically in the midst of socialist debates at the turn of the twentieth century, in which unity—even if imposed "from above"—produced unexpected diversity. To gloss a text I quoted earlier, these "hitherto unknown or little-known nationalities" have been given a "new life and a new development."[46]

Conclusion: A multinational utopia?

I close with two questions. First, what is the driver of unity in the overarching narrative? The nationality in question clearly becomes distinct through retrofitted religious (and thereby cultural) features—a version of monotheism, a legal code,

---

43. A foretaste already appears in Gen. 10:17 and 15:19, with Hivites, Arkites, Sinites, Arvadites, Zemarites, Hamathites, Kenites, Kenizzites, Kadmonites, Perizzites, and Girgashites.

44. Or as the Book of Mormon puts it, with unwitting insight, "any manner of -ites" (4 Nephi 1:17).

45. Skinner, *Commentary of Genesis*, 214.

46. Stalin, "Political Tasks," 141.

institutions, material structures, leadership, and so on. This drive to identity may be regarded as one imposed "from above," an effort to find unity among diversity. The catch is that the more unity is pressed, the more diversity appears. But we may also espy a legendary, if not mythical "history" that stems not merely from Abraham but from the first moments of creation what I have elsewhere called a political myth.[47] This entails the effort to develop a stable community (first in the wilderness), territory (even if conquered), language (of the text), and even an economy that may be described primarily as a subsistence regime, with a late but marginal effort at a palatine estate system.[48] These are of course the terms I noted earlier in the definition of nationality, with the notable absence of ethnicity.[49] Running through all of this is the determining feature of a spiritual or "psychological storehouse [*sklada*] manifested in a common culture."[50]

Second, how is this utopian? It is neither the much sought-after unity of the people, closed off from others, which would then run into the dystopia of Kings-Chronicles and the prophetic condemnations, nor some form of liberal multiculturalism based on a limited European notion of human rights.[51] Instead, the text seems to suggest that it is the very openness, diversity, and incompletion that arises first in the move to unity (the patriarchal and matriarchal narratives) but even more in the effort to produce a national unity, the desired final articulation of which is itself utopian. This effort produces ever greater diversity, internally and externally, in what may be called—with allusion to actually existing socialism—as "actually existing Israel."[52]

---

47. R. Boer, *Political Myth: On the Use and Abuse of Biblical Themes* (Durham, NC: Duke University Press, 2007).

48. Boer, *The Sacred Economy of Ancient Israel*.

49. F. Crüsemann, "Human Solidarity and Ethnic Identity: Israel's Self-definition in the Genealogical System of Genesis," in *Ethnicity and the Bible*, ed. M. Brett (Leiden: Brill, 2002), 66–68.

50. See also ibid., 69.

51. C. Westermann, *Genesis*, trans. D. Green (London: T&T Clark, 1988), 249–50; M. Brett, *Genesis: Procreation and the Politics of Identity* (London: Routledge, 2000).

52. D. Boer, *Delivery from Slavery: Attempting a Biblical Theology in the Service of Liberation*, trans. R. Pohl (Historical Materialism Book Series; Leiden: Brill, 2015 [2009]).

CONTRIBUTORS

Carolyn Alsen is an educator and researcher in the areas of religious and biblical studies. Her main interest is in Hebrew Bible scholarship using postcolonial, feminist, and ideological criticisms. Particularly, she is engaged in narratological research using the gaze and seeing to re-read and reconstruct Israelite identity in the Hebrew Bible. She also has research experience in biblical Semitic linguistics, critical theory and the Bible, and field work in contextual readings for liberation and Bible translation. She is an Honorary Postdoctoral Associate and Acting Director of Learning and Teaching at the University of Divinity, Australia.

Roland Boer is Distinguished Professor of Literature at Renmin University of China, Beijing. His current research focuses on comparative Marxism and the philosophical basis of socialism in power.

Jeremiah W. Cataldo is Associate Professor of History in the Frederik Meijer Honors College at Grand Valley State University. His research currently focuses on the early formation of monotheism and the place of the Bible in cultural criticism.

Matthew J. M. Coomber is Associate Professor of Biblical Studies at St. Ambrose University, an Episcopal priest, and a director at the Center and Library for the Bible and Social Justice. He researches the intersections of Bible and systemic poverty in ancient and modern contexts. In addition to journal articles and book chapters, he is the author of *Re-Reading the Prophets through Corporate Globalization* (Gorgias), editor of *Bible and Justice: Ancient Texts, Modern Challenges* (Routledge), and co-editor of *Fortress Commentary on the Bible: Old Testament and Apocrypha*. Coomber is currently writing *Amos and Micah through the Centuries* (Wiley Blackwell), and is editing a six-volume series, *The Cascade Companion to Bible and Economics* (Cascade Books).

Bradley L. Crowell is Associate Professor of Religious Studies and Chair of the Department of Philosophy and Religion at Drake University in Des Moines, Iowa. He received his Ph.D. in Ancient Near Eastern Studies and the Hebrew Bible from the University of Michigan. His publications have appeared in the *Journal for Ancient Near Eastern Religions*, the *Bulletin for the American Society of Oriental Research*, *Zeitschrift für die alttestamentliche Wissenschaft*, *Currents in Research: Biblical Studies*, and *Biblical Interpretation*. He is also the co-editor of *Excavating Asian History: Interdisciplinary Studies in Archaeology and History* with Norman Yoffee.

Kyong-Jin Lee is Associate Professor of Old Testament Studies at Fuller Theological Seminary. Her research explores the social, political, and theological contexts in which the Hebrew Bible/Old Testament developed and attained its authoritative status during the Persian and Hellenistic periods.

Mark Sneed is Professor of Bible at Lubbock Christian University. His work combines expertise in the biblical wisdom literature and social theory, especially the honor-shame cultural perspective. He is best known for challenging the notion of a wisdom tradition that reflects an idiosyncratic worldview within the Hebrew Bible. He is currently working on a reception history of Behemoth and Leviathan.

Ehud Ben Zvi is Professor Emeritus in the Department of History and Classics at the University of Alberta, Canada. He has written extensively on social memory in ancient Israel and the latter's past-shaping texts, especially prophetic literature, "historical" books, and particularly Chronicles. For a list of publications see https://sites.ualberta.ca/~ebenzvi/ebz-publications.html

BIBLIOGRAPHY

Abbott, Andrew. *Department & Discipline: Chicago Sociology at One Hundred*. Chicago, IL: University of Chicago Press, 1999.

Abrahams, Roger D. "A Rhetoric of Everyday Life: Traditional Conversational Genres." *Southern Folklore Quarterly* 32 (1968): 44–54.

Abrahams, Roger D. "Proverbs and Proverbial Expressions." In *Folkflore and Folklife: An Introduction*, edited by Richard M. Porson, 117-27. Chicago, IL: University of Chicago Press, 1972.

Adams, Karin. "Metaphor and Dissonance: A Reinterpretation of Hosea 4:13-14." *JBL* 127 (2008): 291–305.

Adelman, Rachel. "Seduction and Recognition in the Story of Judah and Tamar and the Book of Ruth." *Nashim: A Journal of Jewish Women's Studies and Gender Issues* 23 (2012): 87–109.

Ahlström, Gösta W. *The History of Ancient Palestine*. Minneapolis, MN: Fortress Press, 1993.

Albertz, Rainer. *A History of Israelite Religion in the Old Testament Period*. London: SCM Press, 1994.

Alter, Robert. *The Art of Biblical Narrative*. New York: Basic Books, 1981.

Alter, Robert. *The Art of Biblical Poetry*. New York: Basic Books. Ansberry, 1985.

Amer, Sahar. *What Is Veiling? Islamic Civilization and Muslim Networks*. Chapel Hill, NC: The University of North Carolina Press, 2014.

Amit, Yairah. "Hidden Polemics in the Story of Judah and Tamar (Genesis 38:1-30)." *Shnaton: An Annual for Biblical and Ancient Near Eastern Studies* 20, no. 1 (2010): 11–25.

Amit, Yairah. "Narrative Analysis: Meaning, Context and Origins of Genesis 38." In *Method Matters: Essays on the Interpretation of the Hebrew Bible in Honor of David L. Petersen*, edited by Joel M. LeMon and Kent Harold Richards, 271–92. Atlanta, GA: Society of Biblical Literature, 2009.

Amit, Yairah. *Hidden Polemics in Biblical Narrative*. Biblical Interpretation Series 25. Leiden; Boston, MA: Brill, 2000.

Anderson, Benedict. *Imagined Communities*. Revised ed. London: Verso, 1991.

Anthonioz, S. "Adummatu, Qedar and the Arab Question in Neo-Assyrian Sources." *Duma 3: The 2012 Report of the Saudi-Italian-French Archaeological Mission at Dumat Al-Jandal (Saudi Arabia)* 2015: 35–36.

Arera, E. O., and Alan Dundes. "Proverbs and the Ethnography of Speaking Folklore." *American Anthropologist* 66, no. 6 (1954): 70–85.

Assmann, Jan. *Moses the Egyptian: The Memory of Egypt in Western Monotheism*. Cambridge, MA: Harvard University Press, 1997.

Barajas, Elías Domínguez. *The Function of Proverbs in Discourse: The Case of a Mexican Transnational Social Network*. Edited by Joshua A Fishman. Vol. 98. Contributions to the Sociology of Language. Berlin: De Gruyter Mouton, 2010.

Barrick, W. B. "Dynastic Politics, Priestly Succession, and Josiah's Eighth Year." *ZAW* 112 (2000): 565–66.

Barstad, Hans M. "After the 'Myth of the Empty Land': Major Challenges in the Study of Neo-Babylonian Judah." In *Judah and the Judeans in the Neo-Babylonian Period*, edited by Oded Lipschits and Joseph Blenkinsopp, 3–20. Winona Lake, IN: Eisenbrauns, 2003.

Barzel, Yoram. "Property Rights and the Evolution of the State." In *Conflict and Governance*, edited by Kai A. Konrad and Amihai Glazer, 135–61. Heidelberg: Springer, 2003.

Bauer, Otto. *The Question of Nationalities and Social Democracy*. Edited and translated by Joseph O'Donnell. Minneapolis, MN: University of Minnesota Press, 2000 [1907].

Becking, B. "The Enigmatic Garden of Uzza: A Religio-Historical Footnote to 2 Kings 21:18, 26." In *Berürungspunkte: Studien Zur Sozial- Und Religionsgeschichte Israels, Festschrift Für Rainer Albertz Zu Seinem 65. Geburtstag*, edited by I. Kottsieper, R. Schmitt, and J. Wohrle, 383–91. Münster: Ugarit-Verlag, 2008.

Begg, C. "Jotham and Amon: Two Minor Kings of Judah According to Josephus." *Bulletin for Biblical Research* 6 (1996): 1–13.

Berlinerblau, Jacques. "Ideology, Pierre Bourdieu's Doxa, and the Hebrew Bible." *Semeia* 87 (1999): 193–214.

Bird, Phyllis A. "The Harlot as Heroine: Narrative Art and Social Presupposition in Three Old Testament Texts." *Semeia* 46 (1989): 119–39.

Bird, Phyllis A. *Missing Persons and Mistaken Identities: Women and Gender in Ancient Israel*. Overtures to Biblical Theology. Minneapolis, MN: Fortress Press, 1997.

Blenkinsopp, Joseph. "Theme and Motif in the Succession History (2 Sam xi 2ff.) and the Yahwist Corpus." In *Volume du Congres: Geneve, 1965*, edited by P. A. H.de Boer, 44–57. Leiden: E.J. Brill, 1966.

Blenkinsopp, Joseph. *Ezra-Nehemiah : A Commentary*. 1st ed. The Old Testament Library. Philadelphia, PA: Westminster Press, 1988.

Bloch, Ernst. *Heritage of Our Times*. Edited and translated by Neville Plaice and Stephen Plaice. London: Polity, 1991 [1935].

Bloch, Ernst. *The Principle of Hope*. Edited by Stephen Plaice, Neville Plaice, and Paul Knight. Cambridge, MA: MIT Press, 1995.

Bloch, Ernst. *The Spirit of Utopia*. Edited and Translated by Anthony A. Nassar. Stanford, CA: Stanford University Press, 2000.

Bloch, Ernst. *Traces*. Edited and Translated by Anthony A. Nassar. Stanford, CA: Stanford University Press, 2006 [1930].

Boer, Dick. *Delivery from Slavery: Attempting a Biblical Theology in the Service of Liberation*. Edited and Translated by Rebecca Pohl. Historical Materialism Book Series. Leiden: Brill, 2015 [2009].

Boer, Roland. *Political Myth: On the Use and Abuse of Biblical Themes*. Durham, NC: Duke University Press, 2007.

Boer, Roland. *The Sacred Economy of Ancient Israel*, Library of Ancient Israel. Louisville, KY: Westminster John Knox, 2015.

Bourdieu, Pierre, and Randal Johnson. *The Field of Cultural Production*. Edited by Randal Johnson. New York: Columbia University Press, 1993.

Bourdieu, Pierre. *Distinction: A Social Critique of the Judgment of Taste*. Translated by Richard Nice. Routledge Classics. London: Routledge, 2010.

Bourdieu, Pierre. *Outline of a Theory of Practice*. Translated by Richard Nice. Vol. 16. Cambridge Studies in Social and Cultural Anthropology. Cambridge: Cambridge University Press, 1977.

Bourdieu, Pierre. *Practical Reason: On the Theory of Action*. Stanford, CA: Stanford University Press, 1998.

Bourdieu, Pierre. *Sociology in Question*. Translated by Richard Nice. Theory, Culture & Society. London: Sage, 1993.
Bradley, Katherine, and Robert Rector. "Hunger and Food Programs: Reforming the Food Stamp Program," 2012. http://www.heritage.org/node/12241/print-display. Accessed March 3, 2019.
Bradley, Katherine, and Robert Rector. "Interpreting Ethnicity: Method, Hermeneutics, Ethics." In *Ethnicity and the Bible*, edited by Mark Brett, 3–22. Leiden: Brill, 2002.
Bradley, Katherine, and Robert Rector. *Genesis: Procreation and the Politics of Identity*. London: Routledge, 2000.
Brodie, Thomas. *Genesis as Dialogue: A Literary, Historical, and Theological Commentary*. Oxford: Oxford University Press, 2001.
Brown, William P. *Character in Crisis: A Fresh Approach to the Wisdom Literature of the Old Testament*. Grand Rapids, MI: Eerdmans, 1996.
Brudny, Yitzhak M. *Reinventing Russia: Russian Nationalism and the Soviet State, 1953-1991*. Cambridge, MA: Harvard University Press, 1998.
Bunge, Mario. "Ten Modes of Individualism-None of Which Works-and Their Alternatives." *Philosophy of Social Science* 30 (2000): 384–406.
Bureau of Labor Statistics. "Employment by Major Industry Sector," 2015. https://www.bls.gov/emp/ep_table_201.htm. Accessed March 3, 2019.
Carneiro, Robert L. "Chiefdom: Precursor of the State." In *The Transition to Statehood in the New World*, edited by Grant D. Jones and Robert R. Kautz, 37–75. Cambridge: Cambridge University Press, 1981.
Carruthers, Bruce G. *City of Capital: Politics and Markets in the English Financial Revolution*. Princeton, NJ: Princeton University Press, 1996.
Carter, Charles E. *The Emergence of Yehud in the Persian Period: A Social and Demographic Study*. Sheffield: Sheffield Academic Press, 1999.
Carter, Rita. "The Limits of Imagination." In *Human Nature: Fact and Fiction: Literature, Science and Human Nature*, edited by Robin Headlam Wells and Johnjoe McFadden, 128–43. New York: Continuum, 2006.
Cataldo, Jeremiah W. *Breaking Monotheism: Yehud and the Material Formation of Monotheistic Identity*. LHBOTS 565. London: Bloomsbury, 2009.
Chalcraft, David J. "Sociology and the Book of Chronicles: Risk, Ontological Security, Moral Panics, and Types of Narrative." In *What Was Authoritative for Chronicles?*, edited by Ehud Ben Zvi and Diana Vikander Edelman, 201–27. Winona Lake, IN: Eisenbrauns, 2011.
Chalcraft, David J. "Biblical Studies and the Social Sciences: Whence and Wither?" In *Methods, Theories, Imagination: Social Scientific Approaches in Biblical Studies*, edited by David J. Chalcraft, Frauke Uhlenbruch, and Rebecca S. Watson, xiii–xxxv. Sheffield: Sheffield Phoenix, 2014.
Chaney, Marvin L. *Peasants, Prophets, and Political Economy*. Eugene, OR: Cascade Books, 2017.
Chapman, Cynthia R. *The House of the Mother: The Social Roles of Maternal Kin in Biblical Hebrew Narrative and Poetry*. New Haven, CT: Yale University Press, 2016.
Christopher, B. "What Does Jerusalem Have to Do with Athens? The Moral Vision of the Book of Proverbs and Aristotle's Nicomachean Ethics." *HS* 51 (2010): 157–73.
Civil, Miguel. "Enlil and Ninlil: The Marriage of Sud." *Journal of the American Oriental Society* 103, no. 1 (1983): 43–66.
Clifford, Richard J. *The Wisdom Literature*. IBT. Nashville, TN: Abingdon Press, 1998.

Cohen, Ted. "Metaphor and the Cultivation of Intimacy." *Critical Inquiry* 5, no. 1 (1978): 3–12.
Coomber, Matthew J. M. "Seeking Community in a Capitalist Age: A Collective Response to Poverty and Debt from the Bible to Today." *Journal of Religion and Society* 16 (2018): 92–108.
Coomber, Matthew J. M. *Re-Reading the Prophets through Corporate Globalization.* Piscataway, NJ: Gorgias, 2010.
Coote Robert B., and Keith W. Whitelam. *The Emergence of Early Israel in Historical Perspective.* Sheffield: Almond, 1987.
Cornell, Drucilla. "The Secret behind the Veil: A Reinterpretation of 'Algeria Unveiled.'" *Philosophia Africana* 4, no. 2 (2001): 27–35.
Cross, F. M., and D. N. Freedman. "Josiah's Revolt against Assyria." *JNES* 12, no. 1 (1953): 56–58.
Crüsemann, Frank. "Human Solidarity and Ethnic Identity: Israel's Self-Definition in the Genealogical System of Genesis." In *Ethnicity and the Bible*, edited by Mark Brett, 57–76. Leiden: Brill, 2002.
Currie, Greg. "Imagination and Learning." In *The Handbook of Philosophy of Imagination*, edited by Amy Kind, 407–19. New York: Routledge, 2016.
Davies, Philip. *In Search of "Ancient Israel."* Sheffield: Sheffield Academic, 1995.
Day, Peggy L. "Adulterous Jerusalem's Imagined Demise: Death of a Metaphor in Ezekiel XVI." *VT* 50, no. 3 (2000): 285–309.
Deutsch, Karl W. *Nationalism and Social Communication.* 2nd ed. Cambridge, MA: MIT Press, 1966.
Dexter Callender, Jr. "Fear and Foreign Bodies: The Bible and 'Post-Racial' American Identity." *Political Theology* 13, no. 5 (2012): 536–67.
Diduk, Susan. "Twinship and Juvenile Power: The Ordinariness of the Extraordinary." *Ethnology* 40, no. 1 (2001): 29–43.
Dillon, Michael. *China's Muslim Hui Community: Migration, Settlement and Sects.* London: Routledge, 1999.
Doniger, Wendy. *The Bedtrick: Tales of Sex and Masquerade.* Chicago, IL: Chicago University Press, 2000.
Doniger, Wendy. *The Woman Who Pretended to Be Who She Was: Myths of Self-Imitation.* Oxford: Oxford University Press, 2005.
Dube, Musa W. "Toward a Post-Colonial Feminist Interpretation of the Bible." In *Hope Abundant*, edited by Kwok Pui-lan, 89–102. Maryknoll, NY: Orbis Books, 2010.
Durand, Jean-Marie. *Archives Épistolaires Du Palais de Mari.* Vol. 3. Littératures Anciennes Du Proche-Orient. Paris: Cerf, 2000.
Durkheim, Émile. *The Division of Labor in Society.* New York: Free Press, 1802.
Edelman, Diana. "Identities within a Central and Peripheral Perspective: The Use of Aramaic in the Hebrew Bible." In *Centres and Peripheries in the Early Second Temple Period*, edited by E. Ben Zvi and C. Levin, 109–31. Tübingen: Mohr-Siebeck, 2016.
Egry, Gábor. "Social Democracy and the Nationalities Question." In *Regimes and Transformations: Hungary in the Twentieth Century*, edited by Istvan Feitl and Balázs Sipos, 95–118. Budapest: Napvilág Kiadó, 2005.
Elayi, Josette, and Jean Sapin. *Beyond the River: New Perspectives on Transeuphratene.* Edited and translated by J. Edward Crowley. Sheffield: Sheffield Academic Press, 1998.
Elliott, John H. *Beware the Evil Eye: The Evil Eye in the Bible and the Ancient World.* Vol. 1. Cambridge: James Clarke & Co, 2016.

Elman, R. *Service Origins of the State and Civilization: The Process of Cultural Evolution.* New York: Norton, 1975.
Engels, Friedrich. "Socialism: Utopian and Scientific." In *Marx and Engels Collected Works*, Vol. 24, 281–325. Moscow: Progress Publishers, 1880 [1989].
Fanon, Frantz. "Algeria Unveiled." In *The New Left Reader*, edited by Carl Oglesby, 161–85. New York: Grove, 1969.
Fanon, Frantz. *Black Skin White Masks.* Edited and translated by Charles Lam Markmann. London: Pluto, 2008.
Faundez, Julio. "Douglass North's Theory of Institutions: Lessons for Law and Development." *Hague Journal on the Rule of Law* 8, no. 2 (2016): 373–419.
Faust, Abraham. "Settlement Dynamics and Demographic Fluctuations in Judah from the Late Iron Age to the Hellenistic Period and the Archaeology of Persian-Period Yehud." In *A Time of Change: Judah and Its Neighbours in the Persian and Early Hellenistic Periods*, edited by Yigal Levin, 23–50. London: T&T Clark, 2007.
Faust, Abraham. *Israel's Ethnogenesis: Settlement, Interaction, Expansion and Resistance.* London: Equinox, 2006.
Federal Reserve Board of Governors. "Report on the Economic Wellbeing of U.S Households in 2015," 2016. https://www.federalreserve.gov/2015-report-economic-wellbeing-us-households-201605.pdf. Accessed March 3, 2019.
Fine, Gary Alan. *Sticky Reputations: The Politics of Collective Memory in Midcentury America.* New York: Routledge, 2012.
Finkelstein, Israel. "The Archaeology of the Days of Manasseh." In *Scripture and Other Artifacts: Essays on the Bible and Archaeology in Honor of Philip J. King*, edited by J. C. Exum, L. E. Stager, P. J. King, M. D. Coogan, 169–87. Louisville, KY: Westminster John Knox Press, 1994.
Finkelstein, Israel, and Amihai Mazar. *The Quest for the Historical Israel: Debating Archaeology and the History of Early Israel.* Leiden: Brill, 2007.
Finkelstein, Israel, and Neil Asher Silberman. *The Bible Unearthed: Archaeology's New Vision of Ancient Israel and the Origin of Its Sacred Texts.* New York: Free Press, 2001.
Fitzpatrick-McKinley, Anne. *Empire, Power and Indigenous Elites: A Case Study of the Nehemiah Memoir.* Leiden: Brill, 2015.
Flanagan, James W. "Chiefs in Israel." In *Social Scientific Old Testament Criticism: A Sheffield Reader*, edited by David J. Chalcraft, 136–61. Sheffield: Sheffield Academic Press, 1997.
Fletcher, Natalie M. "Imagination and the Capabilities Approach." In *The Handbook of Philosophy of Imagination*, edited by Amy Kind, 392–404. London: Routledge, 2016.
Fontaine, Carole. "Proverb Performance in the Hebrew Bible." *JSOT* 32 (1985): 87–103.
Fox, Michael V. "Ethics and Wisdom in the Book of Proverbs." *HS* 48 (2007): 75–88.
Frame, G. "The Inscription of Sargon II at Tang-I Var." *Or* 68, no. 1 (1999): 31–57.
Frankel, Jonathan. *Prophecy and Politics: Socialism, Nationalism and the Russian Jews, 1862–1917.* Cambridge: Cambridge University Press, 1981.
Fried, L. S. "The 'Am Ha'Aretz in Ezra 4: 4 and Persian Imperial Administration." In *Judah and the Judeans in the Persian Period*, edited by Oded Lipschits and Manfred Oeming, 123–45. Winona Lake, IN: Eisenbrauns, 2006.
Fry, Richard. "The Growing Economic Clout of the College Educated." *Pew Research Center*, 2013. http://www.pewresearch.org/fact-tank/2013/. Accessed March 3, 2019.
Frymer-Kensky, Tikva S. *In the Wake of the Goddesses: Women, Culture, and the Biblical Transformation of Pagan Myth.* New York: Maxwell Macmillan, 1992.

Gabler, Neal. "The Secret Shame of Middle-Class Americans." *Atlantic*, May 2016. https://www.theatlantic.com/magazine/archive/2016/05/my-secret-shame/476415/. Accessed March 3, 2019.

Gandhi, Leela. *Affective Communities: Anticolonial Thought, Fin-de-Siècle Radicalism, and the Politics of Friendship*. Durham, NC: Durham University Press, 2006.

Gellner, Ernest. *Nations and Nationalism*. Ithaca, NY: Cornell University Press, 1983.

George A. Akerlof, and Rachel E. Kranton. "Economics and Identity." *Quarterly Journal of Economics* 140, no. 3 (2000): 715–53.

Gladney, Dru. *Muslim Chinese: Ethnic Nationalism in the People's Republic*. Cambridge, MA: Council on East Asian Studies, Harvard University, 1991.

Go, J. *Patterns of Empire: The British and American Empires, 1688 to the Present*. Cambridge: Cambridge University Press, 2011.

Goering, Greg Schmidt. "Attentive Ears and Forward-Looking Eyes: Disciplining the Senses and Forming the Self in the Book of Proverbs." *JJS* 66, no. 2 (2015): 242–64.

Goering, Greg Schmidt. "Honey and Wormwood: Taste and the Embodiment of Wisdom in the Book of Proverbs." *HBAI* 5 (2016): 23–41.

Golka, Friedemann. *The Leopard's Spots: Biblical and African Wisdom in Proverbs*. Edinburgh: T&T Clark, 1993.

Goodkind, Nichole. "Trump's Food Stamp Cuts Will Leave More Americans Hungry." *Newsweek*, 2018. https://www.newsweek.com/trump-food-stamps-snap-hunger-815327. Accessed March 3, 2019.

Gottwald, Norman K. "Early Israel as an Anti-Imperial Community." In *Social Justice and the Hebrew Bible: Volume Two*, edited by Norman Gottwald, 3–19. Eugene, OR: Cascade Books, 2017.

Gottwald, Norman K. *The Tribes of Yahweh: A Sociology of Liberated Israel 1250-1050 BC*. Reprint with new Preface ed. Sheffield: Sheffield Academic Press, 1999 [1979].

Grabbe, Lester L. "Joseph Smith and the Gestalt of the Israelite Prophet." In *Ancient Israel. The Old Testament in Its Social Context*, edited by Philip F. Esler, 111–27. Minneapolis, MN: Fortress Press, 2006.

Grabbe, Lester L. "The Kingdom of Judah from Sennacherib's Invasion to the Fall of Jerusalem: 'If We Had Only the Bible....'" In *Good Kings and Bad Kings*, edited by Lester L. Grabbe, 78–122. London; New York: T&T Clark International, 2005.

Grabbe, Lester L. *Ezra-Nehemiah*. New York: Routledge, 1998.

Grabbe, Lester L. *Priests, Prophets and Diviners, Sages: A Socio-Historical Study of Religious Specialists in Ancient Israel*. Valley Forge, PA: Trinity Press International, 1995.

Grace, Daphne. *The Woman in the Muslim Mask: Veiling and Identity in Postcolonial Literature*. London; Sterling, VA: Pluto Press, 2004.

Gray, J. "The Desert God 'Attr in the Literature and Religion of Canaan." *JNES* 8 (1949): 72–83.

Gray, J. *I & II Kings*. OTL. Philadelphia, PA: Westminster John Knox Press, 1963.

Greenstein, Edward. "Reading Strategies in the Book of Ruth." In *Women in the Hebrew Bible: A Reader*, edited by Alice Bach, 211–31. London; New York: Routledge, 1999.

Gruber, Mayer I. "Hebrew Qĕdēšāh and Her Canaanite and Akkadian Cognates." *Ugarit Forschungen* 18 (1986): 133–48.

Guins, George C. *Soviet Law and Soviet Society*. The Hague: Martinus Nijhoff, 1954.

Halpern, B. "Jerusalem and the Lineages in the Seventh Century BCE: Kinship and the Rise of Individual Moral Liability." In *Law and Ideology in Monarchic Israel*, edited by B. Halpern and D. W. Hobson, 11–107. Sheffield, 1991.

Hardt, Michael, and Antonio Negri. *Multitude: War and Democracy in the Age of Empire*. New York: Penguin, 2004.

Harrison, T. P., and J. F. Osborne. "Building XVI and the Neo-Assyrian Sacred Precinct at Tell Tayinat." *JCS* 64 (2012): 125–43.
Hayek, Friedrich A. "The Use of Knowledge in Society." *American Economic Review* 35 (1945): 519–30.
Hayek, Friedrich A. *Law, Legislation and Liberty: A New Statement of the Liberal Principles of Justice and Political Economy*. New York: Routledge, 2012.
Hayek, Friedrich A. *The Constitution of Liberty*. Chicago, IL: University of Chicago Press, 1960.
Hayek, Friedrich A. *The Road to Serfdom*. Chicago, IL: University of Chicago Press, 1944.
Heim, Knut Martin. *Poetic Imagination in Proverbs: Variant Repetitions and the Nature of Poetry*. Winona Lake, IN: Eisenbrauns, 2013.
Hens-Piazza, G. *1-2 Kings*. Nashville, TN: Abingdon Press, 2006.
Hiltzik, Michael. "Sen. Joni Ernst Learned to 'Live within Her Means'—on the Taxpayer's Dime." *LA Times*, 2015. https://www.latimes.com/business/hiltzik/la-fi-mh-sen-joni-ernst-learned-20150123-column.html. Accessed March 3, 2019.
Hoglund, Kenneth. "The Material Culture of the Persian Period and the Sociology of the Second Temple Period." In *Second Temple Studies III: Studies in Politics, Class and Material Culture*, edited by John M. Halligan and Phillip R. Davies, 14–18. London: Sheffield Academic Press, 2002.
Horwitz, Steven. "Hayek and Freedom," n.d. https://fee.org/articles/hayek-and-freedom/. Accessed March 3, 2019.
Houlberg, Marilyn. "Two Equals Three: Twins and the Trickster in Haitian Vodou." In *Twins in African and Diaspora Cultures: Double Trouble, Twice Blessed*, edited by Philip M. Peek, 271–89. Bloomington: Indiana University Press, 2011.
Hume, David. "Of Some Further Considerations with Regard to Justice." In *An Inquiry Concerning the Principles of Morals, Sec III*, 357–64. Edinburgh: James Clarke, 1809.
Jackson, Melissa. *Comedy and Feminist Interpretation of the Hebrew Bible: A Subversive Collaboration*. Oxford: Oxford University Press, 2012.
Jaén, Isabel, and Julies Jacques Simon, eds. *Cognitive Literary Studies Current Themes and New Directions*. Austin, TX: University of Texas Press, 2012.
Jameson, Fredric. *Archaeologies of the Future: The Desire Called Utopia and Other Science Fictions*. London: Verso, 2005.
Jameson, Fredric. *The Ideologies of Theory*. London: Verso, 2008.
Jevons, William Stanley. *The Theory of Political Economy*. London: Macmillan and Co, 1888.
Johnson, Allen, and Timothy Earle. *The Evolution of Human Societies: From Foraging Group to Agrarian State*. 2nd ed. Stanford, CA: Stanford University Press, 2001.
Kahn, D. "The Inscription of Sargon II at Tang-I Var and the Chronology of Dynasty 25." *Or* 70, no. 1 (2001): 1–18.
Kammen, Michael G., and A. Machine. *That Would Go of Itself: The Constitution in American Culture*. New Brunswick, NJ: Transaction Publishers, 2006.
Kang, Youwei. *Ta T'ung Shu: The One-World Philosophy of K'ang Yu-Wei*. Edited and translated by Lawrence G. Thompson. London: Routledge, 1958.
Kasperkevic, Jana. "Occupy Activists Abolish $3.85m in Corinthian Colleges Students' Loan Debt." *The Guardian*, 2014. https://www.theguardian.com/money/2014/sep/17/occupy-activists-student-debt-corinthian-colleges. Accessed March 3, 2019.
Kautsky, Karl. "Die Moderne Nationalität." *Die Neue Zeit* 5, no. 392–405; 442–451 (1887). http://library.fes.de/cgi-bin/neuzeit.pl?id=07.00427&dok=1887&f=1887_0392&l=1887_0405. Accessed March 3, 2019.

Kautsky, Karl. "Nationality and Internationality, Part 1." *Critique: Journal of Socialist Theory* 37, no. 3 (1907 [2009]): 371–89.
Kautsky, Karl. "Nationality and Internationality, Part 2." *Critique: Journal of Socialist Theory* 38, no. 1 (1907 [2010]): 143–63.
Kim, Uriah. "Uriah the Hittite: A (Con)Text of Struggle for Identity." *Semeia* 90/91 (2002): 69–85.
Kincaid, Harold. "Methodological Individualism and Economics." In *Elgar Companion to Economics and Philosophy*, edited by Jocken Runde, John Davis, and Alain Marciano, 299–314. Cheltenham: Edward Elgar, 2004.
Kind, Amy. "Imagining under Constrains." In *Knowledge through Imagination*, edited by Amy Kind and Peter Kung, 145–59. Oxford: Oxford University Press, 2018.
Kind, Amy, and Peter Kung, eds. *Knowledge through Imagination*. Oxford: Oxford University Press, 2016.
Kippenberg, H. G. *Religion Und Klassenbildung Im Antiken Judäa*. Göttingen: Vandenhoeck und Ruprecht, 1978.
Klein, Lillian R. "Honor and Shame in Esther." In *Feminist Companion to Esther, Judith and Susanna*, edited by Athalya Brenner, 149–75. Sheffield: Sheffield Academic Press, 1995.
Knauf, E. Axel. "The Glorious Days of Manasseh." In *Good Kings and Bad Kings*, edited by L. L. Grabbe, 164–88. London: T&T Clark, 2005.
Knauf, E. Axel. "King Solomon's Copper Supply." In *Phoenicia and the Bible. Proceedings of the Conference Held at the University of Leuven on the 15th and 16th of March 1990*, edited by E. Lipiński, 167–86. Leuven: Peeters, 1991.
Knight, Nick. *Mao Zedong on Dialectical Materialism: Writings on Philosophy*. Armonk: M.E. Sharpe, 1990.
Knight, Nick. *Marxist Philosophy in China: From Qu Qiubai to Mao Zedonf, 1923-1945*. Dordrecht: Springer, 2005.
Knoppers, Gary. "Saint or Sinner? Manasseh in Chronicles." In *Rewriting Biblical History: Essays on Chronicles and Ben Sira in Honour of Pancratius C. Beentjes*, edited by J. Corley and H. van Grol, 223–25. Berlin: Walter de Gruyter, 2011.
Kovacs, Brian W. "Is There a Class-Ethic in Proverbs." In *Essays in Old Testament Ethics*, edited by James L. Crenshaw and John T. Willis, 173–89. New York: Ktav, 1974.
Kovacs, Brian W. "Sociological-Structural Constraints upon Wisdom: The Spatial and Temporal Matrix of Proverbs 15:28-22:16." Ph.D. diss., Vanderbilt University, 1978.
Kowal, E. "Sociology and Empire." *Postcolonial Studies* 17, no. 4 (2014): 415–17.
Kraus, M., and D. Keltner. "Signs of Socio-Economic Status: A Thin-Slicing Approach." *Psychological Science* 20 (2009): 99–106.
Kraus, Michael, and Paul Piff. "Social Class, Solipsism, and Contextualism: How the Rich Are Different from the Poor." *Psychological Review* 119, no. 3 (2012): 546–72.
Lafont, Bertrand. "The Women of the Palace at Mari." In *Everyday Life in Ancient Mesopotamia*, edited by Jean Bottéro, 127–40. Edinburgh: Edinburgh University Press, 2001.
Lambe, Anthony J. "Judah's Development: The Pattern of Departure—Transition—Return." *JSOT* 83 (1999): 53–68.
Lamont, Michèle. *The Dignity of Working Men: Morality and Boundaries of Race, Class, and Immigration*. Cambridge, MA: Harvard University Press, 2002.
Laniak, Timothy S. *Shame and Honor in the Book of Esther*. Vol. 65. SBLDS. Atlanta, GA: Scholars Press, 1988.

Latimer, Joanna, and Beverley Skeggs. "The Politics of Imagination: Keeping Open and Critical." *The Sociological Review* 59 (2011): 393–410.
Leeuwen, Neil Van. "The Imaginative Agent." In *Knowledge through Imagination*, edited by Amy Kind and Peter Kung, 85–110. Oxford: Oxford University Press, 2018.
Lemos, T. M. "Shame and Mutilation of Enemies in the Hebrew Bible." *JBL* 125 (2006): 224–25.
Lenin, V. I. "Philosophical Notebooks, Vol. 38." In *Collected Works*. Moscow: Progress Publishers, 1914–1916 [1968].
Liddle, Celeste. "Molly Hadfield Social Justice Oration." In *City of Darebin Molly Hadfield Oration*, Preston, Victoria, Australia, March 10, 2016.
Lim, Jason, and Alexandra Fanghanel. "'Hijabs, Hoodies and Hotpants'; Negotiating the 'Slut' in Slutwalk." *Geoforum* 48 (2013): 207–15.
Lipschits, Oded. "Achaemenid Imperial Policy, Settlement Processes in Palestine, and the Status of Jerusalem in the Middle of the Fifth Century B.C.E." In *Judah and the Judeans in the Persian Period*, edited by Oded Lipschits and Manfred Oeming, 19–52. Winona Lake, IN: Eisenbrauns, 2006.
Lipschits, Oded, and Oren Tal. "The Settlement Archaeology of the Province of Judah: A Case Study." In *Judah and the Judeans in the Fourth Century B.C.E.*, edited by Rainer Albertz, Oded Lipschits, and Gary N. Knoppers, 33–52. Winona Lake, IN: Eisenbrauns, 2007.
Little, David. "The Heterogeneous Social: New Thinking about the Foundations of the Social Sciences." In *Philosophy of the Social Sciences: Philosophical Theory and Scientific Practice*, edited by C Mantzavinos, 154–78. Cambridge: Cambridge University Press, 2009.
Longman Jr., Tremper. *The Fear of the Lord Is Wisdom: A Theological Introduction to Wisdom in Israel*. Grand Rapids, MI: Baker Academic, 2017.
Losurdo, Domenico. *Il marxismo Occidentale: come nacque, come morì, come può rinascere*. Rome: Editori Laterza, 2017.
Luckenbill, D. *Ancient Records of Assyria and Babylon, Volume 2: Historical Records of Assyria from Sargon to the End*. Chicago, IL: University of Chicago Press, 1927.
Mackerras, Colin. *China's Ethnic Minorities and Globalisation*. London: RoutledgeCurzon, 2003.
Macpherson, C. B. *The Political Theory of Possessive Individualism*. Oxford: Clarendon Press, 1962.
Malamat, Abraham. "The Historical Background of the Assassination of Amon, King of Judah." *IEJ* 3, no. 1 (1953): 26–29.
Malamat, Abraham. "Mari and the Bible: Some Patterns of Tribal Organizations and Institutions." *Journal for the American Oriental Society* 82 (1962): 143–50.
Mao, Zedong. "On Contradiction." In *Selected Works of Mao Tse-Tung, Vol. 1*, 311–47. Beijing: Foreign Languages Press, 1937 [1965].
Martin, Terry. "Modernization or Neo-Traditionalism? Ascribed Nationality and Soviet Primordialism." In *Stalinism: New Directions*, edited by Sheila Fitzpatrick, 348–67. London: Routledge, 2000.
Martin, Terry. "An Affirmative Action Empire: The Soviet Union as the Highest Form of Imperialism." In *A State of Nations: Empire and Nation-Making in the Age of Lenin and Stalin*, edited by Ronald Grigor Suny and Terry Martin, 67–90. Oxford: Oxford University Press, 2001.
Martin, Terry. *The Affirmative Action Empire: Nations and Nationalism in the Soviet Union, 1923-1939*. Ithaca, NY: Cornell University Press, 2001.

Marx, Karl, and Friedrich Engels. *The Communist Manifesto*. New York: Penguin Classics, 1848/1967.
Mayshar, Joram. "Who Was the Toshav?" *JBL* 133, no. 1 (2014): 225–46.
Mbembe, Achille. "Provisional Notes on the Postcolony." *Africa* 62, no. 1 (1992): 3–37.
Mbembe, Achille. *On the Postcolony*. Vol. 41. Studies on the History of Society and Culture. Berkeley: University of California Press, 2001.
McLennan, G. "Complicity, Complexity, Historicism: Problems of Postcolonial Sociology." *Postcolonial Studies* 17, no. 4 (2014): 451–64.
Meek, Theophile J. "Middle Assyrian Laws." In *Ancient Near Eastern Texts Relating to the Old Testament*, edited by James Bennett Pritchard, 180–87. Princeton, NJ: Princeton University Press, 1969.
Messenger, John. "The Role of the Proverb in a Nigerian Judicial System." *Southwestern Journal of Anthropology* 15 (1959): 64–73.
Meyers, Thomas A. "Open Letter from Thomas A Myers to Occupy Wall Street." *Journal of International Business Ethics* 5, no. 1 (2012): 50–59, 63.
Miles, Johnny. "Re-Reading the Power of Satire: Isaiah's 'Daughters of Zion,' Pope's 'Belinda', and the Rhetoric of Rape." *JSOT* 31, no. 2 (2006): 193–219.
Miller, J. M., and J. H. Hayes. *A History of Ancient Israel and Judah*. Philadelphia, PA: Westminster, 1985.
Mitchell, Lawrence E. *Stacked Deck: A Story of Selfishness in America*. Philadelphia, PA: Temple University Press, 1998.
Moghadam, Valentine M. *Modernising Women: Gender and Social Change in the Middle East*. London: Lynne Reiner, 1993.
Moors, Annelies. "The Affective Power of the Face Veil: Between Disgust and Fascination." In *Things: Religion and the Question of Materiality*, edited by Dick Houtman and Birgit Meyer, 282–95. New York: Fordham University Press, 2012.
Morrow, W. S. "Were There Neo-Assyrian Influences in Manasseh's Temple? Comparative Evidence from Tel-Miqne/Ekron." *CBQ* 75 (2013): 53–73.
Moulier, Yann. "Introduction." In *The Politics of Subversion: A Manifesto for the Twenty-First Century*, 1–44. Cambridge: Polity, 2005.
Myers, Jacob. *Ezra.Nehemiah*. Edited by William Foxwell Albright and David Noel Freedman. Vol. 14. Anchor Bible. Garden City, NY: Doubleday & Co., 1965.
Na'aman, N. "Josiah and the Kingdom of Judah." *TA* 18 (1991): 27–28.
Na'aman, Nadav. "In Search of Reality behind the Account of David's Wars with Israel's Neighbours." *IEJ* 52 (2002): 200–24.
Newsom, Carol. "Rhyme and Reason: The Historical Résumé in Israelite and Early Jewish Thought." In *Israel's Prophets and Israel's Past: Essays on the Relationship of Prophetic Texts and Israelite History in Honor of John H. Hayes*, edited by B. E. Kelle and M. B. Moore, 293–310. LHBOTS 446; New York: T&T Clark, 2006.
Nicholson, E. "The Meaning of the Expression 'Am Ha'Aretz in the Old Testament." *JSS* 10 (1965): 59–66.
Niditch, Susan. "The Wronged Woman Righted: An Analysis of Genesis 38." *Harvard Theological Review* 72, no. 1–2 (1979): 143–49.
Niditch, Susan. *Underdogs and Tricksters: A Prelude to Biblical Folklore*. New Voices in Biblical Studies. San Francisco, CA: Harper & Row, 1987.
Niditch, Susan. *The Responsive Self: Personal Religion in Biblical Literature of the Neo-Babylonian and Persian Periods*. Anchor Yale Bible Reference Library. New Haven, CT: Yale University Press, 2015.
Niesiolowski-Spano, L. *Goliath's Legacy: Philistines and Hebrews in Biblical Times*. Wiesbaden: Harrassowitz, 2016.

Nirenberg, David. "A Time of Mind," 2016. http://eventbeat.org/the-527th-convocation-ad dress-the-university-of-chicago/. Accessed March 3, 2019.
Nissinen, Martti. *Ancient Prophecy: Near Eastern, Greek, and Biblical Perspectives*. Oxford: Oxford University Press, 2018.
North, Douglass C. "Epilogue: Economic Performance through Time." In *Empirical Studies in Institutional Change*, edited by Douglass C. North, Lee J. Alston, and Thrainn Eggertsson, 342–56. Cambridge: Cambridge University Press, 1996.
North, Douglass C. *Institutions, Institutional Change and Economic Performance*. Cambridge: Cambridge University Press, 1990.
North, Douglass C. "Institutions." *The Journal of Economic Perspectives* 5, no. 1 (1991): 97–112.
North, Douglass C. "Economic Performance through Time." *The American Economic Review* 84, no. 3 (1994): 359–68.
North, Douglass C. "Markets." In *The Oxford Encyclopedia of Economic History, Volume 3*, edited by Joel Mokyr, 432–33. Oxford: Oxford University Press, 2003.
North, Douglass C. *Structure and Change in Economic History*. New York: W. W. Norton & Company, 1981.
North, Douglass C. *Understanding the Process of Economic Change*. Princeton, NJ: Princeton University Press, 2005.
Oden, Robert A. *The Bible without Theology: The Theological Tradition and Alternatives to It*. New Voices in Biblical Studies. San Francisco, CA: Harper & Row, 1987.
Olson, Dennis. "Literary and Rhetorical Criticism." In *Methods for Exodus*, edited by Thomas Dozeman, 13–54. Cambridge: Cambridge University Press, 2010.
Olyan, Saul M. "Honor Shame, and Covenantal Relations in Ancient Israel and Its Environment." *JBL* 115 (1996): 201–18.
Overholt, Thomas W. *Channels of Prophecy: The Social Dynamics of Prophetic Activity*. Minneapolis, MN: Fortress Press, 1989.
Overholt, Thomas W. *Cultural Anthropology and the Old Testament*. Minneapolis, MN: Fortress Press, 1996.
Overholt, Thomas W. "Prophecy: The Problem of Cross-Cultural Comparison." *Semeia* 21 (1982): 55–78.
Parker, B. J. "Power, Hegemony, and the Use of Force in the Neo-Assyrian Empire." In *Understanding Hegemonic Practices of the Early Assyrian Empire: Essays Dedicated to Frans Wiggermann*, edited by B. S. During, 287–97. Leiden: Brill, 2015.
Peled, Ilan. *Masculinities and Third Gender: The Origins and Nature of an Institutionalized Gender Otherness in the Ancient Near East*. Alter Orient und Altes Testament 435. Münster: Ugarit-Verlag, 2016.
Petersen, Kirsten Holst, and Anna Rutherford. *A Double Colonization: Colonial and Post-Colonial Women's Writing*. Mundelstrup: Dangaroo Press, 1986.
Piff, Paul K. "Does Money Make You Mean?" 2013. https://www.ted.com/talks/paul_piff _does_money_make_you_mean. Accessed March 3, 2019.
Piff, Paul K. "Wealth and the Inflated Self: Class, Entitlement, and Narcissism." *Personality and Social Psychology Bulletin* 40, no. 1 (2014): 34–43.
Piff, Paul K., Andres G. Martinez, Daniel M. Stancato, and Michael W. Krau. "Class, Chaos, and the Construction of Community." *Journal of Personality and Social Psychology* 103, no. 6 (2012): 949–62.
Piff, Paul K., Daniel M. Stancatoa, Stéphane Côtéb, Rodolfo Mendoza-Dentona, and Dacher Keltnera. "Higher Social Class Predicts Increased Unethical Behavior." *Proceedings of the National Academy of Sciences of the United States of America* 109, no. 11 (2012): 4086–91.

Pinkus, Benjamin. *The Jews of the Soviet Union: A History of a National Minority*. Cambridge: Cambridge University Press, 1988.

Pipes, Richard. *The Formation of the Soviet Union: Communism and Nationalism, 1917-1923*. Cambridge, MA: Harvard University Press, 1964 [1954].

Provan, I. W. *1 and 2 Kings*. NIBC. Peabody, MA: Hendrickson, 1995.

Purves, Pierre M. "Commentary on Nuzi Real Property in the Light of Recent Studies." *JNES* 4, no. 2 (1945): 68–86.

Rakowska-Harmstone, Teresa. "The Dialectics of Nationalism in the USSR." *Problems of Communism* 23, no. 3 (1974): 1–22.

Ranger, Johannes. "Institutional, Communal, and Individual Ownership or Possession of Arable Land in Ancient Mesopotamia from the End of the Fourth to the End of the First Millennium B.C." In *Symposium on Ancient Law, Economics, and Society, Part II*, edited by Geoffrey P Miller, Martha Roth, James Whitman, James Lindgren, and Laurent Mayali, 269–319. Chicago: Chicago-Kent College of Law and Illinois Institute of Technology, 1995.

Reddit, Paul L. *Introduction to the Prophets*. Grand Rapids, MI: Eerdmans, 2008.

Renfrew, Colin. "Beyond a Subsistence Economy: The Evolution of Social Organization in Prehistoric Europe." In *Reconstructing Complex Societies: An Archaeological Colloquium*, edited by Charlotte B. Moore, 69–88. Cambridge, MA: ASOR, 1974.

Ro, Johannes Unsok. "The Theological Concept of YHWH's Punitive Justice in the Hebrew Bible: Historical Development in the Context of the Judean Community in the Persian Period." *VT* 61, no. 3 (2011): 406–25.

Robinson, Ira. "Bepetah Enayim in Genesis 38:14." *JBL* 96, no. 4 (1977): 569.

Roth, Martha T. *Babylonian Marriage Agreements: 7th-3rd Centuries B.C.* Edited by Manfred Dietrich, Kurt Bergerhof, and Oswald Loretz. Alter Orient Und Altes Testament 222. Neukirchen-Vluyn: Neukirchener Verlag, 1989.

Roth, Martha T., Harry A. Hoffner, and Piotr Michalowski. *Law Collections from Mesopotamia and Asia Minor*. Vol. 6. Writings from the Ancient World. Atlanta, GA: Scholars Press, 1995.

Rudman, D. "A Note on the Personal Name Amon (2 Kings 21, 19-26 II 2 Chr 33, 21-25)." *Biblica* 81, no. 3 (2000): 403–05.

Rutenberg, Jim, and Ashley Parker. "Romney Says Remarks on Voters Help Clarify Position." *NY Times*, 2012. https://www.nytimes.com/2012/09/19/us/politics/in-leaked-video-romney-says-middle-east-peace-process-likely-to-remain-unsolved-problem.html. Accessed March 3, 2019.

Sasson, Jack M. "The Servant's Tale: How Rebekah Found a Spouse." *JNES* 65, no. 4 (2006): 241–65.

Schäder, J. "Patronage and Clientage between God Israel and the Nations: A Social-Scientific Investigation of Psalm 47." *Journal for Semitics* 19 (2010): 235–62.

Schneider, Tammi J. *Mothers of Promise: Women in the Book of Genesis*. Grand Rapids, MI: Baker Academic, 2008.

Schott, Liz, and Dottie Rosenbaum. "'Superwaiver' Bill Threatens Key Low-Income Programs." *Center on Budget and Policy Priorities*, 2017. https://www.cbpp.org/research/poverty-and-inequality/superwaiver-bill-threatens-key-low-income-programs. Accessed March 3, 2019.

Schwarzenberg, Sarah J., A. Kuo, J. Linton, and P. Flanagan. "Promoting Food Security for Children." *Pediatrics* 136 (2015): 1431–38.

Scrivner, Joseph. "Wisdom as Cultural Capital: Textuality and Moral-Social Reproduction in Proverbs 1-9." Princeton Theological Seminary, 2008.

Scurlock, Jo-Ann. "Religious Participation: Ancient Near East - Sacred Prostitution." In *The Oxford Encyclopaedia of The Bible and Gender Studies*, edited by Julia M. O'Brien, 205-09. Oxford: Oxford University Press, 2014.

Skinner, John. *A Critical and Exegetical Commentary on Genesis*. The International Critical Commentary. Edinburgh: T&T Clark, 1910.

Smith, Adam. *An Inquiry into the Nature and Causes of the Wealth of Nations*. Edited by Edwin Cannan. New York: Modern Library, 1994.

Sneed, Mark R. "The Class Culture of Proverbs: Eliminating Stereotypes." *SJOT* 10, no. 2 (1996): 296-308.

Sneed, Mark R. *The Politics of Pessimism in Ecclesiastes: A Social-Science Perspective*. Vol. 12. SBLAIL. Atlanta, GA: SBL Press, 2012.

Sneed, Mark R. *The Social World of the Sages: An Introduction to the Israelite and Jewish Wisdom Literature*. Minneapolis, MN: Augsburg Fortress, 2015.

Sneed, Mark R. "'White Trash' Wisdom: Proverbs 9 Deconstructed." *JHebS* 7 (2007): Article 5. http://www.arts.ualberta.ca/JHS/Articles/articl_66.pdf.

Spiekermann, H. *Juda Unter Assur in Der Sargonidenzeit*. Göttingen: Vandenhoeck & Ruprecht, 1982.

Stalin, I. V. "Kak Ponimaet Sotsial-Demokratiia Natsional'nyĭ Vopros?" In *Sochineniia*, Vol. *1*, 32–55. Moscow: Gosudarstvennoe izdatel'stvo politicheskoi literatury, 1925.

Stalin, I. V. "Marksizm i Natsional'nyĭ Vopros." In *Sochineniia*, Vol. *2*, 290–367. Moscow: Gosudarstvennoe izdatel'stvo politicheskoi literatury, 1925.

Stalin, I. V. "Marxism and the National Question." In *Works*, Vol. *2*, 300–81. Moscow: Foreign Languages Publishing House, 1925.

Stalin, I. V. "O Politicheskikh Zadachakh Universiteta Narodov Vostoka: Rech' Na Sobranii Studentov KUTV, 18 Maia 1925 G." In *Sochineniia*, Vol. *7*, 133–52. Moscow: Gosudarstvennoe izdatel'stvo politicheskoi literatury, 1925.

Stalin, I. V. "The Political Tasks of the University of the Peoples of the East: Speech Delivered at a Meeting of Students of the Communist University of the Toilers of the East, May 18, 1925." In *Works*, 7:135–54. Moscow: Foreign Languages Publishing House, 1925.

Stalin, I. V. "The Social-Democratic View on the National Question." In *Works*, Vol. *1*, 31–54. Moscow: Foreign Languages Publishing House, 1925.

Stavrakopoulou, F. "Exploring the Garden of Uzzah: Death and Ideologies of Kingship." *Bib* 87 (2006): 1–21.

Steinmetz, G. "Empires Imperial States and Colonial Societies." In *Concise Encyclopedia of Comparative Sociology*, edited by Ekkart Zimmermann, Stephen K. Sanderson, Masamichi Sasaki, and Jack Goldstone, 58–74. Leiden: Brill, 2014.

Steinmetz, G. "Major Contributions to Sociological Theory and Research on Empire, 1830s-Present." In *Sociology and Empire: The Imperial Entanglements of a Discipline*, edited by G. Steinmetz, 1–52. Durham, NC: Duke University Press, 2013.

Steinmetz, G. "Neo-Bourdieusian Theory and the Question of Scientific Autonomy: German Sociologists and Empire, 1890s–1940s." *Political Power and Social Theory* 20 (2009): 100–08.

Stewart, Anne W. *Poetic Ethics in Proverbs: Wisdom Literature and the Shaping of the Moral Self*. Cambridge: Cambridge University Press, 2016.

Stewart, Anne W. "Wisdom's Imagination: Moral Reasoning and the Book of Proverbs." *JSOT* 40, no. 3 (2016): 351–72.

Stokl, Jonathan. *Prophecy in the Ancient Near East: A Philological and Sociological Comparison*. Vol. 56. Culture and History of the Ancient Near East. Leiden/Boston, MA: Brill, 2012.

Sugirtharajah, R. S. *Exploring Postcolonial Biblical Criticism: History, Method, Practice*. Chichester, West Sussex; Malden, MA: Wiley-Blackwell, 2012.

Suny, Ronald Grigor. "Nationalism and Class in the Russian Revolution: A Comparative Discussion." In *Revolution in Russia: Reassessments of 1917*, edited by Edith Rogovin Frankel and Jonathan Frankel, 219–46. Cambridge: Cambridge University Press, 1992.

Suny, Ronald Grigor. *The Revenge of the Past: Nationalism, Revolution, and the Collapse of the Soviet Union*. Stanford, CA: Stanford University Press, 1993.

Swartz, David. *Culture & Power: The Sociology of Pierre Bourdieu*. Chicago, IL: University of Chicago Press, 1997.

Sweeney, M. A. *I & II Kings*. OTL. Louisville, KY: Westminster John Knox Press, 2007.

Tadmor, H., and S. Yamada. *The Royal Inscriptions of Tiglath-Pileser III (744-727 BC), and Shalmaneser V (726-722 BC), Kings of Assyria*. Vol. 1. RINAP. Winona Lake, IN: Eisenbrauns, 2011.

Thames, J. T. "A New Discussion of the Meaning of the Phrase 'Am Ha'Aretz in the Hebrew Bible." *JBL* 130, no. 1 (2011): 109–25.

Thareani-Sussely, Y. "The 'Archaeology of the Days of Manasseh' Reconsidered in the Light of Evidence from the Beersheba Valley." *PEQ* 139, no. 2 (2007): 69–77.

Thurnwald, R. C. "The Crisis of Imperialism in East Africa and Elsewhere." *Social Forces* 15, no. 1 (1936): 84–91.

Toorn, Karel van der. "Female Prostitution in Payment Vows in Ancient Israel." *JBL* 108, no. 2 (1989): 193–205.

Toorn, Karel van der. "The Significance of the Veil in the Ancient Near East." In *Pomegranates and Golden Bells: Studies in Biblical Jewish, and Near Eastern Ritual, Law, and Literature in Honor of Jacob Milgrom*, edited by David Noel Freedman, Avi Hurvitz, Jacob Milgrom, and David P. Wright, 327–40. Winona Lake, IN: Eisenbrauns, 1995.

USDA. "School Breakfast Program Fact Sheet," 2017. https://www.fns.usda.gov/sbp/fact-sheet. Accessed March 3, 2019.

USDA. "Supplemental Nutrition Assistance Program Participation and Costs," 2016. https://www.fns.usda.gov/pd/supplemental-nutrition-assistance-program-snap. Accessed March 3, 2019.

Van Ree, Erik. *The Political Thought of Joseph Stalin: A Study in Twentieth-Century Revolutionary Patriotism*. London: Routledge Curzon, 2002.

Vermeule, Blakey. *Why Do We Care about Literary Characters?* Baltimore, MD: John Hopkins University Press, 2010.

Wang, Long, and J. Keith Murnighan. "Money, Emotions, and Ethics across Individuals and Countries." *Journal of Business Ethics* 125, no. 1 (2014): 163–76.

Warner, Megan. "'Therefore a Man Leaves His Father and His Mother and Clings to His Wife': Marriage and Intermarriage in Genesis 2:24." *JBL* 136, no. 2 (2017): 269–88.

Watson, Sophie, and Anamik Saha. "Suburban Drifts: Mundane Multiculturalism in Outer London." *Ethnic and Racial Studies* 36, no. 12 (2013): 2016–34.

Weeks, Theodore R. "Stalinism and Nationality." *Kritika: Explorations in Russian and Eurasian History* 6, no. 3 (2005): 567–82.

Weheliye, Alexander G. *Habeas Viscus: Racializing Assemblages, Biopolitics, and Black Feminist Theories of the Human*. Durham, NC: Duke University Press, 2014.

Westenholz, Joan Goodnick. "Tamar, Qĕdēšā, Qadištu, and Sacred Prostitution in Mesopotamia." *Harvard Theological Review* 82, no. 3 (1989): 245–65.

Westermann, Claus. *Genesis*. Edited and translated by David Green. London: T&T Clark, 1988.

Whitelam, Keith. *The Invention of Ancient Israel: The Silencing of Palestinian History*. London: Routledge, 1997.
Whybray, R. N. *Wealth and Poverty in the Book of Proverbs*. Sheffield: JSOT Press, 1990.
Williamson, Hugh G. M. *Ezra, Nehemiah*. Vol. 16. Waco, TX: Word Books Publisher, 1985.
Wilson, Robert R. *Prophecy and Society in Ancient Israel*. Philadelphia, PA: Fortress Press, 1980.
Wolf, Mark J. P. *Building Imaginary Worlds: The Theory and History of Subcreation*. Routledge: New York, 2012.
Wright, Jacob L. *Rebuilding Identity: The Nehemiah-Memoir and Its Earliest Readers*. Vol. 348. BZAW. Berlin: de Gruyter, 2004.
Yamauchi, Edwin. "Two Reformers Compared: Solon of Athens and Nehemiah of Jerusalem." In *The Bible World: Essays in Honor of Cyrus H. Gordon*, edited by Gary A. Rendsburg, Ruth Adler, Milton Arfa, and Nathan H. Winter, 269–92. New York: Ktav Publishing House, 1980.
Yee, Gale A. "'I Have Perfumed My Bed with Myrrh': The Foreign Woman ('Iššâ Zārâ) in Proverbs 1-9." *JSOT* 43 (1989): 53–68.
Yekelchyk, Serhy. "Stalinist Patriotism as Imperial Discourse: Reconciling the Ukrainian and Russian 'Heroic Pasts', 1939–45." *Kritika: Explorations in Russian and Eurasian History* 3, no. 1 (2002): 51–80.
Yoffee, Norman. *Myths of the Archaic State: Evolution of the Earliest Cities, States, and Civilizations*. Cambridge: Cambridge University Press, 2004.
Žižek, Slavoj. *Revolution at the Gates: Žižek on Lenin: The 1917 Writings*. London: Verso, 2002.
Žižek, Slavoj. "A Leninist Gesture Today: Against the Populist Temptation." In *Lenin Reloaded: Towards a Politics of Truth*, edited by Stathis Kouvelakis, Sebastian Budgen, and Slavoj Žižek, 74–98. Durham, NC: Duke University Press, 2007.
Zvi, E. Ben. "Chronicles and Its Reshaping of Memories of Monarchic Period Prophets: Some Observations." In *Prophets, Prophecy, and Ancient Israelite Historiography*, edited by Mark J. Boda and Lissa M. Wray Beal, 167–88. Winona Lake, IN: Eisenbrauns, 2013.
Zvi, E. Ben. "Re-Negotiating a Putative Utopia and the Stories of the Rejection of the Foreign Wives in Ezra-Nehemiah." In *Worlds That Could Not Be. Utopia in Chronicles, Ezra and Nehemiah*, edited by Steven J. Schweitzer and Frauke Uhlenbruch, 105–28. LHBOTS 620; London: Bloomsbury T&T Clark, 2016.
Zvi, E. Ben. "Reading Chronicles and Reshaping the Memory of Manasseh." In *Chronicling the Chronicler: The Book of Chronicles and Early Second Temple Historiography*, edited by P. S. Evans and T. F. Williams, 121–40. Winona Lake, IN: Eisenbrauns, 2013.
Zvi, E. Ben. "Clio Today and Ancient Israelite History: Some Thoughts and Observations at the Closing Session of the European Seminar for Historical Methodology." In *"Even God Cannot Change the Past": Reflections on 16 Years of the European Seminar in Historical Methodology*, edited by Lester L. Grabbe, 20–49. London: Bloomsbury T&T Clark, 2018.

AUTHOR INDEX

Abbott, A.   9 n.1
Abrahams, R.   119 n.42
Adams, K.   70 n.55
Adelman, R.   77, 77 nn.87, 89, 91, 80 n.95
Ahlström, G.   39 n.38, 41 n.45
Albertz, R.   30 n.10, 43 n.1, 47 n.4
Alter, R.   76, 111, 111 n.1, 116, 116 n.27, 119, 119 n.43, 122, 122 n.46
Amer, S.   62 n.12
Amit, Y.   59 n.3, 74 nn.72–3
Anderson, B.   1–3, 5–7, 28 n.4, 60 n.7, 64 n.21, 81, 81 n.98, 112, 112 n.7, 117 n.32, 118, 118 n.39, 124 n.49, 127 n.1, 133 n.19, 139, 139 n.40, 140–1, 141 n.48, 142, 145 n.1, 146, 146 nn.4–5, 147, 149 nn.17, 19, 154
Anthonioz, S.   32 n.15
Arera, E.   117 n.34
Assmann, J.   156 n.41

Barajas, E.   117, 117 nn.35, 37, 118, 118 n.40, 119–20, 122
Barrick, W.   30 n.7
Barstad, H.   37 n.32
Barzel, Y.   51, 51 n.21
Bauer, O.   150, 150 n.21
Becking, B.   30 n.10
Begg, C.   27 n.1, 33, 34 n.20
Ben Zvi, E.   16 n.18, 18 n.22, 19 nn.23–4, 20 nn.28–9, 21 n.30, 24 n.36, 32 n.13
Berlinerblau, J.   78 n.93
Bird, P.   60 n.5, 71 n.60
Blenkinsopp, J.   43 n.1, 80 n.96
Bloch, E.   146–8, 147 nn.7, 9
Boer, R.   88 n.15, 96 n.28, 153 n.32, 159 nn.47–8
Bourdieu, P.   6, 78 n.93, 113–16, 113 n.12, 114 nn.16, 19, 115 nn.22–3, 123, 125
Bradley, K.   108 n.53
Brodie, T.   156 n.40

Brown, W.   111–12, 112 n.6
Brudny, Y.   150 n.19
Bunge, M.   48 n.8

Carneiro, R.   12, 12 n.8
Carruthers, B.   55 n.34
Carter, C.   13 n.9, 47 n.4
Carter, R.   11 n.4
Cataldo, J.   63 n.18, 132 n.11, 133 n.17, 139 n.41
Chalcraft, D.   12 n.5, 64, 64 nn.19–20
Chaney, M.   88 n.15, 93–4
Chapman, C.   10 n.3
Civil, M.   69 n.45
Clifford, R.   117, 117 n.31
Cohen, T.   71 n.57
Coomber, M.   97 n.31, 106 n.46
Coote, R.   155 n.47
Cornell, D.   66, 66 n.28
Cross, F.   33, 33 nn.17–18, 34
Crüsemann, F.   159 n.49
Currie, G.   11 n.4

Davies, P.   47 n.3, 155 n.37
Day, P.   71 n.58
Deutsch, K.   149 n.19
Diduk, S.   75 n.77
Dillon, M.   153 n.33
Doniger, W.   80 n.95
Dube, M.   60 n.9
Dundes, A.   117 n.34
Durand, J.   67 n.31
Durkheim, E.   85, 85 n.5

Earle, T.   97 n.31
Edelman, D.   22, 22 n.31, 23, 23 n.33, 64 n.19
Egry, G.   150 n.21
Elayi, J.   47 n.3
Elliott, J.   75 n.78
Engels, F.   85 n.5, 145 n.2

Fanghanel, A.   60 n.6
Fanon, F.   61 n.10, 62–3, 63 nn.14–15, 66, 66 n.27, 79
Faundez, J.   53 n.25
Faust, A.   47 n.4, 155 n.37
Fine, G.   19 n.25
Finkelstein, I.   29 n.6, 155 nn.36–7
Fitzpatrick-McKinley, A.   43 n.1
Flanagan, J.   11 n.5, 13, 13 n.9
Fletcher, N.   11 n.4
Fontaine, C.   117 n.36
Fox, M.   112 n.5
Frame, G.   40 n.42
Frankel, J.   150 n.22, 152 n.27
Freedman, D.   33–4, 33 n.17, 59 n.2
Fried, L.   27 n.2, 37 n.35, 139 n.38
Fry, R.   102 n.36
Frymer-Kensky, T.   70 n.54

Gabler, N.   103 n.38
Gandhi, L.   66 n.29
Gellner, E.   149 n.19
Gladney, D.   153 n.33, 154 n.34
Go, J.   35 n.24
Goering, G.   114, 114 nn.14, 17–18, 20
Golka, F.   116 n.28
Goodkind, N.   106 n.47
Goodnick Westenholz, J.   69 nn.44, 47, 70 n.52, 72 n.63
Gottwald, N.   88 n.15, 94, 94 n.26, 154, 155 n.35
Grabbe, L.   15 nn.12, 15–16, 16, 18, 37 n.33
Grace, D.   61 n.11
Gray, J.   31 n.10, 33, 33 n.19
Greenstein, E.   77, 77 nn.88, 90
Gruber, M.   70 n.53
Guins, G.   151 n.27

Halpern, B.   36 n.31
Hardt, M.   147 n.8
Harrison, T.   38 n.37
Hayek, F.   46, 49–51, 49 n.11, 50 nn.12–13, 15–16, 51 n.17, 53, 55, 56 n.35, 58
Hayes, J.   30, 30 n.9
Heim, K.   111, 111 n.3
Hens-Piazza, G.   27 n.1
Hiltzik, M.   106 n.48
Hoglund, K.   46 n.2
Horwitz, S.   50 nn.15–16

Houlberg, M.   75 n.77
Hume, D.   50, 50 n.14

Jackson, M.   59 n.1
Jaén, I.   26 n.38
Jameson, F.   146–7, 146 nn.4, 6
Jevons, W.   55–6, 55 n.33
Johnson, A.   97 n.31

Kahn, D.   40 n.42
Kammen, M.   21 n.30
Kang, Y.   148, 148 n.15
Kasperkevic, J.   103 n.37
Kautsky, K.   149, 150 n.20
Keltner, D.   88 n.17
Kincaid, H.   48 n.8
Kind, A.   11 n.4
Kippenberg, H.   43 n.1
Klein, L.   10 n.3
Knauf, A.   12 n.7, 29 n.6
Knight, N.   148 n.16
Knoppers, G.   32 n.13
Kovacs, B.   123–5, 123 n.48, 124 n.50, 125 n.52
Kowal, E.   35 n.25
Kraus, M.   85–7, 85 n.6, 87 n.12, 88 n.17, 90

Lafont, B.   67 n.35
Lambe, A.   73 n.71
Lamont, M.   88, 88 nn.16, 18, 102, 102 n.34
Laniak, T.   10 n.3
Latimer, J.   11 n.4
Lemos, T.   10 n.3
Lenin, V.   148 n.13
Liddle, C.   79 n.94
Lim, J.   60 n.6
Lipschits, O.   47 n.4
Little, D.   9 n.1
Longman, T.   116, 116 n.30
Losurdo, D.   145 n.3
Luckenbill, D.   41 n.44

Mackerras, C.   153 n.32
McLennan, G.   35 n.25
Macpherson, C.   54–5, 54 n.29
Malamat, A.   27, 31–4, 31 n.11, 32 n.14, 33 n.16, 97 n.30

Mao, Z. 148–9, 148 nn.12, 14
Martin, T. 151 n.27, 153 n.30
Marx, K. 85 n.5, 145 nn.2–3
Mayshar, J. 76 n.82
Mbembe, A. 65, 65 nn.23–4
Meek, T. 67 nn.32, 36, 68 n.37, 69 n.46, 70 n.50
Messenger, J. 117 n.33
Meyers, T. 107 n.50
Miles, J. 67 n.34, 68 n.39
Miller, J. 30 n.9
Mitchell, L. 108, 108 n.54
Moghadam, V. 61 n.11
Moors, A. 80 n.97
Morrow, W. 29 n.6
Moulier, Y. 147 n.8
Murnighan, J. 92 n.24
Myers, J. 57 n.42, 139 n.38

Na'aman, N. 12 n.7, 30 n.8
Negri, A. 147 n.8
Newsom, C. 20 n.27
Nicholson, E. 27 n.2, 37 n.34
Niditch, S. 59 n.1, 60 n.5, 65, 65 n.22, 71 n.60
Niesiolowski-Spano, L. 40 n.43
Nirenberg, D. 11 n.4
Nissinen, M. 16 n.19, 18 n.21
North, D. 45, 48–9, 48 nn.6–7, 49 nn.9–10, 51–3, 52 nn.22–4, 53 nn.25–6, 55–8, 57 nn.37–41, 58 n.43

Oden, R. 71 n.59
Olson, D. 156 n.42
Olyan, S. 10 n.3
Osborne, J. 38 n.37
Overholt, T. 15 nn.12, 14

Parker, A. 108 n.52
Parker, B. 28 n.3
Peled, I. 72 n.62
Petersen, K. 60 n.9
Piff, P. 85–7, 85 n.6, 86 nn.7–9, 11, 87 n.12, 89–90, 89 n.20, 90 n.23, 92, 100–1, 109
Pinkus, B. 151 n.27
Pipes, R. 151 n.27
Provan, I. 27 n.1

Rakowska-Harmstone, T. 152 n.27
Ranger, J. 97 n.29
Rector, R. 108 n.53
Reddit, P. 15 n.11
Renfrew, C. 11 n.5, 13 n.9
Ro, J. 47 n.4
Robinson, I. 73 n.68
Roth, M. 67 n.34, 69 n.48
Rudman, D. 34, 34 n.21
Rutenberg, J. 108 n.52
Rutherford, A. 60 n.9

Saha, A. 60 n.6
Sapin, J. 47 n.3
Sasson, J. 68, 68 n.41, 69 n.43
Schäder, J. 10 n.3
Schneider, T. 72 n.61
Schwarzenberg, S. 103 n.40
Scrivner, J. 114
Scurlock, J. 70 nn.51, 55
Skeggs, B. 11 n.4
Skinner, J. 156 n.39, 158 n.45
Smith, A. 51 n.18
Sneed, M. 17 n.20, 121 n.45, 123 n.47
Spiekermann, H. 27 n.1
Stalin, J. 143 n.53, 151–2, 151 nn.24–7, 152 nn.28–9, 158 n.46
Stavrakopoulou, F. 31 n.10
Steinmetz, G. 34 n.24, 35 n.29
Stewart, A. 112–13, 112 n.8, 113 n.11, 116, 116 n.26
Stokl, J. 15 n.13
Sugirtharajah, R. 7, 7 n.2, 60 n.9, 131, 131 nn.7–10, 135 n.26, 137 n.33, 138 n.35, 140 n.43, 141
Suny, R. 149 n.19, 152 n.27
Swartz, D. 113 n.12, 115 n.22
Sweeney, M. 34, 34 n.22

Tadmor, H. 39–40, 39 n.40, 40 n.41
Tal, O. 47 n.4
Thames, J. 27 n.2, 37 n.36
Thareani-Sussely, Y. 29 n.6
Thurnwald, R. 35–6, 35 nn.28–9, 36 n.30
Toorn, K. 59 n.2, 68, 68 nn.38, 42, 70 n.56, 76 n.83

Van Leeuwen, N.   11 n.4
Van Ree, E.   152 n.27
Vermeule, B.   26 n.38

Wang, L.   92 n.24
Warner, M.   60 n.4
Watson, S.   60 n.6
Weeks, T.   152 n.27
Weheliye, A.   63 n.16
Westermann, C.   159 n.51
Whitelam, K.   155 n.37
Whybray, R.   116, 116 n.29

Williamson, H.   43 n.1
Wilson, R.   14 n.11
Wolf, M.   26 n.38
Wright, J.   43 n.1

Yamada, S.   39, 39 n.40, 40 n.41
Yamauchi, E.   43 n.1
Yee, G.   76 n.85, 88 n.15
Yekelchyk, S.   152 n.28
Yoffee, N.   14 n.10

Žižek, S.   145 n.3

SUBJECT INDEX

Ammon(ites)   40, 77, 156–7
Assyrian empire   28–9, 28 n.3, 32–4, 36, 38–42, 142
authority   37, 63 n.18, 98, 106, 113, 118, 140

Babylonian Empire   28, 45 n.2
belief   1, 49, 53, 57, 98, 140

chaos   24, 80 n.96, 86 nn.9, 11
Chronicler   31–2, 32 n.13
citizen   37, 53, 102–9, 132, 137, 142
  citizenship   108 n.51, 136
colonialism   34, 132
community   1–7, 9, 13 n.9, 15, 18, 20, 24–5, 24 n.37, 28, 44–5, 46 n.3, 47 n.4, 49, 53–60, 61 n.11, 64, 71 n.57, 79 n.94, 86 nn.9, 11, 88, 93, 94 n.26, 98, 102, 106 n.46, 107, 128–30, 129 n.3, 132–3, 135–42, 135 n.25, 137 n.31, 142 n.51, 145–6, 149, 151–2, 153 n.33, 154, 157, 159

David(ic)   12, 12 n.7, 13 n.9, 29, 33, 50, 64–5, 71, 74, 76–7, 83, 88, 91, 93, 97, 100–1, 109, 117, 119–20, 157
diaspora   37, 75 n.77, 139 n.39
discourse   6, 25, 35, 58, 63 n.18, 108, 117 n.35, 128, 130, 133, 134–8, 138 n.35, 141, 143, 152 n.28

Egypt(ian)   22, 28–9, 32–4, 37, 39–41, 45 n.2, 47, 123, 142, 155, 156 n.41, 157
Elisha   14, 14 n.11, 16–17
exile   32, 37, 139, 141
Exodus   22, 76, 156, 156 n.42, 157
Ezra   20, 27, 36–7, 43, 46, 57, 63–4, 81, 138–42, 139 nn.38, 39, 140–2, 157

faith   91, 101
  faithful   62, 138, 154

God   7 n.3, 10 n.3, 16, 24 n.36, 31 n.10, 34, 57–8, 57 n.42, 94, 96, 101 n.33, 109, 130, 132, 135–6, 136 n.28, 138–40, 143, 143 n.54, 154, 157
good (substantive)   52–3, 55, 95, 107, 125, 129
government   44–5, 47–50, 107–8, 121, 150
Greco-Roman   47 n.5

Hellenistic Period   14, 19 nn.23–4, 22 n.33, 47 n.4

identity   1–5, 13 n.9, 20, 21 n.30, 22, 22 n.33, 23 n.33, 25 n.37, 31, 36, 43 n.1, 46, 54–5, 55 n.32, 59–66, 61 n.11, 63 n.18, 66 n.30, 69, 73–81, 80 n.95, 112, 117–18, 126–30, 132–3, 135–42, 136 n.29, 139 n.38, 146, 151 n.23, 154–7, 155 n.38, 159
imperialism   27, 29, 31, 33–7, 35 n.28, 36 n.30, 39, 41–2, 61, 151 n.27
individual   2–5, 9, 11, 18, 36 n.31, 48–9, 52, 54–8, 86–93, 97–101, 97 n.29, 106–8, 130, 137, 143
intermarriage   60 n.4, 74 n.73, 139, 139 n.38, 153–4
Isaiah   14 n.11, 68, 140
Israel(ite)   1, 3, 5–7, 9–10, 9 n.2, 10 n.3, 11 n.5, 12 n.7, 13, 13 n.9, 14 n.11, 15, 15 nn.12, 16, 16, 16 n.18, 17, 18, 19 n.23, 20 n.27, 21, 21 n.30, 22–3, 24 n.36, 25, 26, 30–1, 30 nn.9–10, 33, 36 n.31, 38–40, 43 n.1, 56, 59–61, 60 n.5, 63–6, 70–81, 70 n.56, 74 n.73, 76 n.83, 91, 94–100, 94 n.26, 96 n.28, 111, 113–14, 116–17, 116 n.30, 120–1, 123, 125–6, 128–30, 134, 138–9, 141, 143, 145–6, 152–9, 155 nn.35–7, 159 n.48

Jeremiah 16, 33
Jeroboam 39
Jews 44, 46, 58, 150, 150 n.22, 151 n.27
Josephus 27 n.1, 33, 34 n.20
Josiah 3, 27–8, 30 nn.7–8, 31, 33–4, 33 n.17, 37
Judah(ite) 3, 5, 7, 13, 16–17, 19 n.24, 23, 27–34, 27 nn.1–2, 29 n.6, 30 nn.8–9, 31 n.11, 32 n.14, 33 n.16, 36–8, 37 n.32, 40–2, 46 n.3, 47 n.4, 59 n.3, 60–1, 64, 66, 68–9, 71–6, 72 n.61, 73 n.71, 76 n.86, 77 n.87, 78–80, 100, 132 n.11, 140, 156
Judaism 21 n.30, 130
Judean 3, 7, 27 n.2, 30, 34, 36, 37 n.32, 46 n.3, 47 n.4, 59, 64, 142, 155
Judeo-Christianity 6, 127, 129, 133, 136–7

land 22, 27–8, 30, 34, 48, 51, 54, 58, 84, 93–8, 97 n.29, 129, 132, 134, 139, 156 n.42, 157
  homeland 46, 139 n.39
  landowner 44
  landscape 16, 19 n.24, 56, 105
  people of the land 30–3, 36, 41, 141, 158
law 4, 9, 12, 13 n.9, 36 n.31, 46, 49–50, 50 n.15, 51 n.17, 52, 52 n.24, 53 n.25, 54–7, 59 n.2, 67–70, 74–5, 77, 80–1, 83, 90–1, 93–8, 97 n.29, 105–6, 108–9, 118, 124, 133 n.17, 137, 151 n.27, 154
  daughter-in-law 156
  father-in-law 79, 156–7
liberation 50, 127–9, 127 n.2, 133, 135 n.25, 136 n.28, 138, 138 n.35, 154, 159 n.52

Mesopotamia(n) 47 n.5, 67 n.35, 69 nn.44, 48, 70, 72 n.62, 81, 97 n.29, 123
minority 2, 5, 22, 23 n.33, 128–35, 133, 134 n.23, 135 n.25, 137, 137 n.33, 139–40, 142, 151 n.27, 153, 153 n.32
monarchy 1, 13 n.9, 30, 37
monotheism 63 n.18, 132 n.11, 133, 139 n.41, 156 n.41, 158
Moses 76, 155–8, 156 nn.41–2

Nehemiah 4, 20, 43 n.1, 44–7, 49, 51–8, 57 n.42, 63 n.18, 109, 139, 139 nn.38–9, 140, 142
Neo-Babylonian Period 37 n.32, 65, 65 n.22

order 1, 6, 25, 27–8, 33, 35, 38–40, 43–5, 50, 52–5, 58, 62–3, 66, 68–9, 72, 78, 80, 100, 104, 112, 114, 117, 120, 122, 133, 142–3, 148–9, 153–5
other (the) 129, 131–2, 135–8, 142

Palestine 39 n.38, 41 n.45, 46 n.3, 47 n.4, 143, 157
perception 4, 54, 60–1, 72, 80 n.97, 83, 85, 87, 90, 125, 130, 136, 140
Persian (Achaemenid) Empire 44–5, 139
Persian Period 14, 17, 19 nn.23–4, 21, 27, 37, 43–4, 46–7, 65, 94
postcolonialism 127 n.2, 128, 131, 134 n.23, 141
power 4–5, 28 n.3, 29, 35–9, 35 n.29, 41–2, 43 n.1, 44–6, 46 n.3, 47 n.3, 49–54, 60, 64–6, 68 n.39, 75, 75 n.77, 79–80, 80 n.95, 85, 88, 94, 96, 98–101, 113, 113 n.12, 115, 115 n.22, 116, 121, 123–5, 129, 136–7, 138 n.35, 139–40, 147
  powerlessness 43, 48
prophecy 14 n.11, 15, 15 nn.12–14, 16 nn.18–19, 18 n.21, 150 n.22
prophet 9, 14–20, 14 n.11, 15 nn.12, 15–16, 16 n.18, 18 n.22, 19 n.23, 20 n.27, 23, 23 n.24, 29, 93 n.25, 97, 100, 158
prophetic 10 n.3, 14–16, 15 n.14, 18–20, 19 n.23, 20 n.27, 71, 91, 109, 159

religion 31 n.10, 36, 43 n.1, 62–3, 65, 65 n.22, 80 n.97, 106 n.46, 131, 134, 142, 153
  religiones 131 n.8
  religionsgeschichte 30 n.10
remnant 139, 140
restoration 1, 1 n.1, 129, 133 n.17
revelation 22, 75, 93, 122, 132, 136, 136 n.28
Roman Empire 132

Ruth 67 n.34, 74 n.73, 76–7, 77 nn.87–8, 90, 157

sacred 38, 69 nn.43, 46–7, 70 nn.51–2, 55–6, 72 n.63, 95, 96 n.28, 128, 140, 155 n.36, 159 n.48
Saul 12, 13 n.9, 91, 119
social memory 3, 9, 14, 17, 20–2, 21 n.30, 24–5, 24 n.36
social world 2–3, 9, 61, 63–5, 68, 71–2, 75, 128
society 1–4, 6, 13 n.9, 14 n.11, 29, 35–6, 41–2, 44, 45 n.2, 46–50, 50 n.13, 51–6, 56 n.36, 58, 61, 61 n.11, 65, 65 n.23, 71 n.60, 74 n.72, 85 n.5, 92, 97 nn.29–30, 99, 101, 103, 106 n.46, 113, 113 nn.12–13, 116, 120, 125–6, 136 n.28, 145, 151 n.27
Solomon 12, 12 n.7, 22, 31, 37, 117, 130, 157
symbolic order 66, 80

temple 9, 12, 22, 22 n.31, 29 n.6, 32 n.13, 33, 46–7, 46 n.3, 70, 70 n.56, 108 n.54, 139 n.38, 157
Torah 48, 96, 154

Yahweh 29–30, 32, 42, 129, 130, 138–40, 139 n.38, 155 n.35
Yehud 3–4, 19, 21, 37, 43–8, 47 n.4, 53–8, 63 n.18

Zechariah 19, 39

BIBLICAL INDEX

Genesis
3:16	130
3:21	73 n.70
10:17	158 n.43
11:30	130
11:31	155
12:3	78
15:16	76
15:18-21	96
15:19	158 n.43
17:12, 16	78
19:30-38	77, 156
19:31	78
20:7	16
21:16-18	78
22:8	78
23	156
23:4	76 n.82
24:4	155
24:65	68
25:9-10	156
25:21	130
25:30	156
26:34	156
27:15	73
27:15-16	69
25:19	155
28:2	156
29	156
29:21-25	68
29:23	79
31:15	76
31:32	73
36	156
36:1	156
36:23	158
36:40	73
37:32-33	73
38	70
38:2	156
38:7	76
38:11	78
38:12, 20	76
38:25	76
38:25-26	73
41:42	73
41:45	156
47:13-26	93
49:29–50:14	156
50-52	156
50:20	76

Exodus
1:7	156
1:8	156
2:1-9, 19	156
2:9	156
2:17	156
2:21-22	156
3:1	156
4:18-20	156
6:15	156
15:20	16
18	156
21:2-11	56
22:25-27	48
23:9	157
23:10-11	56

Leviticus
25:23-24	95
25:25	95
25:26-27	96
25:28	96
25:35-38	48

Numbers
11:24-29	16
33:33-34	30
20:24	156
10:29	156
25	157

Deuteronomy
2:19	156
3:14	158
6:20-25	20
10:7	30
13:2-6	16
13:9	73 n.69
15:1-3	56
15:1-18	48
15:4-5	94
15:8-9	95
15:11	94
15:12-18	56
23:7	156
23:17-18	72
23:19-20	48
23:28	70
24:6, 10	48
25:5-10	74
26:5	157
26:5-9	20
28	84
34:1-8	157

Joshua
6:25	157
12:1-6	158
13:1-6	157
13:11-13	158
15:63	157

Judges
1:16	156
1:19-36	157
3:5	157
4:11	156
8:21	120

13:3	130	8:18	30	Ezra	
14:1, 5	73 n.67	9	31	4:1-5	36
18:3	76	11	37	4:4	27, 37 n.35
		11:1-6	31	6:19	141
Ruth		12:21-22	31	6:19-22	138
2:10	77	13:2, 11	30	6:21	141
3:3	77	14:18-19	31	9-10	20, 157
3:9	67 n.34, 68	14:24	30		
4:17	157	14:56	31	Nehemiah	
22:10	76	15:9, 18, 24, 28	30	5	46
		15:10	39	5:1-5	43
1 Samuel		15:19-20	39	5:1-13	4, 43
9:9	16	17:1-6	40 n.41	5:9	57
10:5	15	17:2	30	5:12-13	58
10:10-13	16	21:1-18	27	6:12	76 n.84
14	119	21:2, 16	30	9:7	155
21:7	157	21:18, 26	30	9:36	129
22:1-2	72 n.64	21:19	30	13:23-27	157
22:2	56	21:19-26	27	13:24	76 n.84
22:3-4	157	21:20-22	30		
22:5	16	21:23-24	30	Job	
22:9	157	22:1-23:30	27	4–11	85
23:7	76	23:7	72	12:5	84, 85, 87, 109
24:13	117, 118	23:30	37	24:2	96
26:6	157	25:19	37	34:19	76
27:8	158			36:14	70, 72
		1 Chronicles			
2 Samuel		7:14	156	Psalms	
6:10-11	157	11:26-47	158	110:1	129
11	157	11:39, 41, 46	157	113:9	130
11:2	80	16:5	157		
11:3	157	25:1	15, 16	Proverbs	
11:4-5	72	25:1-8	18	1-9	116
11:11	100	26:8, 15	157	2:16	76
11-12	91	29:30	18	5:20	76
11-12:25	99			7:5	76
12:13	101	2 Chronicles		9:17	120, 121
23:13	72 n.64	9:29	18	10:1	117, 118, 119
23:24-39	158	12:15	18	10–22:16	111
23:37, 39	157	13:22	18	11:22	122
		20:34	18	12:13	84
1 Kings		23:32	18	15:28–22:16	123
21	92, 98, 99, 101	24:26	157	17:27-28	124
		32:32	18	22:7	56
2 Kings		33:18	18	22:7-8	93
3:2	30	33:19	18	22:28	96
3:15	15	33:22-33	32		
4	56	34:6	33		

23:10	96	Jeremiah		Amos	
23:27	76	19:4	76	2:6	56
25-29	111	24:5	76	5:11	93
26:11	114			8:6	56
		Lamentations			
Isaiah		2:14	16	Obadiah	
3:2	16	4:8	76	1:12	76
3:9	76				
3:18-23	68	Ezekiel		Micah	
3:19	68	16:3	157	2:1-2	109
5:8-10	93, 109	16:24	71	2:2-4	93
10:2	93			3:5	16
28:21	76	Daniel			
47:1-3	68	1:6-7	155 n.38	Sirach	
47:2	68			15	85
50:1	56	Hosea			
61:9	76	4:13-14	71		
63:16	76	4:14	70, 72		

www.ingramcontent.com/pod-product-compliance
Lightning Source LLC
Chambersburg PA
CBHW052046300426
44117CB00012B/1995